The Great American Adventure

THE GREAT
ADVEN

Martin Green

AMERICAN
TURE

BEACON PRESS • Boston

Copyright © 1984 by Martin Green

Beacon Press books are published under the auspices
of the Unitarian Universalist Association
of Congregations in North America,
25 Beacon Street, Boston, Massachusetts 02108

Published simultaneously in Canada by
Fitzhenry & Whiteside Limited, Toronto

Library of Congress Cataloging in Publication Data

Green, Martin Burgess, 1927-
  The great American adventure.

  Bibliography: p.
  Includes index.
  1. Adventure stories, American—History and
criticism. 2. Autobiography. 3. Masculinity (Psychology)
in literature. 4. Nationalism in literature. 5. United
States—Civilization. 6. Men—United States—Books
and reading.   I. Title.
PS374.A35G73   1984   813'.087'09   83-72386
ISBN 0-8070-6356-8

To Helen and José Yglesias,
who appreciate an argument
even as they fight it

FOREWORD

Idid not read adventure tales as a boy. I was not a manly boy, and did not easily identify with heroes who, for instance, dived off towering cliffs into the sea, or picked off howling Indians with a deadly rifle.

It was the domestic novel, about personal relations, that I preferred—of any quality. I can remember that in my first years of self-consciousness as a reader, I worried about the fact that my favorite writer was not Shakespeare but the Scots writer of small-scale domestic comedy, O.Douglas. Her stories feature the cozy fortunes and misfortunes of a minister's family; one is called *The Day of Small Things*. Now O.Douglas was in fact the sister of John Buchan, the author of *The Thirty-nine Steps, Prester John*, and many other adventures. The Buchan brother and sister divided popular literature between them; he wrote books for boys-and-men, she wrote books for girls-and-women. But I, as an adolescent, betrayed my pledged faith to "literature" with romances, not adventures.

I came to adventure late, in my forties. In a sense, I arrived when everyone else was leaving—during the Vietnam war, when even Hollywood stopped making westerns. I began to study adventures because of my interest in Gandhi and Tolstoy and their politics of peace. Convinced by their radical criticism of the West—as a society obsessed by and addicted to the lust for power, I asked myself in what way I could teach literature and stay true to that politics.

I had been trained in an English school of criticism, whose major present exponent is Raymond Williams; it looks at literature with strong political and social concerns of a left-wing kind.

This kind of criticism, and the kinds of fiction and poetry that correspond to it, can be called a resistance movement within literature; they resist those tendencies in literature which tie it to the interests of the ruling class, and which make a poet (as Tolstoy once said) only a superior milliner or *sommelier*—that is, someone who adds a new *frisson*, a new flavor to one's experience, for the benefit of people whose palates are jaded. There is no denying that, socially speaking, literature *is*—must be—a pleasure garden for the socially privileged, one of their fantasy islands. And only a radical literary criticism such as Williams offers can make it also something more serious.

However, from the point of view of Tolstoy and Gandhi, even literary political radicalism does not go deep enough or wide enough. It does not include the religious truths of man's experience or the experience of humanity outside Europe and North America. One result of both partialities is the evasive treatment of war and violence by left-wing thinkers (including Marx and Engels), who are ready to accuse their enemies of employing violence—as if it were a crime against humanity—but are themselves implicitly ready to employ it on their own side of the quarrel. They too give an equally inadequate account of imperialism, condemning self-proclaimed "empires," but endorsing the expansion of Western culture over the rest of the globe. The domestic processes of capitalism, industrialism, and the class struggle, they study exhaustively, but the cultural conflicts of imperialism seem peripheral to them.

It is a corresponding weakness in literary matters that radical criticism has not directed itself at the adventure tale. The connection may at first seem obscure; but the adventure tale has been the literary form in which war and the warrior virtues were celebrated and analyzed. It has also been the form which reflected and served the West's cult of expansion—political and economic and military expansion, material and spiritual.

Our fatal evasiveness concerning violence and imperialism is, in effect, promoted by literature's habit of turning away from adventure—whether the critic is turning away to prefer purely aesthetic values or to promote that criticism of our industrialized society which we find in the best novels of the domestic kind, like George Eliot's. (When I say "literature" in a sentence like that, I mean primarily criticism; I mean thought about literature—the institutionalized forms of such thought in departments of literature, where adventures are rarely mentioned, and never studied seriously.) Only when we have a criticism that focuses powerfully on the adventure tale will literary criticism, or "the English major," be a satisfactory center to an education. This at least is what I decided when I asked myself what Tolstoy and Gandhi would ask of a teacher of literature; and I began to read accordingly.

So I came to the adventure tale with a heavy load of moral and theoretical predispositions—even prejudices. But I found that I could not merely apply them in depreciation of what the authors offered. These tales exert on any reader their own powerful fascination—which is far from merely narrative. They are themselves full of moral and historical intentions and interpretations, which are not to be despised. The reader of these books has a great deal to notice and to think about, to respond to and to wrestle with; their writers are all men of intelligence and conviction, who have thought about the same issues we have.

I do not think these books should be read to be mocked or dismissed. On the other hand, it goes without saying that they should not be read with total assent or complicit enjoyment. The kind of reading appropriate to the adventure tale is dialectical; it involves denial of the writer's implicit and explicit arguments, but it denies as a way to agree, a way to put as much specific assent and dissent together in as stable a compound as possible. Today's readers will surely not profit by exultantly condemning their cultural fathers; they must sympathetically *understand* that old version of heroism and reluctantly accept their heritage of both privilege and guilt. Nothing will make that complex heritage clearer to them than a dialectical reading of the adventure tale.

CONTENTS

The Great American Adventure

INTRODUCTION
Adventure, Manliness, Nationalism

Adventure can, of course, mean both a certain kind of experience and the literary form built around that kind of experience. It is an adventure, of a passive kind, if your ship gets wrecked in a storm, and you alone of all aboard are thrown up by the waves upon the shores of a desert island. It is also an (active) adventure if you thereupon set to work, and build a hut, tame some animals, grow some vegetables, bake bread, build boats, make your own clothes of skins, set up little outposts all over the island, design your own daily, seasonal, annual routines, and make the island blossom like a rose, your property. But something else we call an adventure is the story of such experience, told even by a man who is making the whole thing up.

Conceptually I would define the adventure experience as a series of events, partly but not wholly accidental, in places far from home—most often also far from civilization—which constitute a challenge to the person they happen to. In the adventure tale, that person responds to that challenge with a series of exploits which make him/her a hero/heroine, that is, eminent in such virtues as courage, fortitude, cunning, strength, leadership, and persistence.

I said him/her, but in fact it nearly is nearly always him (and for that reason I propose to use "him" as the pronoun for the adventure reader). That is, the adventure tale was written almost exclusively for a masculine audience. It has been the main literary means by which males have been taught to take initiatives, to run risks, to give orders, to fight, defeat, and dominate; while females have been taught, both by being ignored by the genre and by being reduced to passive roles within it, *not* to do those things.

Less obviously, but just as importantly, adventure writing has been linked to the expansion of certain political societies. To enjoy adventures was (and is) to prepare oneself in imagination to go out to a frontier, whether it was overseas or in the western part of this continent, and to advance that frontier—against native populations or natural barriers—to extend the domain of civilization. (And "civilization" was usually a pseudonym for one's own country.) Some thrillers, of course, have no connections with this political theme, but, as I hope the rest of this book will show, many *have* such connections, though they are sometimes of a hidden kind.

Thus "adventure" is linked to both "manliness" and "patriotism"; linked as critical concepts, in our minds, now studying the adventure tale, but also linked, as articles of faith, in the minds of those who read these tales with avidity. And I do not mean, by putting these words in quotation marks, to make fun of them. They are ideas that have motivated great historical actions and great moral virtues. I only mean to put them into question.

We think first of all, no doubt, of popular adventure stories; of the paperbacks at the drugstore and the shelves at the public library marked "Mysteries," "Westerns," "Thrillers," and "Spy Stories." "Adventures" are for men what "Romances" are for women; and taking the two together, they amount to a very large part of "American literature," if we understand that phrase sociologically, to include all the books of narrative printed in this country. Books of this sort continue to flow out of the publishing houses and to be bought and read in enormous numbers, as they have for many generations.

But I am interested in literature in that other sense—the books we take seriously because they embody an intelligence equal to our own. There *are* adventures that embody such intelligence and seriousness, although we tend to forget that when we are being literary. But in fact nearly every man reads *some* adventures, and even the best of them have a lot in common with the worst; just as even the most serious novels of, say, Doris Lessing, have a lot in common with the most fomularized Harlequin or Gothic romances. The best and the worst are both parts of the same enterprise, whether they be adventures or romance novels;

and the serious adventure writers are in time imitated by the formula writers—although the reverse also happens sometimes. So I have chosen twelve American adventures which I do take seriously and will try to show how some of the political secrets of America are revealed in the way they are written and in what they borrow from the history of their own times.

We can, of course, distinguish between different kinds of adventure in literature. The most important distinction is between two main kinds; to explain them I must for a moment refer to British authors, because the Americans took their bearings from traditions established by the British. The Robinson Crusoe adventures (of which many have been written since the first one of 1719) are quite unlike the Waverley adventures. (Walter Scott's *Waverley* (1814) tells the story of the 1745 Jacobite Rebellion in Scotland.) One can distinguish the two kinds by the number of participants (Defoe's Crusoe story has one man alone, while Scott's Waverley novels have crowd scenes and, usually, a romantic pair); the kind of setting (the Crusoe story is set on an island, the Waverley story has scenes at court and a generally "historical" flavor); and the kind of narrative (Crusoe's is a plain-man's autobiography, Waverley is elaborately literary and cites historical sources and folklore).

These different adventures address different parts of society as their primary audiences: Defoe's story is written by, about, and for the English merchant; Scott's is by, about, and for the British aristocrat—the bearer of arms, in both senses of arms. But both serve a national purpose, and are aimed at a national audience (the one sees the nation as primarily a trading community, the other sees it as primarily a political organism) and both are versions of the energizing myth of British society, the dream that made young Britons want to go out and spread the empire.

One more distinction must be made to avoid confusion later. The energizing myth of America, like that of the other nations of the modern world-system, has been ambiguous. On the one hand, it has been passionately anti-imperialist; born in rebellion against the British empire, America has detested tyranny, aristocracy, militarism, courts, and castes, and has suspected every elegance that seemed to speak of social privilege, even the purely intellectual. On the other hand, it has been triumphantly imperialist; it has not only spread westwards like a prairie fire to take a whole continent away from its original inhabitants but has spread American styles of technology and discourse all over the world, to displace other indigenous cultures. It has become an empire, relying on its own military caste, while thinking of itself as an egalitarian democracy. Adventure has been the energizing myth of both aspects of America, and thus has recommended both plain, peaceable manliness and triumphant imperial militarism. Usually the first meaning is overt, the second covert (visible only to readers who cannot or will not identify with the audience for whom the story was written); but both meanings are there, and in the long run they are interdependent. In nearly all the narratives I discuss, I shall have to turn from the one meaning to the other.

In all of them, adventure is the energizing myth of empire, taking empire to mean any expanding society dominant over others. This myth most obviously energizes a society when that society is expanding territorially, as the United States was doing throughout the nineteenth century. The American adventure stories represented, in attractive and individualized form, the policies and compromises, the punishments and rewards, and the stresses and problems involved in advancing a frontier at the expense of native populations and against natural obstacles. To read the adventures was to prepare oneself to go west and take part in the national work. Yet such stories are also relevant to the culture of any society which is still expanding economically and politically, even if it has stopped its territorial growth, as the United States has in the twentieth century. On the other hand, adventure stories become less relevant and attractive to a society which has ceased to expand and has begun to repent its former imperialism. Thus Britain after 1918 stopped enjoying adventure stories and told them only ironically and bitterly. (The abrupt decline in Kipling's reputation exemplifies this change.)

Unlike Britain, America in the twentieth century was still—is still—a world power, a world ruler, and a world leader. And America has never *not* been an expanding society; it has been, from its inception and conception, a land of adventure. It was Europe's land of adventure before it was its own. It was the place Englishmen, Germans, Spaniards, and Frenchmen came to, seeking the adventures they could not find in their overcivilized home countries. That is why the adventure story is a peculiarly

American form; although, if we look at the world as a whole, and at literature as a whole, we see that adventure is also a European form, because of the great story of Europe's establishment of hegemony over the rest of the globe. American stories were often written by and for Europeans. Even today, one of most widely read writers of Westerns is the German Karl May, who never saw America. Thus *American* adventure is just the most striking version of this European (or white) form of literature.

Adventure tales are in fact where the two cultures come together. I mean the most important pair of opposed cultures, that of reflection (enshrined in our universities) and that of action or violence (institutionalized in our army, our police, our prisons). I do not mean the cult of violence, but the imaginative preparation to manage, employ, and engage in conflict and force. Because of the split between these two cultures, adventure has been neglected, intellectually. Even though it has been the major imaginative form and educative force for men of action, they have had little help in thinking about it from men or women of reflection. For example, the adventure tale, the literary version of adventure, has been studied, if at all, only in terms of popular culture, and "Popular Culture" is a kind of study that refuses to respond to the writer's intentions in anything like his own language. This book attempts to work out a critical method that takes the significant adventure tales seriously, to create an imaginative context for them equivalent to that we have for "serious literature"—a method that combines form, content, and historical criteria.

Significant literary adventures consist of three elements, the first two of which are frontier anecdote (or seafaring anecdote or shipwreck anecdote) and the long tradition of literary romance. We have adventure when those two elements fuse, and the romance motifs of treachery and revenge, disguise and mystery, a great wrong righted, and true love frustrated and then consummated are interwoven with the specifying details of wigwam and warpaint, the log cabin and the covered wagon, or the ocean and the storm and the footprint in the sand. This fusion becomes significant, can be taken seriously, when a third element is added: when the adventure makes the reader/writer contemplate his/her own status anthropologically. (I use the term *anthropological* to suggest the way adventures compare "civilized people"—that is, people of the writer's own culture—with other groups.) What distinguishes us from the Other? How do we measure up against Him, in warmth of heart, keenness of mind, firmness of courage? How would we measure up to the challenges he meets, as well as those he himself offers? How exactly has our nature changed as a result of this immense modern civilization we have built up around ourselves? And how do we feel about that change? These are the questions that, for instance, *Robinson Crusoe* makes us ask and helps us answer; and obviously they are as serious as any questions raised by what we call serious fiction.

Significant adventure also raises the question of violence, which serious literature (notably the domestic novel) by and large evades. Of course, there are episodes of suffering in novels of all sorts; but there is nothing problematic about violence, however appalling its scope, so long as it is merely suffered. The difficult questions about it are only raised when the reader is asked to engage in it himself, via a character, or an institution with whom he has identified. In many adventures, of course, the violence merely occurs, and is enjoyed—often as a corrupt excitement. But the significant adventure always raises the moral question, even though it usually resolves that question in the affirmative.

That is why adventure (the experience) has been the great rite of passage from boyhood to manhood, as in the Boy Scout movement; and why adventure (in books) has been the ritual of the religion of manliness, which was the unofficial religion of the nineteenth century, if not of the twentieth. In mainstream books it quite displaced the Christian values. Adventure experience was the sacramental ceremony of the cult of manhood. (That is why adventure writers put such stress on the coarse food and the rough conditions of sleeping, and so forth—all the experiential and initiatory rituals by which a boy becomes a man.) From Cooper's *The Pioneers* and Bird's *Nick of the Woods* to Mailer's *Why Are We in Vietnam?* a crucial set of images and concepts relates to manhood. The man of the woods—from Natty Bumppo and Nathan Slaughter to Big Luke Fellinka—is more of a man than those he meets, and the genteel heroes of those novels, from Oliver Effingham to Roland Forrester to Randall Jethroe, have to measure up to him, to show themselves worthy to be his heirs.

"Manhood" was also paired with some contrasting term—as the affirmed or superior value—in dozens of polarities of thought. Any male had to strive always to be a man and not a boy, in Hemingway adventures; a man and not an animal, in religious exhortation; a man and not a slave, in slavery narratives; and similarly, a man and not a coward, a man and not a mouse, a man and not a woman. At the same time, manhood also—*being* such a sacred value—spread out to mean all humanity, spread out beyond these antitheses to include the inferior or rejected term in each case; manhood/humanity thus included boys and slaves and women and cowards.

This anthropocentric and androcentric religion penetrated literature gradually during the eighteenth century; there is no sign of it in *Robinson Crusoe,* and in *Waverley* it is mild and modest; but in the American adventure from Cooper on it is evangelical in its fervor. And the political expression of that religion, which was very intimately related to manhood, was nationalism. The political system as a whole was emotionally and spiritually animated by the religion. Congress was an assemblage of national elders, who exerted actual power over the nation's young adventurers, but who—in terms of the national myth—lived in imaginative dependence upon them. The young adventurers were more "American" than any professional politician.

I have defined adventure as the energizing myth of empire (in another book, I develop this idea at length), but it will be to our advantage, here, to use the idea of nationalism as much as, or more than, imperialism; partly because Americans thought of their politics and literature as nationalist and partly for other reasons that will become clear as we look at the specific adventures. In any case, the idea of a nation was closely related to the idea of empire—of the modern world-system. Nationalism was what was talked about, because imperialism was morally shady. "Nations," as the nineteenth century used the term, were the members of that family of states which ruled the modern world-system. It was the British, the Dutch, the French, and so on, who were thought of as nations; and the Germans, the Poles, the Greeks, the Italians, the proto-nations, were summoned to join them, to become nations, to throw off the yoke of the old empires—Turkey, Austria, and Russia—and join us in exploiting the unclaimed world out there—Asia, Africa, Australia, and so on. (The latter areas were not inhabited by *nations.*) This summons was carried by the adventure tales of Scott and his European successors, and nationalism was not felt to be at odds with empire of the modern kind. The Austrian empire was the enemy of the nations it ruled over, but the British empire was the friend of all true nationalism—it ruled only over tribes or mutually hostile groups like Hindus and Muslims. Thus, when Scott showed Scotland how to accept her destiny as a nation, it was as a partner *within* the British empire.

It will perhaps be agreed without much protest that the Anglo-Saxons always felt there to be close natural connections between the love of adventure, the writing of adventures, the progress of democracy, and the expansion of trade, between adventure and, for example, the expansion of the American empire in this modern sense. It will be easily agreed, I suggest, that such activities supported and strengthened each other in the great new republic as much as in the constitutional monarchy of England. That idea was always more or less acknowledged.

To give an example, two sentences from the chapter entitled "The Advocate" in *Moby Dick* will show the close connections which Melville took for granted, between world democracy and commercial enterprises like whale fishing, between free trade and the modern empire that was driving out colonies of the old kind.

> Until the whale fishery rounded Cape Horn, no commerce but colonial, scarcely any intercourse but colonial, was carried on between Europe and the long line of the opulent Spanish colonies on the Pacific coast. It was the whalemen who first broke through the jealous policy of the Spanish crown, touching these colonies; and, if space permitted, it might distinctly be shown how from those whalemen at last eventuated the liberation of Peru, Chili, Bolivia from the yoke of Old Spain, and the establishment of eternal democracy in those parts.[1]

It will be the argument of chapter 6, which primarily examines *Typee*, that Melville was himself an adventure lover and adventure writer, although an ambivalent one; and to suggest that even *Moby Dick* was, at one level of intention, a work of literary propaganda for the modern world-system, a literary version of the energizing myth of the nineteenth century.

It may be more difficult to accept the idea that there is an equally close connection between adventure and caste; adventure was the means by which men of the ruling class justified their claims to represent America. Yet this is true of adventure in both senses: as action and experience, and as literary form.

Adventure (the experience) is always an escape from, an alternative to, settled civilized city life. But settled life has two aspects, which from some points of view are very different; for this reason, adventure, as the alternative to it, also takes on different meanings. On the one hand, settled life is a matter of limitations, rules, and privileges—of hierarchy—and so an escape from it can be a pursuit of egalitarian democracy. On the other, settled life is organized under the aegis of bourgeois commercial work, industriousness and productivity; so that an escape from it can serve the purposes of aristocracy, of the warrior virtues, and of romanticism. Egalitarian democracy and what I shall call the "aristo-military" virtues were usually held to exclude each other; but in this context they did not.

Adventure as a written form has served both these purposes—sometimes *either* one *or* the other, sometimes both in the same story—and Americans have often confused the two, in consequence. But the most interesting adventures from a literary point of view have predominantly served the second purpose, perhaps because literature itself as a social entity is committed to manifesting and conferring high-culture status. Readers and writers are always, willy nilly, members of the ruling class.

Literature is, after all, an activity of one particular class, who can be defined economically as the book buyers. And in America in the early nineteenth century when the book buyers included neither an intelligentsia nor an academia, they could perhaps be named, in terms of their ideology, the responsible class—meaning those who felt themselves responsible for their culture, felt it their duty to look after their country's sense of values, its cultural standards, its ideology. The main geographical locus of this class in nineteenth-century America was, in the first 40 years, Philadelphia, in the later years, Boston. It was no mere accident that these were the publishing centers of America, and the first three of the authors I shall discuss published at Philadelphia; the second three, at Boston. The ideology of this class was nationalist, adventurous, and humanist—meaning that it made a cult of manhood.

Hidden in this ideology—which I shall sometimes call just nationalism—was an antidemocratic tendency that will be important for our argument. A nation was conceived of as, or felt to be, an organic entity; the different groups in society were felt to be natural growths and to be mutually complementary, rather than mutually competitive; it was thus implicitly a caste and not a class theory of society. I use the world "class," by contrast, to signify that sense of society we associate with democracy, in which all social distinctions are felt to be unjust or at least unfortunate, and in which the ideal is universal equality and social mobility—lack of differentiation. Nationalism, however, insisted on differentiation. For instance, "the American nation," as Cooper understood it, assigned an important function to the soldier and the aristocrat, even though society disapproved of them. (I am reporting Cooper's view of America's attitude toward its soldiers and aristocrats. But can we say he was wrong?) According to the strictly economic theory of society, which modern bourgeois experience tends to generate, soldiers and aristocrats are idle consumers and/or destroyers of wealth. Cooper's heroes, however, were soldiers and aristocrats, and he wanted his readers to prefer them to those mean and envious "democrats" among his characters who resented his heroes. Since nationalism connotes relation with other states (as democracy and society do not) and so implies a nation's need for military defense and/or aggression, it reconciles the middle-class reader to the aristo-military caste. (This is why Scott's novels were felt to be so nationalist and were so often imitated, by Cooper in America and by other writers in other countries; because their primary drive was just to bring together the merchant and the soldier.)

Nationalism also carried with it an anti-Christian tendency; that is, a tendency opposed to any form of religious radicalism, any sect (in America the classic example was Quakerism) that renounced war and empire and "the world." The most striking expression of this theme in American adventures is the implicitly hostile treatment of Quakers and Moravians in Cooper, Irving, and Bird. There was a British precedent, in Defoe's *Captain Singleton,* but the theme is much more developed in the American works. No doubt this is because the issue of peace versus patriotism had been sharpened by the War of Independence, when the Quakers of Pennsylvania had refused to fight; Franklin tells some anti-Quaker stories in his autobiography, mocking their pacifism. The relation of this issue to nationalism is thus very clear. Cooper discusses it quite explicitly in the first Natty Bumppo romance, gently criticizing the Quakers and deploring the Moravians' "Christianizing" of the Delawares—which meant their emasculation as a tribe. The message of this novel, and of many others, was that in order to be manly and to become a nation, Americans had to give up the Christian devotion to peace. They could not go on being, as they had been in the seventeenth and eighteenth centuries, a congeries of idealistic sects (seekers of political "alternatives," to use a modern term), refugees from the various European evils of tyranny, hierarchy, luxury, latitudinarianism, and so on. They had to recognize that they too had become a military people and to accept the leadership of an aristo-military caste.

Nineteenth-century fiction as a whole taught this lesson, including the domestic or serious novel, though in a discreet and disguised way. The hero, the man fit to marry the heroine (who, in these novels, is the true center) must be a man of adventures, with a fiery and in some sense aristocratic temperament. He cannot be a Quaker or religious zealot. Scott's treatment of low-church enthusiasts is markedly unsympathetic—they are the enemy for his sensibility. Dickens and Trollope, but also Charlotte Brontë and even George Eliot, consistently drew unfavorable portraits of evangelicals, and preferred ardent young gentlemen, full of natural fire, as their heroes. But the serious novel's values are—in oblique and attenuated form—erotic, not political; only in the adventure is the connection made clear between these fiery heroes and militarism and nationalism.

In nineteenth-century America, above all, it is striking how many adventures (in both senses) served the purposes of its ruling class; most notably, served the purpose of legitimizing its aristo-military function. America had of course an unusual preponderance of "democrat-adventurers" in its population—people in revolt against all social hierarchy. Most frontiersmen thought themselves the opposite of aristocrats. Moreover, the culturally dominant class were ex-Puritans, at least in New England, and hostile to "the men of blood," as their seventeenth-century ancestors had called the aristo-military caste. More than other countries, America needed propaganda on behalf of that caste.

There had been a development away from Puritanism even in New England in the course of the eighteenth century; one that especially affected attitudes towards soldiers. We may date the decline of clerical influence from 1691, when the governors of Massachusetts began to be appointed by the King and voting rights were determined by property ownership, not church membership.[2] Merchants made huge profits in the wars that were so frequent from 1690 to 1715, and the attitude to war changed; it was now said to stimulate inventiveness and manly qualities. Military discipline was seen as moral, and Christianity itself was praised for transforming "effeminate Cowards" into "valiant Heroes." Army officers became culture heroes, a pattern begun in Colonel Church's *Entertaining Passages*.

One striking example of this shift is found in the comment of John Adams, in the middle of the century, that he "longed more ardently to be a Soldier" than a lawyer; at the First Continental Congress, he grew impatient with those who "shuddered at the prospect of blood." He said he would have been a soldier himself had he come from any colony south of New England, "where the martial Spirit is but just awakened and People are unaccustomed to Arms." He described the military regimen as "a mixture of the Sublime and the Beautiful" and declared that an independent America "must adopt the great, manly, and warlike virtues." My source for this account concludes that "now the soldier was idealized, for he had come to embody the masculine and sacrificial virtues which Americans believed essential for maintenance of the new nation and its new republican freedoms."[3] An important change had taken place, but the antimilitary and antiaristocratic feeling stayed strong in New England, and the conflict of loyalties was often renewed.

It was therefore the task of American "culture" to reconcile that conflict, to combine in authoritative images the Brahmin with the aristo-military virtues; and literature, as we shall see, was a major means to that end. So the American adventure, in its written form, was often a gesture of ideological rebellion against Christian tradition (though a gesture also of caste piety) whereby ruling-class men subverted their Brahmin heritage while asserting new claims for it. This was especially true in New England, which took culture most seriously, and we shall see it in the autobiographical narratives of Dana and Parkman, but Cooper and Bird had contributed to the same cause through their fiction. The political-historical climax to this century-long process could be said to be Theodore Roosevelt's career. Roosevelt made himself fit to represent America though born to the upper class, fit to become President—by virtue of his adventures, both enacted and written.

In all these narratives we see the implicit conflict between the claims of different classes to represent adventure (and thus to represent America) as well as the implicit assertion of the claims of the rulers, the responsible or gentlemanly class, over those of the irresponsible or frontier class. In *Dreams of Adventure* I tried to show how Cooper's characterization of Natty Bumppo amounts to such a claim. Natty, Cooper's hero, may be called a definition of the "true American"; Cooper is making a claim on his behalf that it is *this* type that represents America, not the uncultured frontiersman represented by Davy Crockett and other "wild men of the West" (their own phrase). Cooper's hero is a figure of responsibility, a reincarnation of ruling-class, classical, Republican virtues in democratic guise. Crockett's picture of himself, in his autobiography, and in campaign speeches, is culturally anarchic. Dana and Parkman (and most of the other writers I shall discuss) endorse both of Cooper's claims: that the best Americans are gentlemen—that there is no intrinsic conflict between being an American and being a gentleman—and that the gentleman is not essentially Brahmin (that is, a man of peace and learning) but rather a leader, a captain, a hero, a man of fire and fierceness.

Thus Cooper (and his successor, Bird) uses aristocratic terms to explain the workings of command, discipline, courage, and so on. Leaders, even in the wilderness, should be aristocrats. Born gentlemen (or Virginians, or English officers), because they are of the warrior caste, know how to give courage to others, how to impose discipline on a group, and how to maintain its spirit.

Dana and Parkman often use aristocratic terms, too; and they also use an idealized caste-consciousness to the same effect. Men of courage may be low born, but they are *nature*'s gentlemen. This does not mean that snobbery blinded these writers to reality. They present decadent aristocrats and lion-hearted plebians quite insistently, but they see them as anomalies within nature's caste system. They see the phenomena of command as analogous to those of caste, and they understand the former in terms of the latter. Nobility of nature may be found at any social level, but nobility will always be the dominant value. Such "democratic" sentiments (very typical of nineteenth-century liberalism) employ caste terms as a matter of course and imply that, given a chance, nature's aristocrats will end up on top. They will know how to give orders and keep order—as if they were born to it.

Melville, in *Redburn*, describes a sailor (Jackson) who derives his power to command from depths of malignity, not nobility. This upsets the hierarchy I just described. But that is because Melville was in some ways deeply hostile to the adventure ethos. His was quintessentially a divided mind. In other passages, moreover, he says just the reverse. In *White Jacket* he more comfortingly confirms that Virginians make better captains than other Americans, and that English ships are happier than American ones because an English captain belongs—as a captain ought to belong—to the aristo-military caste. (The phrase is mine, but his idea is the same.) The terms of this old-fashioned and chivalric sociology were indeed better adapted than those of progressive democracy to explaining the phenomena of authority and leadership.

Of course, there are differences between what "gentleman" means to different writers. Although all claim to be gentlemen, they do not all define the concept the same way. Melville, like Irving, usually demonstrates a sophistication of taste and a range of reference, especially in literary matters, that establishes him, the writer, as a belletrist, a man of taste, something of a scholar. In his satirical and self-distinguishing way, Twain aims in the same direction. Bird and Cooper, however, are more inclined to assert a noble and spirited temperament, a character implicitly martial and neither bookish nor commercial. Their gentility is not so essentially literary. Their joking references, in letters and so on, to their books as objects of commerce, as commodities with prices and sales sheets may be read as protests against the ignominy of their position. (You find the same sharp-edged jokes in Pushkin and Byron, two arrant aristocrats.) Dana and Parkman too, although they do it more discreetly, stress their own qualities of command, courage, and endurance.

The class idea of the gentleman can thus be assimilated to two different social entities, two different castes, the Brahmins and the warriors; Melville, Irving and Twain incline to the first, the other four to the latter. But in all of their books, the fateful question, gentleman or not-gentleman? is always asked. Both the Brahmins and the warriors are, after all, twice-born castes; the crucial distinction is between them and the once-born laborers, the masses. That alternative is the dynamic of the modern system's disguised caste structure, as much as it is the dynamic of Hinduism; in Europe it can be found forcefully expressed in, for example, Defoe's work. That system has made a basic dynamic out of the drive to become a gentleman and to avoid being the opposite, and literature has been one of the principal mechanisms by which the drive has been transmitted.

Our first three writers ("Three From Philadelphia"), Cooper, Irving, and Bird, wrestle in literary ways with the myths of the frontier, subduing them to the purposes and advantages of the ruling class. (They invented very important lower-class characters, like Natty Bumppo and Nick of the Woods, but their own representative in their books is a romantic-genteel hero.) The second group ("Three From Boston"), Dana, Melville, and Parkman, wrestled with those myths more existentially, risking their lives to conquer them, to acquire them for gentlemen. Dana showed what the life of the common man, as sailor and beachcomber, was really like, and how gentlemen could succeed in that life. Melville showed what cannibals were really like, and how a gentleman could deal with them; Parkman what Indians and emigrants were really like, and how a gentleman could deal with them.

The dates and occasions of the books discussed coincide with the growth of American empire. Dana's voyage of 1839 placed California on the American map; Melville dates his narrative, or his voyage, from the French annexation of the Marquesas Islands in 1841 (and the subtler American-missionary imperialism there); and Parkman's narrative is dated by the Mexican War of 1846, as well as by the land migration to Oregon and California. Each relates obliquely to a further step of empire, and each develops the adventure genre in significant ways.

The next three chapters ("Three Anomalies") deal with figures, Carson, Twain, and Roosevelt, who extend and exemplify this pattern but who are in one way or another exceptions to it. They employ various forms of narrative and none of them are represented by a single literary text. Carson was a man of action, not of letters, and his narrative is less interesting, *as narrative*. Twain, the opposite, is so *much* the man of letters that his relations with adventure are hostile and mocking, as well as enthusiastic. They must be examined thematically throughout his work. Finally, Roosevelt is interesting primarily as a political phenomenon. A self-made man, self-formed in the image of the adventure hero, he coined that lore and legend into political gold; he was the manly leader America had been looking for, at least since *Two Years Before the Mast*.

What they have in common is that all three make the nation-state, as much as the individual, the adventurer or the locus of adventure. The United States as a whole is seen on the move in their narratives. They represent the period in which the historians of Parkman's group were writing the adventure legend of the Anglo-Saxon nations, the white race's epic of world domination. We associate this legend with concern over the closing of the frontier—elucidated in the famous 1893 essay by historian Frederick Jackson Turner, the heir of Parkman—and with the replacement of the frontier as the locus of adventure on foreign soil—the sites of imperialist adventure like Roosevelt's "splendid little war."

The period of Carson, Twain, and Roosevelt was, therefore, militaristic, or at least military, and may be said to have begun with the Civil War and ended with World War I. Even during years of peace between, books made Americans aware that their army was employed in either fighting Indian tribes or enforcing white American policy toward them. These were the decades of Custer and his last stand and of Buffalo Bill Cody—Custer's guide—and his Wild West Show. This was the period, everywhere in the modern world-system, of *militarism* and *imperialism*. The two words were first employed together by critics of Napoleon III's empire and adopted in England in 1864, and in Germany in 1870.

Thus nationalism was transformed into, or unmasked as, imperialism. (When Germany finally achieved national unity in 1870, Bismarck named it the Second Reich, the Second German Empire.) *Imperialism*, however, was a sinister word, which set a moral obstacle between writers and the adventure theme; at the same time it gave the theme a fatal allure for them. At least in politics, and to some degree in literature also, the obstacle was overcome by Theodore Roosevelt.

If we associate Roosevelt with Dana, rather than with Natty Bumppo, it is because he was a Harvard man; it was the gentleman-as-adventurer who finally entered the White House in the twentieth century. This was also the period of the adventure's greatest popularity as reading matter, the period of the dime novel. After his death, partly because of the pendulum movement of taste, and partly because of the Great War's character as nightmare rather than adventure, there was a reaction against the form. In England this led to a complete divorce between adventure and literature, but in America, it led to a new alliance under the aegis of art—an aestheticization of adventure. The evolution began with Crane's *The Red Badge of Courage*, and was carried to triumph by Hemingway, Faulkner, and Mailer ("Three Aesthetes").

It was natural that, as America entered upon her career as a world power, and then world ruler, the character of her written adventures should also change. Her writers became more concerned about the artistic status of their forms; they could write adventure only if it was also myth or metaphor. *Because* they were now the artist-representatives of a world-empire, they had to make their art proud, mysterious, and autonomous. Their rhetoric became more esoteric and aesthetic, and the figure of the adventurer approached that of an artist—and vice versa as they made themselves adventurers-as-artists. Not superficially, but profoundly, this change resembled one that had occurred in English writing at the end of the nineteenth century, when Kipling briefly imposed himself upon the reading public as the bard of empire. The subtler imperialization of American literature occurred fifty years later and corresponded with the transfer of world leadership (or, more exactly, the leadership of the modern world-system) from Great Britain to the United States.

Kipling had no heirs among his fellow-countrymen, but in America he found a follower in Hemingway, as Conrad did in Faulkner. Between 1920 and 1960, after all, America still had a calling to rule the world, which England had lost; and it had no strong tradition of the serious novel to resist adventure. The literary coup d'état, which had failed in Kipling's hands but which had intended to make adventure the dominant genre of fiction, and so of all literature, triumphed in America in the middle of the century.

Despite all these historical changes, a remarkable continuity runs through these narratives, fictional and nonfictional. Similar, even identical, themes and motifs recur, like guns, nature, and Crusoe, in the early narratives. California is described in Dana, the Marquesas Islands in Melville, and both recur in Twain. The hunter's passions and his great animal antagonists appear in Parkman, and again in Faulkner and Hemingway. The ocean and the prairie, the cannibal and the Indian, the whale and the buffalo, the bear and the lion, all clearly manifest the same values in the different narratives.

This sequence of books, moreover, has some claims to be considered the highest achievement of American literature in this 150-year period—that is, in the history of the United States. They are the equivalent of the Great Tradition that British critics found in the line of great novelists beginning with Jane Austen and the concurrent line of culture theorists beginning with Burke.

In England in the nineteenth century adventure was an entertainment genre, as far as literature went. The serious literary work was done in the genre of the novel—stories about marriage and domesticity written in a form of moral realism, and woman-centered whereas adventure was man-centered. The works of Charlotte Brontë, Mrs. Gaskell, George Eliot, and Thomas Hardy will show what I mean. But the nineteenth-century novel was also a function of "culture"—that is, a principled criticism of and resistance to "civilization" (understood as society's aggressive and repressive forces). And culture, at least in the nineteenth century, drew much of its strength from continuities, cyclical rhythms in nature and social life (in, for instance, marriage), which continued from the preindustrial era. Culture seemed to transcend class conflicts and to harmonize all the nation's values. Tolstoy and Lawrence, probably the two greatest writers of the cultural novel, exemplify these characteristics for nineteenth-century Russia and twentieth-century England.

In America, however, because it remained a frontier society (receiving new citizens all the time, changing its physical limits, and acquiring new resources), the serious novel did not establish itself. Continuities were not characteristic of American life. Moreover, at least in nineteenth-century America, the very concept of culture was debased to a slogan or battle cry in the struggle between the two classes that claimed to represent the country: the gentleman and the frontiersman. The frontiersman knew he was not cultured and did not want to be. Culture never escaped the reproach of being sectarian, never seemed to transcend class as it did in England. It was adventure that seemed to transcend class in America and to bring all the conflicting interests of Americans into harmony. In consequence, adventure could command some of the best energies of men of letters. Thus the sequence of books studied here constitutes the central achievement of American literature.

Part One

THREE FROM PHILADELPHIA

Cooper's *The Pioneers* (1823)
Irving's *A Tour on the Prairies* (1832)
Bird's *Nick of the Woods* (1837)

Stories of gentlemen who visited the frontier, encountered a frontiersman, and won the right to be his heir—to inherit America for gentlemen in general.

Chapter 2   COOPER'S
            THE PIONEERS
            (1823)

The first great American adventure hero in literature was James Fenimore Cooper's Natty Bumppo, and *The Pioneers* is the story in which Natty Bumppo first came to life. There American readers first saw him save a young maiden from a panther, show his loyalty to Chingachgook the Delaware, and display his matchless marksmanship and woodcraft. They also learned about the deeper themes of Natty's love of Nature and distaste for civilized life, his unconscious Romanticism, and his need to move on, farther into the forest, as the settlements advanced westwards behind him.

Natty Bumppo was immensely popular. For a century and a half, according to the testimony of many autobiographies, American boys spent their formative years imagining themselves as his disciples and followers, stealing through the forest, skimming down the streams, shooting across the lakes, tracking hostile Indians, protecting white maidens, bringing down eagles and deer with a single shot, pledging deathless love to one redskin comrade. The boys who became America's politicians, businessmen, and soldiers—but also those who became her historians, preachers, writers—prepared themselves for manhood in Cooper's gymnasium of the heart.

This is hard for us to believe now, for Cooper's adventures are no longer at all exciting. Most students cannot be brought to read any one of them through, and those who do complain that they are very bored. Indeed, Cooper's stories were always badly flawed as stories, and there were even in his own lifetime two bodies of dissent to the general enthusiasm I just reported. One criticism came from spiritual rebels like Edgar Allan Poe; the other, from men of the West like Mark Twain. The first found Cooper too American, too philistine, too complaisantly serving up the mythic pabulum his audience asked for. The second found him too European, Eastern, and aristocratic to be an authentic writer of American adventures. But between those two wings of taste stood the center phalanx of readers who loved him—readers like historians Parkman, Prescott, Bancroft, and Motley, all of whom professed a lifelong gratitude to Cooper. Abroad as well, in England, France, Germany, and Russia, he was translated and imitated over and over again.

Thus American adventure in literary form began its career with an injustice, for Cooper had much greater success than far better adventure writers. On the other hand, he had an interesting mind, and he did think seriously about adventure and empire and nationalism; he certainly deserves a chapter in any book on this subject.

Although a New Yorker, he belonged to that Philadelphia school of writers that gave birth to American literature in the generation before Boston established its dominance as a writing and publishing center; a school which was more worldly and aristocratic, less moralistic and modern, than the Bostonians were to be. Philadelphia was the political and publishing capital of Federalistic America. In literary terms, it was the city of Sir Walter Scott and Thomas Moore, or, among American writers, of Charles Brockden Brown and Philip Freneau. The taste it promoted through the books it published was genteel-Romantic. It was not a city of ideas or moral enthusiasms, as Boston was to be; there was no equivalent of the Concord writers in Philadelphia. Like New York, with which it formed an axis, its literature served a mildly epicurean, aristocratic, and cosmopolitan audience, who prided themselves on enjoying a good stirring tale of the frontier without incessant ethical anxiety. Fictional adventure was definitely in the Philadelphia style.

We may take *The Pioneers* as representative of those frontier tales. Although the first of Cooper's Natty Bumppo novels, and so the first of American adventures, it is not, as we shall see, in all ways typical of that genre. In this story, Judge Temple is the main landowner in a settlement called Templeton; on the outskirts of town live Natty Bumppo (an old frontiersman), his Indian comrade, and a mysterious young man called Edwards, who is destined to marry Temple's only child, Elizabeth. It is an

American adventure because Edwards, who is genteel by birth and education, is the rightful heir to the Temple property, but he must earn another right to it by abandoning every privilege and apprenticing himself to his social inferior, Natty, the Man of the Woods, the American Adam. The plot revolves around Temple's land (from whom he got it, to whom he will leave it), but the themes also include the very different kinds of American found in Templeton and their different senses of what it means to be an American.

The settlement's lower classes are hostile to Judge Temple; disliking any kind of social or cultural hierarchy, they resent the kinds of taste (in manners, in architecture, in church services) he brings to Templeton. His elegance of mind and even his integrity of judgment seem un-American to them because they claim to be "superior." Cooper is on Temple's side; he takes no sympathetic interest in the other point of view. The conflict in which he does take a dialectical interest is that between civilized and savage values.

Cooper (and this is typical of all his work) is very direct and simple in presenting this anthropological theme. In the following description of a group of the novel's characters going home after church, he draws broad contrasts between the tame and the wild, the civilized and the savage:

> The clergyman in his dark dress of broad cloth, with his mild, benevolent countenance occasionally turned towards his companions, expressing that look of subdued care, that was its characteristic, presented the first object of this singularly constituted group. Next to him moved the Indian, with his hair falling about his face, his head uncovered, and the rest of his form concealed beneath his blanket. As his swarthy visage, with its muscles fixed in rigid composure, was seen under the light of the moon, which struck his face obliquely, he seemed a picture of resigned old age, on whom the storms of winter had beaten in vain, for the greater part of a century; but when, in turning his head, the rays fell directly on his dark, fiery eyes, they told a tale of passions unrestrained, and of thoughts free as the air he breathed (131).[1]

Such a passage clearly challenges a reader to reflect on his own position within such a group: "Am I like the clergyman or like the Indian?" We soon recognize the firmness and intelligence in Cooper's purpose that we should see important virtues in both contrasting possibilities: "Am I not both fierce in my passions, by nature, and mildly benevolent, by culture?"

This same contrast of tame versus wild has been presented by the British novelists Defoe and Scott. What *The Pioneers* added to the adventure material were two themes derived specifically from the American experience: (1) the establishment of law in the settlements; and (2) the wastefulness of the frontiersmen—the way they despoiled the great resources of nature. The reader is asked to think seriously about the questions raised by these processes. Apropos of the first, the two main thematic characters, Natty and Judge Temple, come into conflict, for the former has become an independent hunter in order to escape from laws and all the impedimenta of civilization; while the latter's vocation is to establish civilization's claims, prohibitions, values, and rewards. This theme (obviously corresponding to the settlement process all over America) reaches a climax when the Judge condemns the hunter to sit in the stocks for breaking new laws against killing animals out of season. Apropos of the second theme of waste, however, the two men are on the same side, feeling equally revolted when a group of townsmen slaughter a huge flight of pigeons by firing a cannon into the flock.

Law and waste are not, however, the themes most readers associate with Cooper. Our images of the stories he tells are more simply adventurous. And the reason is not merely the vulgarization of the Natty Bumppo stories by later writers and film makers. Cooper himself, in his later volumes, moved away from the farmer's frontier to the hunter's frontier, and his stories employed different motifs. In, for example, *The Last of the Mohicans*, the main motifs are the group flight of whites through the wilderness (chased by Indians) and the fate worse than death, the rape of a white woman by an Indian—the mere presence of a white woman in the forest is assumed to set every Indian for miles around aflame with lust. Such images (likely to arouse racist and sexist passions in the white reader) do not appear in Defoe and Scott, and they can be considered to be Cooper's contribution to the genre. They were to provide later writers with powerful motors of plot and feeling. Obviously, these motifs moved the meaning of adventure in directions very different from law and waste.

The latter themes, however, represent something important in Cooper, something that is perhaps his best contribution to the genre—a sense of responsibility, the adventurer's responsibility to the environment and to the generations to come. His best work speaks for that sense of responsibility in a number of ways. Its prime spokesman in *The Pioneer* is Judge Temple, who attracts more of Cooper's affection and esteem than any other character. (This was, in fact, a portrait of Cooper's father, whom he much admired.) The Judge wanted to protect the environment: " 'The first object of my solicitude, friend Jones,' returned [Temple], 'is to protect the source of this great mine of comfort and wealth from the extravagance of the people themselves' " (221).

Later he reflects upon a past time of famine, and his daughter urges him to describe what he did in what must have been his hour of heroism, saying, "Upon thee must have fallen all the responsibility, if not the suffering." (Note her Quaker use of "thee.") " 'It did, Elizabeth,' returned the Judge . . . 'I had hundreds, at that dreadful time, daily looking up to me for bread . . . It was not a moment for inaction. I purchased cargoes of wheat from the granaries of Pennsylvania . . . Seines were made, and the lakes and rivers were dragged for fish. Something like a miracle was wrought in our favor, for enormous shoals of herring were discovered to have wandered five hundred miles through the windings of the impetuous Susquehanna, and the lake was alive with their numbers' " (235). The Judge is a man of peace and not of war—a point the book makes much of—and this incident is a sort of miracle of the loaves and fishes. It is in the name of such experiences of famine and responsibility that the Judge speaks out against waste, and that is why he is one of the novel's heroes.

At the story's end, Natty sets out for the West, away from the settlements, alone. The representative of an earlier and outdated life of freedom, he cannot accommodate himself to the rule of law. History is against him. Judge Temple's time has come, the time of law. Even so, there are ominous signs that the rule of law is still feeble in the hearts and minds of even the best Americans. In one scene of waste we see 2,000 fish brought in with one drag of a net. The Judge calls this "a fearful expenditure of the choicest gifts of providence" (261) and notes that the fish "already begin to disappear, before the wasteful extravagance of man" (263).

Nonetheless, he does not try to prevent the seining. Although a figure of authority in his town, the Judge "appeared to understand that all opposition to the will of the Sheriff would be useless, and he strolled from the place" (270). Indeed, he himself later yields to "the excitement of the moment," and joins in the sport.

A later scene of the same sort depicts a deer hunt out of season and involves Natty, Chingachgook the Indian, and Edwards. At first Natty will not kill the deer, and Edwards—when Natty begins to waver—warns him against doing so. The morally right thing to do is made perfectly clear. But again "the excitement of the moment" takes over. " 'Hurrah!' shouted Edwards, inflamed beyond prudence at the sight" (304). And Chingachgook's dark eye, we are told, was dancing as brightly and wildly as the deer's own. When the killing is complete, Natty laughs and says, " 'This warms a body's blood, old John' " (305); and though the Indian had long been drooping with his years and with the calamities of his race, the "invigorating and exciting sport had caused a gleam of sunshine to cross his swarthy face" (306). It seems that the excitement of killing is too great for even the best men's sense of law and responsibility to restrain it. When such passions are aroused, they will always triumph, even in the morally responsible.

The acknowledgment of such truths is at once the weakness and the strength of the adventure. Compared with the serious novel, it is morally weak. In the latter at its best—in Jane Austen or George Eliot—the moral values are not allowed to slide at the crucial moment. Right is right and wrong is wrong, and the novelist is always demonstrating the truth of that proposition. In the adventure, however, moral values *are* allowed to slide; the hero goes against his or the writer's professed values, and the latter, in effect, shrugs his shoulders.

Robinson Crusoe, in this matter a typical adventure, shows us the hero deciding that it is wrong to make war, even on the cannibal savages who have landed on his island; but when he sees that they have white captives with them, all his former reasoning is forgotten. Indeed, Crusoe's adventure begins and ends in disobedience of the moral law. His father had told him not to go to sea, but to do his duty in that social station to which God had appointed him: the family and town in which he was born. Going to sea, he disobeys both his father and the divine law. But, of course, both Defoe and the reader *want* him to go to sea.

Still the adventure, if morally weaker, is historically stronger than the serious novel, which does not reflect the strength of the forces that triumph over moral values; or it reflects them only in the pedagogical form of evil or in the exotic form of tragedy. The adventure shows the struggle between these forces and moral values in all its ordinariness; and with the ordinary defeat of the latter, it shows the limits of morality and art.

Cooper's moral intention in *The Pioneers* is as clear and firm as it ever is in adventure, although his morality is in some ways very different from that of serious readers today. His sense of values is based on adventure, manliness, and patriotism, and he gives Americans a picture of their society that assigns a leading part to the aristo-military caste that embodies these values. Thematically speaking, this is the story of how a piece of land (representing America as a whole) passes from the hands of a Quaker merchant into those of a military family. Edwards, the aristocrat, will rule what Temple the Quaker once owned; just as the United States of America will march its armies into the wilderness where once traders and missionaries wandered at their will. This meaning is complicated by the fact that that military family, the Effinghams or Edwards, were the original owners of the land, before it was Temple's. They had received it as a gift from the Delaware Indians and had owned it under the British. Thus Edwards, the scion of that family, represents the British and the Indians, as well as the American aristocracy. When he marries Elizabeth Temple, the heiress of the Quaker merchant, the land returns to its right and original owners in several senses.

Cooper is very bold in evoking the caste feeling. The Effinghams are presented quite approvingly as one of those families who "thought it a degradation to its members to descend to the pursuits of commerce; and who never emerged from the privacy of their domestic life, unless to preside in the councils of the colony, or to bear arms in her defence . . . [As soldiers, moreover, they felt that] they were entitled to receive the greatest deference from the peaceful occupants of the soil" (17). Young Effingham made friends with Marmaduke Temple at school, and even became his sleeping partner in a commercial enterprise; but he kept the fact secret: "To the descendant of a line of soldiers, commerce, even in that indirect manner, seemed a degrading pursuit" (20).

During the War of Independence, while Effingham is first a soldier and then a refugee, the nonviolent merchant, Temple, "never seemed to lose sight of his own interests"; he bought up Effingham's estates at low prices. (This is offered as in some sense sordidly typical of a Quaker merchant, although it later turns out that Temple's motives were pure.) He remains something of a Quaker in his use of "thee" and in refusing to hang bells on his sleigh; and at the end of the book he describes his old friend as, like the young Edwards, " 'sometimes hasty and rash.' The Judge continued, in a self-condemning manner, 'Perhaps my fault lies the other way; I may possibly look too far ahead, and calculate too deeply' " (458). This is, to Cooper, a typically mercantile trait, and the comment is characterization by caste. The intention is not entirely clear at first reading because Cooper describes Temple's gentlemanly features rather than his Quaker and mercantile ones. He stresses that Temple is becoming, as a result of living the gentlemanly life, not what he originally was. He is now a judge and not a merchant, an Episcopalian and not a Quaker, and his daughter Elizabeth is clearly of the aristo-military caste, a fit bride for Edwards (the only touch of the Quaker is her use of "thee").

These distinctions of caste are defined as inevitable, biological. We are misled about the Judge's character because he has "a fine manly face" with eyes full of humor (4). In Cooper's vocabulary, this tells us that Temple is a gentleman. Edwards, being incognito, has no external determinants; but he is an aristocrat in every inch of his physique. He is nobly formed, rounded, rich voiced. When he takes off his hat, his head is seen to be "covered with hair that rivalled in color and gloss the locks of Elizabeth . . . there was something noble in the rounded outlines of his head and brow . . . [And when he speaks] the rich manly sounds of a youthful male voice proceeded from the opposite part of the room. Miss Temple knew the tones of the young hunter instantly" (120).

But Edwards is not merely genteel. He is a different kind of gentleman from the Judge, as befits his ancestry. He is aristo-military and owns "fierce and uncontrollable passions" (309), notably the passion for revenge upon the usurper of his family estate. These make him the novel's hero. Elizabeth, though the moralist of the story, is attracted to Edwards *because* of his passions. They are associated for us with his "Indian descent"; he tells Louisa Grant that revenge is a virtue with an Indian. In fact, he has no Indian blood, although his grandfather was made an honorary Delaware, and the idea that he is part-Indian is often rumored in the novel, and welcomed by Elizabeth.

This complex—revenger-aristocrat-Indian—fits smoothly into a pattern prevalent in nineteenth-century fiction, especially adventures and Gothic tales. (Perhaps Dumas's *The Count of Monte Cristo* and Verne's *20,000 Leagues Under the Sea* have the most famous avenger heroes.) The function of this motif is to evoke the "feudal" idea of the feud, the vendetta, which in the nineteenth century belonged, like the duel, to the past and to the aristocracy. That caste and that mode of pursuing quarrels belonged to the premodern world, the world of passion, mystery, and splendor, that was put out of our reach by modern reason. The nineteenth-century avenger is usually a Byronic, dispossessed noble (or he acts like one by virtue of his thirst for revenge). The revenge guarantees that fieriness of temperament that was indispensable to an adventure hero. Politically, it is another piece of propaganda for the aristo-military caste.

Cooper draws marked physical distinctions between the people of this caste—who have the right shape and size—and members of the other castes, who are physically exaggerated or contorted in a caricatural way, like drawings by Hogarth or a cartoonist. Aristocrats are rounded, while nonaristocrats are not. Thus Remarkable Pettibone, for example, has a "tall, meagre, shapeless figure, sharp features, and a somewhat acute expression in her physiognomy" (51). Elnathan Todd stands six feet four inches, with shoulders "so narrow that the long dangling arms that they supported seemed to issue out of his back" (61). Mr. Doolittle "belonged physically to a class of his countrymen, to whom nature has denied, in their formation, the use of curved lines" (452). And Cooper denies them full human sympathy; he has Natty shoot Doolittle in the behind for our amusement. When we are told that Louisa Grant's face excited deep interest by its sweet and perhaps melancholy expression (120), we cannot but reflect that however sad Remarkable Pettibone might get, her face would never be recommended to us as interesting.

This recommendation of the aristo-military caste is harmoniously allied to a repudiation of radical Christianity, as represented by Quakerism and Moravianism. Radical religion is the ultimate enemy of caste thinking because it imposes one identical moral and social duty on every group; it is especially hostile to the aristo-military caste, which derives its high status and moral justification only from war. Major Effingham, we are told, hated the Quakers of Pennsylvania because "the safety of himself and his troops were jeopardized by the peaceful policy of that colony" (17). Natty tells us that Chingachgook's life was ruined when he was Christianized by the Moravians, " 'who was always over intimate with the Delawares . . . It's my opinion that had they [the Delawares] been left to themselves, there would be no such doings now' " (151).

Later on, Chingachgook tells Elizabeth that the Delawares had given their land—now the Temple estate—to Major Effingham because " 'He was strong, and they were women, and he helped them' " (415). They had turned into women because Christian ministers had persuaded them to give up making war. According to the values of the adventure, with its cult of manliness, emasculation is an ultimate evil, and Cooper clearly follows that value scheme rather than the Christian one. At the story's end, Major Effingham's epitaph describes him as a man of valor and chivalry, then adds his Christianity as something extra: "To these virtues he added the graces of a Christian" (471).

This treatment of the Quakers and Moravians is supported indirectly by the satire aimed at the New England "Dissenters"— the Templeton settlers who come from "the *moral* states of Connecticut and Massachusetts" [91; my emphasis]. In the religious spectrum, the opposite of the religious radicalism of the Quakers is Episcopalianism, the Christianity of warriors, bishops, and kings. This is what Cooper prefers, among the Christian sects, although his own fundamental religious position in the novel is Romantic pantheism.

The New England sects are presented as tending away from Episcopalianism, even though not committed to peace. They are moral and religious enthusiasts. Cooper distastefully describes New England as "a people who owed their very existence, as a distinct nation, to the doctrinal characters of their ancestors" (124), and he confidently expects all his readers to join him in his distaste. Jotham, one of the New Englanders in Templeton, is said to have "a discontented expression of countenance, and with something extremely shiftless in his whole air. Thus spoken to, after turning and twisting a little, by way of preparation, he made a reply" (154). It is clear that this twisting and writhing had the same significance for Cooper as it was to have for Dickens, who used the same symbolism in his portrait of Uriah Heep in *David Copperfield.* It is the sign of something dishonorable and unmanly in these low-caste, low-church figures, whom the reader is expected to join the writer in detesting. They are recusants from the religion of manliness; they lack form and fire, nobility and force.

This idea is expressed again in the criticism of American settlement life that takes up so many pages of *The Pioneers'* comic writing. The settlements lack social hierarchy, and so they lack organic form. American doctors, American lawyers, American architecture, American church services—much of the novel is a series of humorous complaints about the eccentricity, provinciality, formlessness of all these people and institutions. Their characters are parodies of the real thing (which is to be found, of course, in England).

None of this is adventure writing, of course, for Natty Bumppo was not originally designed to be a hero of adventure, and *The Pioneers* has only a few episodes that are really adventurous. Leon Howard has said that Cooper originally set out to become the Maria Edgeworth of the American frontier; and that formula fits the author of *The Pioneers,* though the later Natty stories are nothing like Maria Edgeworth's.[2] What forced the change was presumably the mythic vitality of the idea Cooper had stumbled across, and the readers' enthusiasm for Natty.

It seems likely that the reader was originally intended to identify more completely with Judge Temple; for in the early passages Natty is presented in caricatural terms that align him with the other low-caste characters. After his first speech, he "drew his bare hand across the bottom of his nose, and again opened his enormous mouth with a kind of inward laugh" (7). He is tall and thin to the point of emaciation, with a single tooth (tusk), and makes a thick hissing noise when he laughs. When he walks, at every step, "his body lowered several inches, his knees yielding with an inclination inward" (15). He is thus like Elnathan Todd and Mr. Doolittle. By page 367, however, he is the vehicle of a noble rhetoric: "What would ye have with an old and helpless man?" he asks; and by the end he is a poet: "Why lad, they tell me, that on the Big Lakes, there's the best of hunting, and a great range, without a white man on it, unless it may be one like myself. I'm weary of living in clearings, and where the hammer is sounding in my ears from sunrise to sundown" (473).

Here he is being associated (implicitly) with Daniel Boone and the other great American pioneers. In the last sentence of the book we are told that "He had gone far towards the setting sun,—the foremost in that band of Pioneers, who are opening the way for the march of our nation across the continent" (476). But he is also dissociated from certain other frontier figures— from the anarchic, comically ebullient frontier heroes like Davy Crockett. The dissociation becomes clearer in later stories, but even here it is implicitly conveyed by the contrast drawn between Natty and Billy Kirby, "the noisy, boisterous, reckless lad," who takes a lead in the wasting of natural resources (188). Cooper is much concerned to assign to Natty, the noble solitary, the virtue of embodying America; and to assign to Edwards, the aristocrat, the right to inherit settled America from him, once Natty has to "move on." Billy Kirby, like Davy Crockett, is outside the line of inheritance.

The Maria Edgeworth story of culture in the settlement, in any case, Cooper did not write, at least successfully; and we can say that nobody else wrote it either. America's readers were more interested in the hunter's frontier than in the farmer's. Cooper's attempt at that kind of settlement genre was ruined not only by the presence of Natty Bumppo, but also by that of Elizabeth Temple, also a strong mythic character in her own different way. Yet if Natty had to be given the adventure novel for his setting, Elizabeth should have been given the domestic novel. (Cooper did in fact write domestic novels about the Effinghams, and they include several strong female characters.) Both these genres proved stronger than the story of the settlements.

Elizabeth embodies the values of her genre (let us call it the Jane Austen novel) so fully, even fiercely, that she makes everything in this story—everything in Templeton—ridiculous; as a consequence, the reader feels out of sympathy with her and her fond creator. Cooper asks us to take Templeton seriously, but if we see it through her eyes, we cannot. By her standards, Templeton is pathetic. If we compare her with Edith, the corresponding figure in *Nick of the Woods,* we see how much more seriously Cooper could take women than Bird could. Cooper had more talent than Bird for the serious domestic novel; perhaps, in fact, he had a more natural predilection for that than he had for the adventure. But regardless of his personal talent and predilection, the times called for the adventure, and richly did his country reward him for answering that cultural vocation. No literary career shows as clearly as Cooper's the power of the adventure genre in America—in this case, its power to deflect a talent from a more natural path.

Elizabeth is the supreme object-of-value of the culture her father is trying to establish. It is so that every man may have a daughter or a bride like her that the settlements must become cultured, that the army of progress marches westward. At the beginning of the novel, when she enters her father's house after a long absence at school, the dog looks wistfully at the door that closed behind her and "laid himself in the kennel that was placed nigh by, as if conscious that the house contained something of additional value to guard" (52). But besides being an object-of-value, she is an incarnate sense of values. When Templeton's comic German and Frenchman meet the Temples' sled outside the town, their comic patter fills the air until her voice "sounded in the clear air of the hills like tones of silver," saying exactly the right thing, light, graceful, spirited, and gracious (37). And she remains the social and moral tuning fork for the rest of the narrative.

Her fierceness (which makes her an interesting character, although destructive to the adventure form of this novel) is revealed by the reactions of other characters to her. Remarkable Pettibone "felt a little appalled, when . . . the large black hood was removed, and . . . the sweet but commanding features of the young lady [were] exposed to view (55) . . . As the last shawl fell aside, and she [Elizabeth] stood, dressed in a rich blue riding habit that fitted her form with the nicest exactness . . . and with every feature of her speaking countenance illuminated by the lights which flared about her, Remarkable felt that her own power had ended" (56).

How right she was! Wherever Elizabeth may be, she will be in charge, because she knows best. She terrifies the other characters. Thus when Elnathan Todd enters the Temples' house, to act as doctor, he sees "Elizabeth in her riding habit, richly laced with gold cord, her fine form bending towards him, with her face expressing deep anxiety in every one of its beautiful features. The enormous bony knees of the physician struck each other with a noise that was audible" (66).

Nonetheless, the settlement novel could not accommodate so powerful an incarnation of values as Elizabeth. Indeed, Cooper's attraction to values (a theme carrying with it an affinity for hierarchical social situations) always hampered his attempts to write Natty Bumppo adventures, because there was in them no active role for a woman to play, nor for any male arbiter of manners either. Cooper was at his best in nautical adventures, at least partly because in a ship, even if there is no Elizabeth, the men live in a clearly hierarchical social system in which correct behavior is both important and easily measured.

In his preface to *The Pilot*, Cooper expressed the hope that the public interest his books have aroused in the plight of sailors may "tend to a melioration of their condition," for his love of sailors was profound if paternalist. Expressing this hope, however, leads him on to a couple of pages of social commentary that are very characteristic of Cooper: "With several hundred rude beings confined within the narrow limits of a vessel, men of all nations and of the lowest habits, it would be to the last degree indiscreet to commence their reformation by relaxing the bonds of discipline, under the mistaken impulses of a false philanthropy." The issue of the flogging of American sailors he dismisses with a reference to the tens of thousands of Americans ashore who "would be greatly benefited by a judicious flogging." He urges the public to trust "the experience of those who have long governed turbulent men," and he deplores the reform, peace, and temperance societies that have replaced the churches as moral law-givers.[3]

In these attitudes Cooper was a traditional adventure writer and (by his own standards) a democrat. The navy had always been regarded in England as the bulwark of liberty and the opposite of a standing army. In the late seventeenth century, Blackstone wrote, in his famous *Commentaries on the Law*, that the navy was England's best defense, because it was "an army from which, however strong and powerful, no damage can be apprehended to liberty." For the danger to liberty could come from below as well as from above, as the Civil War of the seventeenth century had just demonstrated; from the mob as well as from the throne; the navy was a bulwark of discipline as well as freedom. This was also Cooper's attitude in the nineteenth century, and it was shared by his most enthusiastic readers, like Parkman, Prescott, and Dana, the last of whom took up the same themes and developed them in *Two Years Before the Mast.* Thus the nautical novel was distinguished, among the other forms of adventure, as being the most clearly a gentleman's genre. It always maintained a clear distinction between captain and crew and their respective caste characteristics.

The frontier, as we shall see, presented more difficult problems for the novelists who tried to write adventures that would be true both to America—the land of freedom—and to literature—the guarantor of culture and gentility. This conflict is why Cooper's forest adventures are inferior to his sea novels. Of course, it was the forest adventure that won Cooper his fame and that concerns us here, and he made an important contribution to it, in *The Pioneers,* in the development of several adventure motifs. Natty's rifle, for example, although it did not receive the stress here that Cooper gives it in later novels, has an important symbolic function in the plot. Cooper tells us, as Defoe told us, that white culture is built on guns and explosives. Natty asks Elizabeth to buy him some gunpowder and to bring it to him on the mountaintop. She finds Chingachgook there instead and hands it to him, whereupon he tells her: "Daughter, the Great Spirit gave your fathers to know how to make guns and powder, that they might sweep the Indian from the land" (418). In the forest fire, a chance spark ignites the explosive, and the gunpowder causes his death.

By his imaginative development of such motifs Cooper won his place in the long line of adventure writers that began with Defoe (whose Crusoe also has a rifle of great symbolic value). He put together the three essential ingredients of significant adventure: frontier anecdote (although his is rather thin), literary romance (rather too rich), and anthropological concern (about the nature of white Americans). This combination is enough to explain and even justify his immense popularity, which is, after all, sufficient reason for considering him. At the time of his death in 1851, Cooper was, according to Leon Howard, the most widely read of all American novelists, and he remained so for more than a century afterwards (v). America wanted adventures, and the book-buying class wanted stories in which an American gentleman was the adventurer. They wanted them with such fierceness of appetite that they would even swallow Cooper's crude concoctions.

Chapter 3   IRVING'S
              A TOUR ON
              THE PRAIRIES
              (1832)

This book tells the story of Washington Irving's 1832 sojourn on the prairie in Indian Territory, which later became the state of Oklahoma. He served there as secretary to Henry Ellsworth, one of the three commissioners to the western Indians, the federal officials assigned to help in the resettlement of the Indians forced to move west from their homes east of the Mississippi. Irving was in no personal danger during those months, nor did he perform an adventurer's feats of skill, cunning, or leadership. But he did live in the land of adventure, every day seeing hunts, wild animals, Indians, and white adventurers.

If we were to pass directly from Cooper to Bird, we would find the same plot expressing the same political and social preoccupations. *Nick of the Woods* is also about the inheritance of a piece of land and also has a genteel hero who has to abandon his privileges and apprentice himself to an uneducated Man of the Woods in order to become a true American. That is the American adventure plot, as America's fiction writers told it. But American adventure was not just fiction; it was also autobiography. In that genre the plot told how the writer (necessarily himself genteel) went West or went to sea, exposed himself to that natural and social roughness, and reported back (now both tough and sensitive) to city readers what it was like out there. The first of the writers to work this vein was Washington Irving.

Irving was not, however, an adventure writer. Indeed, he was primarily the opposite—a man of letters, the most famous man of letters in the America of his time (whose literary capital was Philadelphia). Representing literature at its purest, he might well have been hostile to the adventure, for there was a dialectic within the world of literature that tended to drive the two apart. The man of letters is often a man of peace, to whom the warrior-adventurer is an enemy. Parkman, for example, described Cooper as a writer for men of action, and so the opposite of Hawthorne, the man of letters—and Poe described Cooper as the opposite of a writer like himself, the Romantic Artist. Irving, however, belonged to a party—similar to the one led by Scott in England—called the Knickerbocker School, which reconciled the two interests and wrote to please both men of action and men of taste. Although we tend to identify him with works of literary whimsy, he also wrote three books that were in some sense adventures—*A Tour on the Prairies, Astoria*, and *Captain Bonneville*—which I shall discuss in this chapter.

As no one of the three is clearly superior for our purposes, we can use *A Tour* as representative of Irving's other writings in this genre; it can also represent works of literature to come, like those by Dana and Parkman. *Astoria* and *Bonneville*, on the other hand, are treatments of historical documents, and have influenced historians more than men of letters.

Irving is an important figure to consider in the argument about adventure for various reasons. First, he makes a very clear connection between adventure and nationalism; his historical heroes are both adventurers and extenders of the national boundaries. More importantly, although *the* American writer of his day, he did better in the humble adventure genre than in the more prestigious literary forms for which he is better known. He is therefore an example of the way the adventure form brought to fruition the talents of American writers. Above all, he shows us the important social ideas that stiffen and structure the exciting narrative—ideas of nationality, class, and social function that consort naturally with that of adventure. For adventure was not just exciting narrative, it was also an ideology—the energizing myth of empire.

Earlier, in 1815, Irving had gone to Europe and stayed for seventeen years. By then he was famous as a writer but anxious about his reputation at home, for Americans were hypersensitive to the disloyalty of expatriation, especially on the part of writers. On his return he immediately made this trip to Indian Territory and described it in *A Tour on the Prairies*, which was written in

1832 and published in 1835. The long introduction, in which he discusses his expatriation, gives the impression that he undertook this expedition in expiation. Subsequently he wrote, in quick succession, *Astoria* (1836) and *The Adventures of Captain Bonneville* (1837), which are also western adventures and have a clear connection to national expansion. More clearly in Irving than in any other American writer, we can see how the individual adventure contributes to national adventure and how literature pays tribute to nationalism.

The introduction to *Astoria*, however, makes the claim that his interest was of long standing, not something fabricated in the 1830s to serve his literary career. He tells us that as long ago as 1803, in Canada, he had known "men who had passed years remote from civilized society, among distant and savage tribes, and who had wonders to recount of their wide and wild peregrinations, their hunting exploits, and their perilous adventures and hairbreadth escapes among the Indians. I was at an age when the imagination lent its colouring to everything, and the stories of the Sinbads of the wilderness made the life of a trapper and fur trader perfect romance to me . . . [such stories] . . . have always been themes of charmed interest to me; and I have felt anxious to get at the details of their adventurous expeditions" (*A*xiv).[1]

This is, of course, very much the language of the Romantic man of letters talking of "the age when the imagination lent its colouring to everything" and of "perfect romance" and "charmed interest." Irving was more literary than Cooper, and so he was more "Romantic." This literariness is his special contribution to American adventure; he translates it into Romantic terms. In *Captain Bonneville*, for example, he says: "It is not easy to do justice to the exulting feelings of the worthy captain, at finding himself at the head of a stout band of hunters, trappers, and woodmen; fairly launched on the broad prairies, with his face to the boundless West. The tamest inhabitant of cities, the veriest spoiled child of civilization, feels his heart dilate and his pulse beat high, on finding himself on horseback in the glorious wilderness." (*CB*14).

Irving makes a Romantic cult of freedom, for example in his frequent passages about the wild horses of the plains and their superiority to tame ones. Sometimes he invokes the image of the Romantic bandit, who is already familiar in Byronic drama and in opera, to explain the Indians and the hunters: "Such is the glorious independence of man in a savage state," he says in *A Tour on the Prairies*, "We of society are slaves, not so much to others as to ourselves" (*T*34). If all this sounds rather loose or "literary," we are reassured by the concluding lines of the passage from *Astoria*; for Irving wanted to get at the *details* of the hunters' adventures, and he does in fact deal in facts. What he describes in that passage is a real cult of adventure; and the reader's imagination is pressed into contact with the facts as well as the feelings of this legendary Americanism.

Astoria was the trading post the New York millionaire John Jacob Astor planned to establish at the mouth of the Columbia River in Oregon in order to control the fur trade of the continent in the interests of the United States. The British, the Canadians, and the Russians were also competing for the trade. Irving's *Astoria* is a history of that trading post. As he says at the beginning of the first chapter,

> Two leading objects of commercial gain have given birth to wide and daring enterprise in the early history of the Americas; the precious metals of the south, and the rich peltries of the north. While the fiery and magnificent Spaniard, inflamed with the mania for gold, has extended his discoveries and conquests over those brilliant countries scorched by the ardent sun of the tropics, the adroit and buoyant Frenchman and the cool and calculating Briton have pursued the less splendid . . . [traffic in furs] (*A*5).

This paragraph embodies the ideas of adventure as it had developed from Elizabethan times on. Most importantly, it sets in opposition the two forms of empire that adventure writers always talked about: on the one hand, the complex of traditional (Spanish) imperialism, the tropics, fire, gold, mania, glory; and on the other, the complex of modern and modest (British and French) enterprise, animals, furs, the North, river traffic, cool calculation, and skillful buoyancy. That polarity can be found in *Robinson Crusoe* itself, and in a thousand other documents of modernist ideology, fictional and nonfictional.

Astor was a merchant, a private citizen who traded for his own profit, but the interest he took in this enterprise was also nationalistic and patriotic. Irving, besides being Astor's friend, was eager to have access to the documents of exploration the fur trader had accumulated. Astor's use of those documents was, in some ways, like that of the East India Company 200 years before; both were commercial companies, promoting individual enterprise in the name of the whole nation. And what Irving did in writing *Astoria* was comparable (on a smaller scale) with what the Hakluyts had done for the East India Company in the early seventeenth century, when they compiled and published various narratives of the East India Company's sea voyages and adventures in commercial enterprise. The company put a copy of the *Voyages* in the cabin of every captain in their employ, and a hundred years later the narratives were a major source for Defoe. Indeed, *Robinson Crusoe* crystallized them into a single mythic narrative. Irving can be said to be doing the same thing in *Astoria*. He says that he gave Astor's documents "that unity so much sought after in works of fiction, and considered so important to the interests of history" (*A*4). Irving was, however, a more self-conscious and ambitious literary artist than Defoe—closer to Scott or Lamb in the elegance of his style and form.

Nonetheless, the title *Astoria* announces a factual narrative and a simple (nationalist and adventurous) motive, and the promise is kept. There are two narratives, as Astor's men made two journeys to Oregon: one by sea, around Cape Horn, and the other by land, over the continent. The book ends with the failure of the enterprise in 1813; an English naval squadron causes the American traders to retreat, and Astoria becomes Fort George. The last words of the book are Irving's regret that the American government had failed to take full possession and initiate empire.

Chapter 1 shows Irving's strong sense of the anthropological interest of his subject. He is especially interested in the exotic and lavish life-styles of those engaged in the fur trade in the eighteenth century, portraying them in picturesque terms appropriate to adventure. Thus the merchant at his trading post "had a little world of self-indulgence and misrule around him . . . his harem of Indian beauties, and his troop of half-breed children; nor was there ever wanting a loutish train of Indians" (*A*8). When in New York these men bought lavishly at the goldsmith's, showing "a gorgeous prodigality, such as was often to be noticed in former times in Southern planters, and West Indian Creoles, when flush with the profits of their plantations" (*A*11). In Montreal, he tells us, the merchants cleared a 200 percent profit from the naked Indians who had sold them their furs; and he quotes La Hontan on the extravagance of the Coureurs des Bois: "The bachelors act just as our East India men and pirates are wont to do; for they lavish, eat, drink, and play all away as long as the goods hold out" (*A*7). Back in the woods they lived like Indians, or worse, and impeded the influence of the missionaries.

These picturesque terms are not trivial in significance. They signify a social theory we shall meet often in later adventures, an intellectually challenging theory that modern readers tend to overlook because it is so unlike the social theories we now take seriously. Irving sees a nation, we might say, in terms of its castes—as a mosaic of social contrasts—as incompatible but complementary types; and he rejoices in their incompatibility in a way that is implicitly treacherous to the democratic faith. The contrasting castes Irving sees making up the nation have conflicting interests. He does not take seriously the egalitarian populism that is the basic political piety of the modern world-system. He believes in the nation rather than in democracy, and so he believes in the caste system which is the organic structure of a nation. He sees his fellow Americans as soldiers or merchants or robbers or priests, fundamentally unlike each other, and he rejoices in each equally; that is why the American scene often sounds, in his descriptions, like a medieval principality or a city in the Orient.

He tells us, for example, that after the North West Company was founded in the 1780s, two opposite social types emerged, the clerks and the partners. The former came mostly from the lowlands of Scotland and were full of perseverance, thrift, and fidelity—the mercantile virtues. But the partners "ascended the rivers in great state, like sovereigns making a progress; or rather, like highland chieftains navigating their subject lakes. They were wrapped in rich furs . . . [and they brought] cooks and bakers, together with delicacies of every kind." They liked to entertain English aristocrats as their guests. Their councils in Fort William were held in great state, like meetings of the House of Lords in London, and "these grave and weighty councils were alternated by huge feasts and revels like some of the old feasts described in highland castles . . . While the chiefs thus revelled in hall, and made the rafters resound . . . their merriment was echoed, and prolonged, by a mongrel legion of retainers [voyageurs and Indians]" (*A*12–13).

Quite apart from the specific allusions (to highland castles and to making the rafters resound) one sees that Irving has learned from Scott the general lesson of the Waverley novels: he has learned to root romance in historical reality; to present as existent in the present, modes of splendor, mystery, and passion, that belong to the past. He does this without asking his readers to give up their grip on reality: "But we are talking of things that are fast fading away! The march of mechanical invention is driving everything poetical before it. The steamboats . . . subdue the world into commonplace" (*A*29).

Chapter 2 introduces Astor as a hero of commerce who does what the government desires done, what it had itself impotently designed to advance America's interests in Oregon. Astor got Jefferson's approval for his scheme; and in 1809 got from the state of New York a charter for his American Fur Company (funded by a million dollars of his own money). "He considered his projected establishment at the mouth of the Columbia as the emporium to an immense commerce; as a colony that would form the germ of a wide civilization; that would, in fact, carry the American population across the Rocky Mountains and spread it along the shores of the Pacific; as it already animated the shores of the Atlantic" (*A*23).

Irving tells us that Astor much regretted that "the true nature and extent of his enterprise and its national character and importance had never been understood . . . [he wanted the world to know] . . . of the fur-trade; of its remote and adventurous enterprises, and of the various people, and tribes, and castes, and characters, civilized and savage, [that] affected its operations" (*A*3).

It is worth noting the word "caste" here, for it is one that recurs. Irving describes the Canadian voyageurs as "one of those distinct and strongly marked castes or orders of people, springing up in this vast continent, out of geographical circumstances" (*A*28). The word obviously implies that these groups are identified each by a way of life so idiosyncratic that its members are separated off from their fellow citizens; less obviously, perhaps, it implies that the writer rejoices in these picturesque separations and likes to see society in caste terms.

Irving characterizes the American castes with an almost theatrical vividness that so stresses difference as to subvert the ordinariness, the generic humanity valued by pure democrats. Thus he tells us that in the streets of St. Louis you could see "the hectoring, extravagant, bragging boatmen of the Missouri, with the gay, grimacing, singing, good-humored Canadian voyageurs; vagrant Indians of various tribes loitered about the streets; now and then a stark Kentucky hunter" (*A*92–93). These groups live each according to its own ethos, which is radically unlike the others.

In *Captain Bonneville* he describes how some rangers "came dashing forward at full speed, firing their fusees, and yelling in Indian style. Their dark sunburnt faces, and long flowing hair, their leggins, flaps, mocassins, and richly dyed blankets, and their painted horses gaily caparisoned, gave them so much the air and appearance of Indians . . . and a day it was, of boast, and swagger, and rodomontado" (*A*48). When such types or groups are put together, as they are in the streets of St. Louis or at a trappers' rendezvous, you get a motley mosaic, which can be compared with accounts of travelers to cities in India. The comparison is an appropriate one, for the viewer understands them, and they understand themselves, not as the American nation united in one democratic faith, but as a juxtaposition of incompatible but complementary castes. This was a characteristic vision of adventure, in England as well as in America.

It is no surprise, therefore, to find that Irving often reminds us of Cooper. He takes, for instance, the same lofty and ironic attitude toward New Englanders—whose vision of America was not picturesque because they were religious radicals and "democrats" by origin. He implies that New Englanders cut a rather ludicrous figure on the frontier or on an adventure. In *Captain Bonneville*, Irving describes Mr. Wyeth's "party of regular 'down-easters,' that is to say, people of New England, who, with the all-penetrating and all-pervading spirit of their race, were now pushing their way into a new field of enterprise" (*CB*37). In *A Tour on the Prairies*, he describes Commissioner Ellsworth as having spent his life in "the society of deacons, elders, and select men, on the peaceful banks of the Connecticut; when suddenly he had been called to mount his steed, shoulder his rifle, and mingle among stark hunters, backwoodsmen, and naked savages, on the trackless wilds of the Far West" (*T*12).

More strikingly, Irving shares Cooper's attitude toward Quakers and the emasculation of Indian tribes by religion. In *Captain Bonneville* he compares the Nez Percés Indians with Quakers. The Captain, he tells us, was at first amazed by this tribe's "unaffected tenderness and piety," because he had been "accustomed to find the wretched Indian revelling in blood, and stained by all the vices which can degrade human nature" (*CB*57). The Nez Percés had heard of Christianity from missionaries; "in fact, the anti-belligerent policy of this tribe, may have sprung from the doctrines of Christian charity . . . These have become blended with their own wild rites . . . On the Sabbath, men, women, and children array themselves in their best style, and assemble around a pole erected at the head of the camp. Here they go through a wild fantastic ceremonial; strongly resembling the religious dances of the Shaking Quakers; but from its enthusiasm, much more striking and impressive" (*CB*58).

He saw something similar in a related tribe, the Pends Oreilles or Hanging Ears: "This tribe, like the Nez Percés, evince strong and peculiar feelings of natural piety. Their religion is not a mere superstitious fear, like that of most savages; they evince abstract notions of morality; a deep reverence for an overruling Spirit, and a respect for the rights of their fellow-men. In one respect, their religion partakes of the pacifist doctrines of the Quakers. They hold that the Great Spirit is displeased with all nations who wantonly engage in war" (*CB*, 62). But they have to fight, at least defensively, against their hereditary enemies, the Blackfeet (a fierce tribe whom Irving calls the *banditti* of the mountains), and naturally they suffer many defeats.

Bonneville, at first much impressed by these natural Christians, for a time tried to be a "pacificator" between them and the Blackfeet. That failed, and he began to grow disturbed at their constant defeats and dismal future. He urged on them the need for "vigorous and retributive measures" to defend themselves: "Unless you rouse yourselves from your apathy and strike some bold and decisive blow, you will cease to be considered men" (*CB*75). They replied, however, that the Great Spirit had given them a heart for peace, not one for war. Bonneville rejoined that He had also given them "an arm to strike your enemies. Unless you do something to put an end to this continual plundering, I must say farewell . . . my property is too unsafe here . . . I and my people will share the contempt you are bringing upon yourselves, and will be thought, like you, poor-spirited beings" (*CB*76).

This is clearly the same philosophy of manliness/militarism that Cooper urged in *The Pioneers;* it is a superficially regretful but imperative recommendation of war. Otherwise, Bonneville and his white Americans ("I and my people") will leave the Pends Oreilles, for fear they too will "lose their character as men."

The same message is conveyed more obliquely by Irving's account of how the frontiersmen adopt Indian ways—"Indian" being identified with the warlike tribes, with the Blackfeet, not the Nez Percés. Men have to become Indian in this sense, in order to survive on the frontier. Many of the voyageurs, he tells us in *Captain Bonneville,* "looked more like Indians than white men, in their garbs and accoutrements . . . [They give] . . . Indian yells and war-whoops, or regale them with grotesque feats of horsemanship, well suited to their half-savage appearance" (*CB*14–15). Of free trappers, he says: "It is a matter of vanity and ambition with them to discard everything that may bear the stamp of civilized life, and to adopt the manners, habits, dress, gesture, and even walk of the Indian. You cannot pay a free trapper a greater compliment, than to persuade him that you have mistaken him for an Indian brave; and, in truth, the counterfeit is complete" (*CB*47). It is savagery, not Christianity, that exerts an overwhelming attraction on the men of the frontier.

Their virtues are often named as "chivalric," a word also applied to the Indians; it again suggests Scott's and Cooper's aristo-military ideology: "The fur trading companies, in the summer, engaged in contests of skill in running, wrestling, shooting, and running horses; contests between the *chivalry* of the various camps." "Here the free trappers were in all their glory; they considered themselves the 'cocks of the walk,' and always carried the high crests" (*CB* 112). Their moral style was the opposite of mercantile—that is, they were the opposite of prudent or economical: "For a free mountaineer to pause at a paltry consideration of dollars and cents, in the attainment of any object that might strike his fancy, would stamp him with the mark of the beast in the estimation of his comrades. For a trader to refuse one of these free and flourishing blades a credit . . . would be a flagrant affront" (*CB* 112).

Irving also hints, more frankly than Cooper, at the erotic component of this style: "The free trapper combines, in the eye of an

Indian girl, all that is dashing and heroic in a warrior of her own race, whose gait, and garb, and bravery he emulates, with all that is gallant and glorious in the white man" (*CB*258). He talks freely of the trappers' plurality of "wives" and the fidelity of the latter and the faithlessness of the former. (It is, of course, a crucial point that they are not REAL wives and that there is no true marriage on the frontier.) He thus introduces what we might call the Madame Butterfly motif—the native girl who must be abandoned, and must break her heart—which later is pervasive in imperialist literature.

Perhaps it is more striking that he is willing to allude, even discreetly, to the homoerotic feeling these men have for each other and for the Indians. In *A Tour on the Prairies*, he describes Antoine, a half-breed, as very handsome and spoiled; Commissioner Ellsworth says in his Journal that Antoine habitually stood with his cloak folded tightly about him, gazing on nothing. "In form, he was an object of admiration to us all, and I suspect to himself no less. His body and limbs were most symmetrically moulded. His bust was that of an Antinous" (*T*23). The Indians' nakedness is stressed. The Osages had "fine Roman countenances, and broad deep chests; and, as they generally wore their blankets wrapped round their loins, so as to leave the bust and arms bare, they looked like so many noble bronze figures" (*T*22). Of another Osage, who attached himself to them "as a squire," we are told that his naked bust would have been a model for a statue; and so on.

The original title of *Captain Bonneville* was *The Rocky Mountains: or Scenes, Incidents, and Adventures in the Far West*. It was derived from the captain's journal and several interviews with him. It does not, however, reveal some of the important links between individual adventurer and the federal government. According to William Goetzmann (in *Exploration and Empire*) Bonneville was a military spy sent out by the government to keep an eye on the Indians.[2] And, indeed, his letter of leave from Major General Macomb asks him to report on the numbers of Indian warriors and their methods of making war. Bonneville (as well as Irving and Astor) was apparently close to the political circles of Martin Van Buren and Andrew Jackson, and the modern editor of the Bonneville book speaks of Irving as "an early spokesman for the military-industrial complex . . . who writes [with] . . . the realism of the propagandist for power and order"

(*CB*xxxix, xl). Certainly, Irving presents the captain as successor to Astor in the nationalist or imperialist enterprise.

A Tour on the Prairies is the record of Irving's brief experience, with Commissioner Ellsworth, of supervising Indian resettlement after the Indians were moved west. Ellsworth's expedition was composed of young Rangers, "a raw, undisciplined band, levied among the wild youngsters of the frontier . . . for the sake of roving adventure" (*T*xix), plus some upper-class equivalents, notably the Swiss Comte de Portales, "scarce twenty-one years of age, full of talent and spirit, but galliard in the extreme, and prone to every kind of wild adventure" (*T*13).

Irving introduces several themes later writers develop, such as the Rangers' imitations of all sorts of animals—in fact, their self-assimilation to animals. (We see this again in Bird and in Twain.) But the most interesting figure he describes is the half-breed guide, Pierre Beatte, who is compared to Napoleon. His features were like Napoleon's, only sharpened up with high Indian cheekbones; and his dusky greenish complexion made him look like an old bronze bust. "He had, however, a sullen, saturnine expression, set off by a slouched woollen hat, and elf locks that hung about his ears" (*T*25). Cold and laconic, he thought himself superior to the rest of them, and Irving gradually comes around to the same opinion. Beatte becomes the hero of the book—Irving's equivalent of Natty Bumppo, the man of the West to whom the young easterner submits himself as apprentice. The Napoleonic touches evince only a slightly different version of America's general reverence for "the old guide." Cooper makes John Paul Jones a sort of Napoleon in *The Pilot*, but later adventure writers failed to develop the theme, even though West Point made a cult of Napoleon, and Andrew Jackson was sometimes labeled the backwoods Bonaparte. It is true that Napoleon was an ambivalent figure for nineteenth-century America, being literally an emperor; to be compared to him was a doubtful compliment. Yet it is significant that there was an impulse to link the frontiersman with that other—European—ebullition of "natural force."

Irving attributed to prairie life an expansion of all the appetites and a reversion to the primitive. "Man is naturally an animal of prey; and, however changed by civilization, will readily relapse into his instinct for destruction. I found my ravenous and san-guinary propensities daily growing stronger upon the prairies" (T90). The remark is lightly said, but it is not trivial. It is an aspect of the frontier legend beyond Cooper's scope, although later writers took it up. We might call this aspect an adventure atavism, which is more than merely Romantic. Parkman scorned Rousseau and Wordsworth and even Thoreau; but he wrote, in his novel *Vassall Morton:* "Take the most polished of mankind, turn him into the wilderness, and forthwith the dormant savage begins to appear. Hunt him with enemies, gnaw him with hun-ger, beat him with wind and rain, and observe the result; how the delicate tissues of civilization are blown away, how rude passions start into life, how his bodily cravings grow clamorous and im-portunate, how he grows reckless of his own blood and the blood of others."[3] This theme is not fully developed until the end of the century, by Norris and London. Of the three, *Astoria* was the most substantial. And it was recognized and praised by con-temporaries as a book of the same sort and quality as *Robinson Crusoe.* It was said to combine commercial enterprise and aggres-sive adventure as vividly as Defoe's masterpiece. *The Knicker-bocker Magazine,* for instance, praised its "exciting expeditions and adventures by land and sea"; and the *London and Westmins-ter Review* said it was no romance but a plain description of a mercantile speculation, one "which had rather the air of a daring and wild expedition of a hunting tribe than the calculating pro-ceeding of a cool and thrifty merchant."[4] In our terms, it presents social and political issues within the matrix of adventure.

In summary, one can say that Irving brought to the frontier subject and the adventure narrative a breadth of intelligence and a liveliness of sensibility, and above all a flexibility that were be-yond Cooper's reach. He paints a broader and more colorful panorama of the prairies and shows more sides of the frontiers-man's personality. What he does not include we shall realize when we turn to Bird, who depicts this other element vividly; for Irving (like Cooper and Scott) evades the violence of his subject matter, the constant killing of man and animals and the lust for slaughter that animates adventure. This was the great stumbling block in the way of literature's approach to this subject matter; literature was dedicated to the rational and the moral. Some writers rationalized the violence as being in the cause of progress; some left it in, passing it off as merely careless or exuberant. Irving, all his deepest loyalties those of a man of letters, evaded the moral and emotional issue and diminished his subject matter in order to fit it under the ornamental awning of belles lettres.

Chapter 4　　BIRD'S *NICK OF THE WOODS* (1837)

Ⓘf it was Cooper who first embodied adventure in the form of the three-volume novel in America, from most points of view his adventures were less successful than those of Robert Montgomery Bird. Bird, a Philadelphia doctor and man of letters (born 1806, died 1854) is best remembered for his plays, which were often vehicles for the famous actor Edwin Forrest.

Cooper's work is unreal romance, that is, insufficiently in touch with its setting; and Irivng never escapes the essay form. Bird's *Nick of the Woods* is a story which exemplifies all the strengths—though also many of the weaknesses and the contradictions—of American adventure. These contradictions can be summed up as conflicts between the conventions of romance and those of adventure, for though the two forms have much in common in terms of cultural meaning, their politics are significantly different. Adventure is more democratic than romance—it pays tribute to the virtues of the people—whereas romance always has a genteel (usually an aristocratic) hero and heroine. In its nonliterary forms, adventure can be quite simply antiaristocratic. Literary adventure is a combination of the two in which there is always some conflict.

These conflicts had troubled even Scott, and he discussed them in his General Preface to the Waverley novels. Bird's "Preface to the First Edition" takes up the same topics as they affected American subject matter. He begins by saying that "a peculiarly romantic interest has ever been attached to the name and history of Kentucky" and goes on to speak of the "ramblings of the solitary Boone" (27), thus promising that what follows will be a

Scott-Cooper romance.[1] However, the next paragraph begins: "But apart from the charm the history of Kentucky possesses for the romantic, it has an interest scarcely inferior for the grave and reflecting. This is derived from the character of the men who" founded that state. They were heroes of democracy and the frontier—idiosyncratically American heroes. Obviously democracy is a more serious value than romance. "They were, with but few exceptions, men drawn from what, in our vanity, we call the humbler spheres of life." There were among them some men "of education and refinement," but only a few. "The true fathers of the State were such persons as we have described, ignorant but ardent, unpolished and unpretending, yet brave, sagacious, and energetic" (28). Such men, obviously, would be heroes of adventure, not of romance. Like Scott, Bird is announcing a split, in historical types and in his literary loyalties, and is stating his preference for adventure.

Of course, the language in which he makes this announcement (e.g., "ignorant but ardent") might be called—and this is an ominous paradox—the language of romance. The frontier characters he depicts, such as Ralph Stackpole and Nathan Slaughter, cannot really be called unpretending or sagacious. Bird is applying a literary, not to say falsifying, rhetoric to his subject, even though he is trying to be realistic.

His preface to the revised edition of 1853 attacks both Cooper and the French novelist Châteaubriand, for romanticizing the American frontier: "Atala and Uncas [characters in stories by Cooper and Châteaubriand] are beautiful unrealities and fictions merely, as imaginary and contrary to nature as the shepherd swains of the old pastoral school of rhyme and romance" (32). Bird seems to be promising us plain, unvarnished truth. Yet as soon as his narrative begins, the reader finds that romance, in the Cooper-Châteaubriand sense, is again dominant.

The first scene presents a "long train of emigrants" on their way to Kentucky; "some seven or eight score individuals in all" (41). They are a large group and represent the many real groups that were part of the historical movement to the frontier. On that level, at least, Bird is dealing in fact.

However, Bird's main character, Roland Forrester, is the only one who does not belong in the group. He is aristocratic, melancholy, and reserved, and a mysterious silence hangs about him.

(His moodiness is later explained by an injustice that was done to him, an intrigue against him, a disinheritance.) He is dressed very plainly, so as to seem no different from his humble companions, but he is distinguished by his "erect military bearing, and the fine blooded bay horse which he rode" (43). In other words, he belongs, as the others do not, to the aristo-military caste; he belongs to romance.

From then on, the events of the novel are seen from the point of view of Roland Forrester, who seems to represent the author and the reader in the events of the novel. He and his cousin Edith (whom he will marry, once he has made his fortune) have come west from Virginia because they have been disinherited by the villainous Braxley. On the frontier their lives are threatened by Indian tribes who have been misled by renegade whites, among them the evil Braxley. In terms of theme as well as plot, Roland is the central figure—but not because he belongs to or represents the frontier. He is definitely alien to it; rather he represents the reader there—and the author—by his gentility: his breeding, polish, nobility, ardor, his power to impress everyone he meets and to impress on them his own standards. Or perhaps not so much his standards as his fiery but well-bred temperament. He is an erotic image, for the reader and for other characters; the women all fall in love with him, and the men all cherish him and submit to his leadership even in situations where he is far less experienced than they are. Each frontier event we encounter, each frontier type, each specimen of frontier rhetoric or reasoning, is measured for us by Roland's reactions to it, or simply by his appearance beside it. That is, the reader is present in the book as a gentleman, and he sees a deep gulf separating the gentleman from the other types. They may be the founding fathers of Kentucky, they may be "brave, sagacious, and energetic," but they are also, in book-readers' terms, decidedly quaint. For instance, their speech, when it is reported, has to be misspelled.

Nick of the Woods nevertheless does celebrate the foundation of Kentucky and, by extension, that of the whole United States. It does attempt, in its easygoing way, to be a foundation epic (or at least a foundation entertainment) like Cooper's and Scott's work. History is often invoked in the course of the novel, and Bird makes important use of historical information from McClung's *Sketches of Western Adventure,* and Marshall's *His-*

tory of Kentucky. He based one of his characters on Simon Girty, a real Kentucky renegade, and another on Simon Kenton, the stealer of Indian horses. He develops the latter character through anecdotes and speech patterns attributed—in various books—to Mike Fink and other actual Salt River roarers. Bird makes more use of this American folk history (at least, more skillful use) than Cooper, or indeed than any contemporary novelist.

There is, moreover, a larger-than-America scope of historial allusion in a passage like the following comment about Indian cruelty: "The familiar of a Spanish Inquisition has sometimes moistened the lips of a heretic stretched upon the rack,—the Buccaneer of the tropics has sometimes relented over the contumacious prisoner gasping to death under his lashes and heated pincers; but we know of no instance where an Indian, torturing a prisoner at the stake, the torture once begun, has ever been moved to compassionate, to regard with any feelings but those of exultation and joy, the agonies of the thrice-wretched victim" (329). The first two examples mentioned were the traditional villains of WASP adventure from its beginnings:* the inquisitor appears in Hakluyt's *Voyages* (which supplied Defoe with his raw materials) and, twenty years after *Nick*, in Kingsley's *Westward Ho!;* and the buccaneers were a common fictional and quasi-fictional subject of that early adventure genre, pirate stories, of which Defoe wrote many. The WASP hero of the modern adventure (typically a trader) was forever falling into the cruel hands of either the Inquisitor or the Buccaneer. Bird was, therefore, in this passage, installing the Indian as the natural heir and representative of this savage Otherness—the climactic apotheosis of their villainy.

Bird had, of course, inherited this image of the Indian as Cooper had, from the captivity narratives written and printed in New England and told and retold along the frontier. *Nick of the Woods* was published in the years between the two groups of Cooper's Leatherstocking novels—between *The Prairie* (1827) and *The Pathfinder* (1840). Bird shares with Cooper all the adventure motifs of the siege: the group flight, the haunted wilderness, the fate worse than death, the scalping hatchet, the torture at the stake, the devilish sinuosity of the Indian's body, the

---

*As the writers and readers of American adventures were predominantly white Anglo-Saxon Protestants, I use the familiar acronym.

nightmarish ferocity of his scream of triumph, his glowing eyes, and his painted face. Bird betrays equally the influence of theater (middlebrow theater, meaning at best Romantic stagings of Shakespeare) that worked so much to the disadvantage of both novelists when they tried to render an adventure convincingly. (Theater in this sense is first cousin to romance.) The form both inherited from Scott was a composite one that combined many kinds of plot and convention; besides the conventions of theater, one can recognize in *Nick of the Woods* the Gothic motifs of revenge, superstition, and Byronism (in heroes and villains), the inheritance plot, the stolen will, the wicked lawyer, the missing heir, and so on. (Bird is put to some pains to insert his kind of action into frontier and wilderness setting—the overhearing of long explanatory conversations does not fall out very naturally in a forest.) This composite form was appropriate to Scott's purposes, which included reconciling Scotland to England, reconciling the military caste to the commercial, and reconciling the modern to more primitive social systems. But in Cooper, and even more in Bird, these purposes were less important and the composite form was less suitable; neither writer was artist enough to resolve formal problems of that magnitude.

The great difference between Cooper and Bird, ideologically, is that the latter is more violent, both in the scenes he paints and in the feelings he evokes about the frontier and the Indians. He declares the Indians to be cruel and desperate villains, not noble or romantic figures. He nearly always shows them burning and scalping and yelling, braining babies and getting drunk on the white man's firewater. Gradually he educates his readers to accept the frontiersman's harsh treatment of them, which even includes scalping them—something Natty Bumppo, for instance, would never do.

Bird was reproached for his anti-Indian ferocity by Harrison Ainsworth, who wrote an introduction for an English edition of *Nick of the Woods* in 1837. Ainsworth, a prolific writer of historical novels, took the milder and more chivalrous line of Scott— and Cooper—about Indians and about the Other in general. Of course, Ainsworth, and even Cooper, lived much farther from the frontier than Bird did.

Artistically, Bird's closeness to the frontier was much to his advantage. He speaks with authority, having much more to tell us about frontier ways of life and frontier technology than

Cooper, whose rudimentary woodcraft is palpably literary, in derivation as well as function. The difference in authenticity is important, for adventures were not only myths about the adventurous modes of life practiced at the frontier, but also news, factual accounts aimed at the reading public. Cooper's news of that kind always carried some taint of fraud (as Twain pointed out) while Bird's was genuine. Bird's presentation of frontier types, like Colonel Bruce, the station commander, Abel Doe, the renegade, and Roaring Ralph, the liar, boaster, prankster, and stealer of Indians' horses, are also more authentic. Cooper handles such figures very stiffly, because he disapproves of them and their frontier cult; he takes his cultural responsibilities as educator very seriously. Bird is much less scrupulous—and more knowledgable. He describes Colonel Bruce in this way: "His stature was colossal, and the proportions of his frame as just as they were gigantic . . . Such men were oft-times, in those days, sent from among the mountain counties of Virginia, to amaze the lesser mortals of the plains, who regarded them as the genii of the forest" (46–47).

In similar terms, Judge Hall remembers the frontiersmen he saw as a boy in the streets of Philadelphia at roughly the same date; he admired "their brawny limbs and sun-burned features . . . the rough hardy air . . . the blanket, bear-skin, and saddlebags—nay, the very oilskin on his hat, and the dirk that peeped from among his vestments . . . He strode among us with the step of an Achilles, glancing with a good-natured superciliousness." He also showed "a spirit quick to resent—he had the will to dare, and the spirit to execute; there was something in his look which bespoke a disdain of control, and an absence of constraint in all his movements."[2] It is clear from the language in both cases that a mythical cult was at work; for such writers and their readers the men from the frontier were the embodiment of nature, beyond good and evil. The cult was to be of the greatest importance in the shaping of American politics.

Colonel Bruce was wearing "a new and jaunty hunting-shirt of dressed deer-skin, as yellow as gold, and fringed and furbelowed with shreds of the same substance, dyed as red as bloodroot would make them . . ." (47). He presented his son, Tom: "Thar's a boy, now, the brute, that comes of the best stock for loving women and fighting Injuns in all Kentucky . . . the young brute did actually take the scalp of a full-grown Shawnee before he was fourteen y'ar old." Tom had gone looking for a neighbor's horse when "what should he see but two great big Shawnees astride of the identicular beast he war hunting! Away went Tom, and away went the bloody villains hard after." When one climbed a tree, " 'A bird in the hand,' said Tom, 'Is worth two in a bush,' and with that he blows out the first feller's brains, just as he is gitting up." Afterwards when his father told him how he could have got the other one too, "he blubbered all night, to think he had not killed them both." Nothing could better catch the tone of frontier callousness and recklessness (50).*

Bird also conveys the tone of that frontier humor that was, taken in its most serious aspect, a cult of energy and vitality and an alternative to the legal and ethical culture of city civilization. One of his characters, Roaring Ralph, a popular entertainer of frontier society, "dancing, leaping, and dodging about, clapping his hands and cracking his heels together" (68) and crowing like a cock. Calling himself an alligator half-breed, he "snorted and neighed like a horse; he bellowed like a bull; he barked like a dog; he yelled like an Indian; he whined like a panther; he howled like a wolf; until one could have thought he was a living menagerie, comprising within his single body the spirit of every animal noted for its love of conflict" (70). This performance, indeed all of Ralph's behavior, is greeted with derisive laughter. He is, nevertheless, enacting the frontiersmen's faith; he is presenting to them, in humorous exaggeration, their cult, which, for obvious reasons, could not be "taken seriously," and found its most intense expression in the popular theater.

Later Ralph makes his way across a dangerous river: " 'If that ar'n't equal to coming down a strick of lightning,' he cried, 'thar's no legs to a jumping bull-frog! Smash away, old Salt!' he continued, apostrophizing with great exultation and self-admiration the river whose terrors he has thus so successfully defied, 'Ar'n't I the gentleman for you?' " (184). At such a moment we see the individual frontiersman absorbing (consciously claiming to absorb) the energies of the natural forces he con-

---

*Buffalo Bill Cody is said to have killed his first Indian at the age of 11— in 1857. His companion reportedly told everyone, "Little Billy's killed himself an Indian, all by himself."

fronts. This is the quasi-religious aspect of the frontier expansion of the spirit—the "philosophy of life" of the American empire.

In his own words, too, Bird was able (as Cooper was not) to enact an equivalent for this performance and capture the spirit. He describes Ralph rushing upon a band of Indians in a skirmish, with "his eyes squinting daggers and ratsbane" (198); and on another occasion, "By magic, as it seemed, the heels of the captain of the horse-thieves were suddenly flying in the air, his head aiming at the earth, upon which it as suddenly descended with the violence of a bomb-shell; and there it would doubtless have burrowed, like the aforesaid implement of destruction, had the soil been soft enough for the purpose, or exploded into a thousand fragments, had not the shell been double the thickness of an ordinary skull" (77). This passage illustrates the essential American humor of self-expansion, self-explosion, and self-mechanization that runs from the South-West humorists to animated cartoons.

Bird's greatest achievement, however, is his conception of Nathan Slaughter, a Quaker much despised in the frontier society of Kentucky because he refuses to take part in violence, even against Indians. For the book-reader, the Brahmin guardian of his culture's higher values, Nathan should, of course, be the object of enthusiastic reverence and respect. Yet he regularly (and psychotically) turns into "Nick of the Woods," a legendary killer of Indians known to the settlers only by his exploits of scalping victims and carving a cross in their flesh. Bird only gradually reveals the identity of these two opposite figures, explaining the episodes by Nathan's history of epilepsy and the fact that his wife and children were murdered by Indians. But what is impressive is neither the narrative suspense nor the characterological study, but the cultural paradox, the enigma Nathan represents; we are all, as white Americans, represented by this schizophrenia, however far behind the frontier we may live. What is the WASP hero we admire, the white adventurer on the frontier? What has he come to America for? He is both Nathan Slaughter, dedicated to peace, humility, forgiveness, making things grow; and Nick of the Woods, avenger, nightmare, devil of cruelty and blood lust, (even though the second identity is involuntary and comes in flashes of madness).

In Chapter 1, discussing the interaction of the old guide and the young genteel hero, I said that Nathan was more of a man than those he met, as all the forest heroes are. But that is not quite true in this case. Especially in the beginning, Roland is no less manly than Nathan. In fact, it is Nathan who acquires manhood in the course of the action; he ceases to be a Christian and becomes, under Roland's tutelage, a man. This exception reinforces our rule, however, for one can see, even within this novel, that Bird is making a tactical error. Roland's position as our representative is unworkable just because he has nothing to learn about manhood—though everything about forest skills. How can Nathan be his teacher, when he is so confused himself? Adventure only makes sense (grand sense) when manhood is a grace bestowed especially on those who learn to live in the forest.

The central thematic action of *Nick of the Woods* is the education of Nathan (seen now as the Quaker, not the Indian killer) into manhood by means of his intercourse with Roland. Although so inept in the forest in every practical way, Roland is an incarnation of military ardor. He is often described as "burning with military ardor" at the thought of attacking his foes; Bird often uses the language of fire about him. (Fire was the emblem of white civilization in its conflict with others; both firearms and firewater brought destruction to the Indians, who could not handle the new intensity of experience brought by these white powers.) Fire was also, of course, a sinister force, even to white readers, and Roland's function is to embody it in an elegant, aristocratic, and traditional form that defends the readers against their fears. Like Cooper's Captain Middleton and Irving's Captain Bonneville, he is an officer in the regular army. The story shows us Nathan, gradually seduced by Roland's manly aristo-military charm, becoming a fighter, taking the gun and playing with fire.

When we first see him, however, he is "hollow of visage," with a melancholy or contemplative twist to his mouth, and staring eyes that beam a "good-natured, humble, and perhaps submissive, simplicity of disposition" (73). He lacks, we might say, the inner principle of fire and forcefulness and is out of place on the frontier. He walks with a "shuffling, awkward, hesitating step," like "a man who apprehended injury and insult," not one who "possessed the spirit to resist them." He lacks form, bodily pride, and the splendor of manhood. He carries the pack his horse should bear, showing a "merciful temper, scarce compatible with the qualities of a man of war and contention." Even his little dog is a coward, creeping along at the horse's heels.

As we read, therefore, we realize that Nathan, however Christian, is not a viable adventure hero. If we are to stay with Bird, we must give up any Quakerish tendencies in ourselves; Bird does not accommodate a possible Quaker reader, any more than he does a possible Indian one. (Cooper does not accommodate Moravians; Twain does not accommodate Mormons. Even within the circle of white Anglo-Saxon Protestants, the world of readers is only a segment.)

When Roland calls on Nathan for help in a fight, the latter declares it "unseemly that one of my peaceful faith should go with fighting men among men of war" (128). His gun is described to us as "that rifle, terrible only to the animals who furnished him subsistence" (129). It was not terrible to men; so it was not, we might say, really a rifle. A few pages later, Roland appeals to him to be a man, but Nathan, in effect, refuses: "I am a man, thee is another; thee has thee conscience and . . . thee thinks thee has a call to battle" (136). But we see that the religion of manhood has begun to seduce him from his Quaker principles. He listens to "the warlike outpourings of the young soldier with a degree of complacency and admiration one would scarcely have looked for in a man of his peaceful character" (138).

When the Indians attack, Roland cannot see one who is crawling toward him, and Nathan says: "I will hold thee gun for thee, and thee shall pull the trigger." The same scene occurs in Defoe's *Captain Singleton,* in which the Quaker William points the gun for his pirate friend. It is a poignant symbol of the involuntary involvement of a man of peace in the wars of his racial comrades. Bird, however, asks his reader to greet the gesture with unambivalent enthusiasm. Roland is delighted with "the happy change in the principles and practice of Nathan, who seemed as if about to prove that he could deserve the nickname of Bloody" (163).

Later Roland is captured and tied up and loses consciousness in horror when a giant Indian falls across his body, killed in the act of killing him. The assailant has in fact been dispatched by Nathan, and when Roland opens his eyes he sees the latter bending over him. "And who, who was it that rescued me? Hah! There is blood on your face! Your hands are red with it! It was *you*, then, that saved me? *You* that killed the accursed cutthroats? Noble Nathan! Brave Nathan! True Nathan! How shall I ever requite thee?" (219). Roland endows Nathan with chivalric epithets for the first time, inducts him into manhood, into knighthood. Nathan, however, is still ashamed of what he has done: "Truly, friend, thee sees it couldn't be helped." He is still undecided.

When, a few pages later, Roland takes a vow "never to pause, never to rest, never to be satisfied with vengeance, while an Indian lives with blood to be shed, and I with strength to shed it," Nathan's response is twofold: " 'Thee speaks like a man!' said Nathan, grasping the soldier's hand, and fairly crushing it in his grip,—'That is to say,' he continued, suddenly letting go his hold, and seeming somewhat abashed at the fervor of his sympathy,—'like a man, according to thee own sense of matters and things' " (228). Nonetheless, he has sealed his conversion with that grasp of hands recently bloodied. A few pages later (discreetly offstage) he scalps his victims and returns to Roland "a new man. His gait was fierce and confident, his countenance bold and expressive of satisfaction" (230).

Nathan has to teach Roland (and the reader) to accept scalping as part of border warfare. Roland is horrified at the idea, seeing it as a betrayal of white culture, a going over to the enemy. " 'Their scalps? *I* scalp them!' cried Roland, with a soldier's disgust; 'I am no butcher' " (238). But Bird tells us that "Such is the practice of the border, and such it has ever been since the mortal feud, never destined to be really ended but with the annihilation, or civilization, of the American race, first began between the savage and the white intruder. It was, and is, essentially a measure of retaliation, compelled, if not justified, by the ferocious example of the red man. Brutality ever begets brutality; and magnanimity of arms can only be exercised in the case of a magnanimous foe" (257).

Soon Nathan is in the position of inspiring Roland to more violence, when the latter has doubts or scruples. When he overcomes them, " 'Thee is a man, every inch of thee!' said Nathan, with a look of uncommon satisfaction and fire: 'thee shall have thee will, in the matter of these murdering Shawnee dogs' "

(250). We notice that Nathan now uses the rhetoric of manliness—with the same significance of killing. When he recommends a surprise attack, it is Roland who has to overcome his conscience by "reflecting that he was fighting in the cause of humanity . . . and marking the fiery eagerness that flamed from Nathan's countenance" (252). Now Nathan too embodies fire, and he goes on to perform a real orgy of killing among the Indians at the end of the story. He has ceased to be a Quaker; he has become a man and an American; and so has the reader, if he has stayed with Bird. The theme introduced by Cooper, and developed by Irving, has become the substance, the main moral substance, of this novel.

That we are talking here about literary conventions rather than personal convictions—that Bird was not simply an Indian hater—is shown by the fact that in letters and even in other literary forms he often took the Indians' side. In letters he shows great sympathy for the Cherokees and the Creeks and their fate, and he wrote a play with an Indian hero. Most strikingly, he wrote a story on the same theme as *Nick of the Woods* with the values reversed; "Awossagame" is a story about an Indian girl who is persecuted in a New England settlement. The story begins: "Our forefathers of New England were strange people. They came as homeless and landless exiles, among a rude but not inhospitable race, whom after a few years they did not scruple to dispossess of their homes and possessions." In this story the Indian hater is an ex-papist, and his victims include Quakers as well; the climax comes when he discovers that Awossagame is really his own daughter. The values are reversed, but the story is the same. And the story is the literary fact, which carries the same meaning, the same instruction—the instruction to contemplate the wildness and savagery on the frontier—however its moral is changed.[3]

It is ironic that Philadelphia houses published the implicitly anti-Quaker books discussed in this section. Two of our three writers, it is true, were New Yorkers, not Pennsylvanians, much less Quakers. But the gesture of attacking Quakerism was nevertheless quixotic; it went against a recent enthusiasm of intellectuals everywhere. The Quakers had been the best of America, the hope of the world, to the philosophers of the late eighteenth century. Yet the attack was in the spirit of the nineteenth century, at least as far as literature was concerned. The new vigorous ideas were nationalism, adventure, and caste, which entailed a sacrifice of religious radicalism. Nineteenth-century novelists and belletrists, even those who published in Philadelphia, clearly did not prepare their books for religious enthusiasts. They expected their readers to join them in gazing *at* Quakers, from as great a distance as they looked at Indians. Readers were defined, implicitly, as manly and gentlemanly.

Part Two

THREE FROM BOSTON

Dana's *Two Years Before the Mast*
(1840)
Melville's *Typee* (1846)
Parkman's *The Oregon Trail* (1849)

Autobiographical narratives by men of letters telling how they made themselves men of action—men with fight in them, true Americans—by engaging in adventures.

Chapter 5

DANA'S *TWO YEARS BEFORE THE MAST* (1840)

W ith the next three adventures, all published in the 1840s, we come to the beginning of Boston's dominance of the American publishing and literary culture. Two of the authors we consider, Richard Henry Dana and Francis Parkman, were from Boston Brahmin families. They engaged in their adventures, and wrote them, to redeem their caste heritage—simultaneously affirming it and changing it. With them American gentlemen became not so much clerisy (as their fathers had been) as captains courageous, men of action and authority. Nonetheless, their narratives, especially when compared with those of the Philadelphia writers, reflect Brahmin and Boston virtues of truthfulness, plainness, firmness, and, above all, seriousness. They are autobiographical narratives in the line begun by Irving, rather than fiction in the line begun by Cooper and Bird.

Melville is something of an anomaly among them—partly because he was *not* very truthful—and his book is discussed in this section partly because of its publication date. Although in character *Typee* belongs to the earlier school of taste associated with Philadelphia and New York, Melville was inspired to some considerable degree by Dana's example; in its equivocal way *Typee* is, like *Two Years Before the Mast* and *The Oregon Trail,* a pursuit of personal truth through risk.

There is no significant polemic against Quakers in these three narratives, but there are traces of that earlier theme. (Later, in *Moby Dick*, Melville developed the motif of the bloody Quaker into the giant figure of Captain Ahab.) Even in *Typee* he continues the earlier writers' polemic against New England moralism and evangelism. Both Dana's and Parkman's adventures were (in a different way) criticisms of New England, of their own forebears, for becoming decadent in their Brahminism, diminished in their vitality. The two young Bostonians were determined not to grow up like their fathers, not to become what Theodore Roosevelt was to call "peace at any price" men. They were determined to become as manly and American as the men of the frontier; to do so they followed the pattern set fictionally by Oliver Effingham and Roland Forrester—they went looking for a Natty Bumppo to teach them.

Two Years Before the Mast tells the true story of a long sea journey in 1839 down the East Coast of North and South America, around Cape Horn, and back up the West Coast to California. The narrator is a Harvard undergraduate who has signed on as a common seaman. In California, moreover, he works on shore, making up a cargo of hides for the return journey. On sea and on land, the work is rough, and the company is even rougher. The young man, delighted to have measured up to the challenges, wrote a book to tell the world how he had achieved manhood.

Richard Dana's adventure was published three years after Bird's *Nick of the Woods*, and it differs from its predecessor in three major ways: by being about the sea as opposed to the land; by being an autobiographical narrative as opposed to a novel; and by being about a peacetime as opposed to a wartime situation. But for those who believe in adventure as a genre, and as one that carried the energizing myth of modern (mercantile) imperialism, the books belong together. We recognize Bird's imaginative imperialism as implicit in Dana, and Dana's moral drive as implicit in Bird. Both books are "Jacksonian"—for the adventure was always Jacksonian, whatever the individual author's politics. Indeed, these two are among the most striking expressions of Jacksonian adventure in American literature.

For Dana's excitement, in the first part of the book, at conquering new psycho-social spaces for himself to expand into, continues naturally into his excitement, in the second part, at finding California a geographical space for his country to expand into—a space so far occupied only by inferior races and nationalities. In the first part he becomes a sailor and an American, and the narrative communicates his excitement to us through the myriad factual details. In the second part he sees and shows us the other coast of our vast continent, empty save for idle, lackadaisical, sauntering, dawdling Mexicans—a people left behind by the tide of history and waiting to be displaced. He shows us, implicitly, that the manifest destiny of the United States is to fill that vacuum.

These are two distinct kinds of excitement: the personal kind, of a Brahmin bursting the limits of his caste, and the historical kind, of the Anglo-Saxons foreseeing their world triumph. But they are continuous, consubstantial; the ego that swells with innocent triumph in the first part is just what is needed to fill the vacancy of the second part. The American gentleman become a man will energize California and the rest of the continent, as, in the last chapter, "Twenty-Four Years After," Dana tells us happened.

Dana's is a discreet and muted version of the energizing myth, a true, sincere, modest story. Consequently, its narrator cannot offer himself as a hero. Although he tells a lot about "how things are done" in the merchant navy, he can only infrequently tell us, as Robinson Crusoe does constantly, "how I did it." Still the spirit of "how to do things" and "do it yourself" (perhaps the major themes of all true adventure) runs through his narrative; and the shaping force of the form, which is especially to be felt in the final chapters, is the adventurer's triumph over opposing forces. In Dana's case, as in Crusoe's, these are the forces of nature. These chapters (31 to 33), in which the ship sails south toward danger and then is driven by powerful winds helter skelter toward its home port, are full of the excitement of fear, challenge, struggle, endurance, and triumph.

The reader identifies with the narrator, who identifies with the ship and the sea, and a self-expansive animation runs from one to the other. (In *Nick of the Woods* the same effect is depicted in Ralph Stackpole's identification with the River Salt.) In the beginning, Dana was surprised to find how much the ship rolled and pitched. "She plunged her head into the sea and then, her stern settling gradually down, her huge bows rose up, showing the bright copper, and her stern and breasthooks dripping, like old Neptune's locks, with the brine" (9).[1] The slightly anomalous and uncharacteristic reference to Neptune reminds us of all the literary archaisms Dana turned away from, in favor of realism.

Toward the end he says: "the ship sprang through the water like a thing possessed. The sail being nearly all forward, it lifted her out of the water, and she seemed actually to jump from sea to sea . . . And when she leaped over the seas, and almost out of the water, and trembled to her very keel, the spars and masts snapping and creaking . . . The mate walked the deck, looking at the sails, and then over the side to see the foam fly by her, slapping his hands upon his thighs and talking to the ship—'Hurrah, you jade, you've got the scent! You know where you're going!'" (279). At such moments, the reader thinks of all the other great icons of organic life in literature—Vronsky's passion for his horse in *Anna Karenina,* for instance. It is power, the power of nature, which both men (or all four men, Tolstoy via Vronsky, and Dana via the mate) are appropriating by an act of their imaginations. That appropriation is the ultimate motive of all adventure. The readers of adventures feel more alive than other people, as do those who succeed in real life adventures. They thrill with the life of the dangers they have outfaced, the lion they have hunted, and the rapids they have shot.

A climactic passage, occurring soon after the one just quoted, portrays this power, paradoxically, in motionlessness. Dana begins by saying that few people have seen a ship in full sail, "with all her sails, light and heavy, and studding sails, on each side, alow and aloft, she is the most glorious moving object in the world" (283). Only once was it given to him to see the ship thus; one night he was sent out to the end of the flying-jib boom and saw, rising from the water and supported only by the small black hull, "a pyramid of canvas, spreading out far beyond the hull, and towering up almost, as it seemed in the indistinct night air, to the clouds . . . And highest of all, the little skysail, the apex of the pyramid, seeming actually to touch the stars, and to be out of reach of human hand. So quiet, too, was the sea, and so steady the breeze, that if those sails had been sculptured marble they could not have been more motionless" (284). The sailor working with Dana said, "half to himself, still looking at the marble sails,—'How quietly they do their work'" (284). This quietude is, of course, impressive because of the turbulent power couched within, power which the spirit of the author expands to meet and match.

This expansion of the self (in the writer, and in the reader by proxy and by contagion) is achieved by an act of identification not only with the force of nature in the ocean but also with the triumph of technology in the ship and with an alien mode of being in the sailors. They are utterly unlike Dana, who comes from a dynasty of lawyers and writers in Boston and has been halfway through Harvard. His family's wealth and position had been won in earlier generations, as had the Parkmans'; both families were, in some sense, decadent Brahmins. Dana's father was a melancholic man of letters, and that destiny hung over his son (indeed, it overcame him in later years).

Recovering his health aboard ship, he also wins his manhood (and a deeper-rooted, bolder-gestured manhood than he would otherwise have attained) by participating in the system of rude and abrasive exchanges that constituted a sailor's life. On the first page of Chapter 1 he describes a sailor's gait and clothes (in the same tone Judge Hall uses to describe the frontiersmen he saw as a boy). Dana's voice betrays nervousness, admiration, a desire to emulate, but fear of exposing himself—all the passion of a spirit stretching out toward something dangerous and alluring.

The sailor's trousers, Dana says, are tight around the hips, but hang thence long and loose; his hat is worn on the back of his head; and he "with a sunburnt cheek, wide step, and rolling gait, swings his bronzed and toughened hands athwartships, half-opened, as though just ready to grasp a rope" (3). Surely Eros is possessing Dana's voice and directing him toward an image of manhood resplendent. In Chapter 13 he draws the picture of a "thoroughbred English sailor," his chest as deep as it was wide, his arm like that of Hercules, and his hand the fist of a tar— "every hair a rope yarn." And to this Popeye caricature is attached some fancy erotics out of a genteel romance: "With all this, he had one of the pleasantest smiles I ever saw. His cheeks were of a handsome brown, his teeth brilliantly white, and his hair, of a raven black, waved in loose curls over all his head and fine open forehead; and his eyes he might have sold to a duchess at the price of diamonds, for their brilliancy. As for their color, every change of position and light seemed to give them a new hue; but their prevailing color was black, or nearly so" (70). The terms "brilliancy," "diamonds," and "duchess"—and the close-up of the sailor's eyes—connote, however ineptly, an intensity of erotic feeling. (I don't, of course, mean that Dana felt sexual desire for this sailor; I mean he felt an intense desire to be like him.)

There was a traditional "handsome sailor" in the contemporary literature of the sea; you find him in, for instance, Cooper's *The Water-Witch*, where he is named Tom Tiller; and he can be found earlier in Charles Dibdin and the English sailor ballads of the eighteenth century. This man's handsomeness is an advertiser's lure thrown out by adventure, a promise to the reader, and a figure in the energizing myth of imperialism. That tradition may suffice to explain Dana's use of "thoroughbred," but there are also details in the description, and in the introductory phrase "the best specimen," which suggest that literal breeding, in genetic and caste terms, was in Dana's mind. (It is notable that Melville's handsome sailor, in *White-Jacket*, is also English; England, being a caste society, was a locus of images of breeding— of men and of horses!) Caste thinking in general was quite American, as we have seen in Judge Hall's *Letters from the West*. Dana's caste thinking, however, is more specific than Hall's; it brings with it the interest in the responsibility, authority, and power of discipline, proper to a gentleman.

This interest in command and discipline was something new. As a primary interest it is absent from Defoe, whose imagination was more purely mercantile; he could leave authority to an aristocratic caste, whereas Dana himself belonged to the republican aristocracy of America. Nonetheless, it is to *Robinson Crusoe* that *Two Years Before the Mast* most often sends us back—in a way that the work of Bird or Melville, Scott or Cooper does not. (The likeness to Defoe was noted at the time by, for instance, Emerson.)

The decisive evidence of Defoe's influence on Dana, or affinity with him, is the passionate attention the latter gives to questions of process and technique, to the virtues of prudence and calculation, and to the praise of purpose and resolution. To this we may add the gestalt that makes these things cohere. D. H. Lawrence said (in *Studies in Classic American Literature*) that "it is in the dispassionate statement of plain material facts that Dana achieves his greatness"; but Dana's statement is not dispassionate.[2] James Joyce noted in his essay on Defoe the organic connection between factuality of that kind and the mercantile gestalt of feeling—the WASP passions. For instance, Dana says:

> During our watches below we overhauled our clothes, and made and mended everything for bad weather. Each of us had made for himself a suit of oil-cloth or tarpaulin, and these we got out, and gave thorough coatings of oil or tar, and hung upon the stays to dry. Our stout boots, too, we covered over with a thick mixture of melted grease and tar. Thus we took advantage of the warm sun and fine weather of the Pacific to prepare for its other face . . . Thick stockings and drawers were darned and patched; mittens dragged from the bottom of the chest and mended; comforters made for the neck and ears; old flannel shirts cut up to line monkey jackets . . . and so forth (239).

This is writing full of emotion—if emotion of a kind unfamiliar to readers of highbrow novels—reflecting the satisfaction taken in prudent forethought and productive work. It is like many passages in *Robinson Crusoe* differing only by being written in the plural—that is, by naming a social practice rather than an individual achievement.

How things get done, mechanical things and social things, is an interest that adventure books like Defoe's and Dana's start from and satisfy. And "how things get done" has a very broad scope when, as in *Robinson Crusoe,* it includes all the features of civilized society and shows us how the castaway can imitate, or rehearse in his limited but sacramental way, all the achievements of civilized western life. Dana's scope is not so broad, but it goes deeper and more existentially into self-discovery and self-realization.

Another example of Dana's likeness to Defoe (less self-evident but more significant) is the long description he devotes to Tom Harris, a sailor he calls "the most remarkable man I had ever seen" (162). This is another icon of manliness, but it is drawn in terms of mind, not body. Harris was remarkable for his memory, which formed "a regular chain, reaching from his earliest childhood up to the time I knew him, without a link wanting . . . for he knew the hoist of every mast, and spread of each sail, on the head and foot, in feet and inches" (163). But Harris was also remarkable for his reasoning powers, and "among all the young men of my acquaintance at college, there is not one whom I had not rather meet in an argument than this man . . . He was a far better sailor, and probably a better navigator, than the captain, and had more brains than all the after part of the ship put together" (164). He was thus a *natural* hero, who did not need the advantages of birth or education. He had picked up the principles of political economy and the steam engine—the two master sciences of the modern system. He embodied that system's characteristic idea of "brains," a significant new word. The only reason Harris had not risen to great heights was his "indomitable obstinacy," which had led him to rebel against his family and go to sea (like Crusoe). Once a drunkard, he had changed his way of life overnight. "The first thing with him was to reason, and then a resolution, and the thing was done" (166). The figure Dana shapes for our admiration combines Crusoe's features with those of the heroes of Samuel Smiles and Twain (e.g., pilot Bixby and the Connecticut Yankee) to make the perfect nineteenth-century WASP.

It comes as no surprise to hear that when *Two Years Before the Mast* appeared in England it won an immediate success, and that large numbers of copies were bought by the British Admiralty, to be distributed on ships of the fleet. The book marked another step forward in that process of amalgamating the mercantile and military virtues, a process that was an essential enterprise of adventure literature. It was, quite simply, propaganda in the interests of modern empire.*

In America, too, books like Dana's were useful to both the mercantile and military castes of the ruling class. In these years the sea story held a uniquely privileged position among adventures. This was because the reader acknowledged the need for authority over sailors and so furnished imaginative space for the captain of the ship—and therefore for the aristo-military caste in society. This space was often begrudged by the frontier adventure, which (as we saw in *Nick of the Woods*) cannot easily ac-

---

*Kingsley's *Westward Ho!* was similarly distributed to English troops in the Crimean War; and a Services Edition of Kipling was issued during World War I. Both Scott and Kipling were given cruises on Royal Navy warships—an honor one can scarcely imagine being offered to Henry James or George Eliot, much less to James Joyce or D. H. Lawrence.

commodate the aristocrat as hero.

What gave Dana's book its special character among sea adventures was its concern with the conditions of the ordinary seaman's life. The most notable expression of this interest in reform comes in Chapter 15, "Flogging"; in it Dana declares his strong revulsion for the act itself and for the arbitrary powers of the captain who ordered it. (Here Dana shows himself to be significantly more liberal than, for example, Cooper.) According to the editor of the Penguin edition, *Two Years Before the Mast* had, fourteen years after the book's publication, some influence on the passage of England's first Merchant Shipping Act.

It was not only particular abuses like flogging that concerned Dana. He was both troubled and pleased by the anomaly constituted by military discipline in a democratic state. How could one justify the autocratic power of a captain over his crew? Yet how could one have a ship—or any other of the great social machines of the nineteenth century—without such autocratic powers? As Melville was to say, the power of a captain over his crew must be quite natural in the Russian merchant navy, because the Russian political system was a tyranny. In an American ship, however, it was completely unnatural. Still, in spite of his objections to flogging, Dana was much more in sympathy with the need for authority, efficiency, and good discipline than Melville (the latter had tendencies to anarchism not shared by Dana). He is on authority's side, but still he continually brings this anomaly to his reader's attention. In Chapter 3, for example, describing life aboard ship, he begins: "The captain, in the first place, is lord paramount"; and his choice of feudal language is obviously deliberate (10). Dana challenges the reader to change either his understanding of naval discipline or his enthusiasm for American democracy, or to give up the idea that the two are congruent. Implicitly he argues for caste thinking, even for caste action, in the merchant navy. The steward, for example, is the captain's *servant*, while the mate is his *prime minister*, and the second mate has no status because "he is obliged to go aloft . . . and to put his hands into the tar and slush with the rest" (11). These are primitive or sacramental criteria of status that are undemocratic in nature.

Nevertheless, this concern of Dana's issues in a straightforward and powerful protest against tyranny. He says that he and the other sailors lived under a tyranny, "with an ungoverned, swaggering fellow administering it" (87). The captain was no gentleman, had no governance, and should not have been entrusted with power. Thus Dana was able to identify his "political" cause with that of the other sailors without identifying himself with them. He was an aristocratic rebel against tyranny; he was a gentleman, and the sailors were not; he was different by his inner nature—and by the bond he makes with the reader. His rebellion against injustice runs parallel with theirs, but at a distance.

On the other hand, at times Dana is able to speak quite directly out of the sailor's identity, as when he and other sailors take the gig to pick up some Mexican passengers who show fear of the sea: "This was nuts to us, for we liked to have a Mexican wet with saltwater . . . and we hoped, as there was no officer in the boat, to have a chance to duck them, for we knew they were such 'marines' that they would not know whether it was our fault or not" (181). This flexible readiness to assume the sailor's identity (on occasion) is a great source of strength to Dana as adventure writer: "Give me a big ship . . . there is more room, better outfit, better regulations, more life, and more company" (159). There is no distance between him and those he is describing at such moments, and the reader suddenly feels deserted, for the author stands aboard ship, and the ocean runs between the two.

Dana's interest was "to present the life of a common sailor at sea," partly as propaganda for reform, but also as a more existential, although also political, encounter with and appropriation of common manhood. In America, more than elsewhere, the idea of the common man was then challenging that genteel section of society, the book-buying public to which Dana belonged. Both frontiersmen and sailors were embodying the expansive powers of the nation more vividly than any other class, and adventure was the genre (of life and letters) in which they could be met and measured up to. Dana's going to sea no doubt had something of that motive behind it. His narrative implies it, and his father's nervous troubles must have been a warning to him.*

---

*Thomas Philbrick, the editor of the Penguin edition (London, 1981), says that Dana chose to be a sailor instead of a passenger because "he needed purpose, some kind of challenge against which he could pit and prove himself" (vii). And the book is full of scenes that suggest a typical nineteenth-century search for struggle and effort.

Indeed, in later years he fell again under the curse of his caste limits, in spite of his heroic effort at self-liberation. His later life, as a Boston lawyer, was inwardly unhappy and outwardly impotent; he was disastrously defeated, in a Boston political election, by the Irishman Ben Butler, who used Dana's Brahmin refinement (his "white gloves") to make him look un-American and ridiculous. So subsequent history gives this book the added interest of being a premature song of triumph, an escape story followed by a recapture.

What he describes is the process whereby a gentleman hardens and changes himself into a likeness of the common man so as to become equally a man, equally an American. (In *Redburn*, Melville describes the same process, but on him it seems not to have taken.) In the first days, Dana is seasick—"making wild vomits into the black night to leeward" (7). But the cook tells him, "You must begin on a new tack—pitch all your sweetmeats overboard, and turn to upon good hearty salt-beef and shipbread, and I'll promise you you'll have your ribs well-sheathed, and be as heart as any of 'em afore you are up to the Horn" (9). After partaking of this sea sacrament, Dana is a new man—long before the Horn. "I cannot describe the change which half a pound of cold salt beef and a biscuit or two produced in me . . . When we went on deck, I felt somewhat like a man, and could begin to learn my sea-duty with considerable spirit" (9). Soon, going out with another sailor to furl the jib, he gets his baptism: "For some time we could do nothing but hold on, and the vessel, diving into two huge seas, one after the other, plunged us twice into the water up to our chins. We hardly knew whether we were on or off; when, the boom lifting us up dripping from the water, we were raised high into the air and then plunged below again" (25). Dana is plainly elated when the other sailor admits that they had been in danger, "which good sailors seldom do when the thing is over" (26). About this time he moves from the steerage to the forecastle: "No man can be a sailor, or know what sailors are, unless he has lived in the forecastle with them—turned in and out with them, and eaten from the common kid" (43). When he sees some passengers seasick, he owns that "there was a pleasant feeling of superiority in being able to walk the deck, and eat, and go aloft, and compare oneself with two poor, miserable, pale creatures, staggering and shuffling about decks, or holding on and looking up with giddy heads, to see us climbing to the mast-heads, or sitting quietly at work on the ends of the lofty yards" (58).

Dana has made the transition they have yet to make; he has joined the hardened men, those exposed to nature and charged with her powers. This process continues throughout the book as a central thread of personal testing, reaching a paradoxical climax in Chapter 31, where, at a moment of greatest danger to the ship, Dana is incapacitated and must stay below in some agony of spirit. Just as the dynamism of wind and water is most vividly realized when the ship is as motionless as marble, so this engagement, this possession of Dana by the sailors' life, is most vividly realized when it is temporarily obstructed. When he arrives home, a Boston acquaintance cannot recognize this " 'rough-alley' looking fellow, with duck trousers and red shirt, long hair and face burnt as dark as an Indian's" (307). This is Dana's triumph; no nineteenth-century writer or reader could be quite at ease as an American until he had passed through being an Indian.

Dana wanted to embody those "natural" or manly qualities that sailors (and Indians and frontiersmen) could claim more plausibly than men of his own class. But the idea of manliness was part of the ruling-class ideology too—for that class was determined to be recognized as American—and Dana gives no hint of repudiating his class identity. When he describes a crew working contentedly under a severe captain, he notes, "Each one knew that he must be a man, and show himself such when at his duty" (153). The vocabulary of manliness suited the owner's and manager's point of view. Dana describes a fight between two boys, in which the smaller and weaker defeats the bigger and more powerful, in the style of *Tom Brown's School Days*.* The bigger boy "had always been master, and had nothing to gain and everything to lose; while the other fought for honor and freedom, and under a sense of wrong" (199). So, of course, the smaller one was bound to win. Such a fable is political as well as moral; when an oppressed class or race stands up for its rights it

---

*Hughes' story is perhaps the British book most comparable to Dana's, taking into account the differences between the two nations. Both are about the self-hardening rituals of the ruling class.

always wins. "It was soon over. Nat gave in—apparently not much hurt—and never again tried to act the bully over the boy" (199). He applies the managerial work ethic to shipboard life; keep the sailors busy all the time, Dana seems to say, and you will have a happy ship and no trouble.

The central issue, the key to Dana's sense of caste identity, is that of discipline and command. Early in the book, he tells us that sailors prefer to "have an officer active, vigilant, and as distant as may be with kindness" (19). And later on he describes their mate as being "a worthy man—a more honest, upright, and kind-hearted man I never saw—but he was too easy and amiable for the mate of a merchantman. He was not the man to call a sailor a 'son of a bitch,' and knock him down with a handspike" (76). Whereas another mate was "a hearty fellow, with a roaring voice, and always wide awake." He was " 'a man, every inch of him,' as the sailors said; and though 'a bit of a horse,' and 'a hard customer,' yet he was generally liked by the crew" (149). Such disciplinarians, not aristocrats themselves, exert power on behalf of gentlemen—they are the noncommissioned officers. In other words, Dana took the same interest in the sources, analogues, and paradoxes of discipline as Kipling did. Both writers built a rhetoric and an iconography in the interests of a ruling class.

That interest was eminently sensible and moderate. Dana was able to employ the criterion of manliness self-critically: "An overstrained sense of manliness is characteristic of seafaring men . . . A man, too, can have nothing peculiar or sacred on board ship; for all the nicer feelings they take pride in disregarding, both in themselves and others" (212–13). Even more clearly, Dana is ready to attack authority in the case of Captain Thomson. At the flogging, a sailor asks, "Can't a sailor ask a question here without being flogged?" "No," shouted the captain. "Nobody shall open his mouth aboard this vessel but myself." And later, "Don't call on Jesus Christ," shouted the captain. *"He can't help you. Call on Frank Thomson! He's the man!"* (85). Dana's blood ran cold, he tells his readers, and he turned away; for here the captain's authority was exerted in defiance of Christianity, in an implicit pact with the Devil.

In the Appendix to the book, written twenty-four years later, Dana tells of Captain Thomson's end, an end worthy of Ahab and a story worthy of Conrad. Having run into trouble trading in Sumatra, he was put in a native jail for a time. When he emerged:

> He sprang into the boat, urged her off with the utmost eagerness, leaped on board, ordered the anchor aweigh, and the topsails set, the four guns, two on a side, loaded with all sorts of devilish stuff, and wore her round, and, keeping as close in to the bamboo village as he could, gave them both broadsides, slam-bang into the midst of the houses and people, and stood out to sea! As his excitement passed off, headache, languor, fever set it—the deadly coast-fever, contracted from the water and night-dews on shore and his maddened temper. He ordered the ship to Penang, and never saw the deck again. He died on the passage and was buried at sea (333).

His supercargo, Dana's cousin, also caught the fever and died; then the chief mate caught it, and the second mate and crew deserted. Thus we see the black and destructive side—the Devil's compact—of WASP adventure and WASP expansion, foreshadowed even in this classic account of its bright achievements. Captain Thomson's "maddened temper" is the shadow version of that expanded self we saw our heroes acquiring.

The other striking way in which *Two Years Before the Mast* continues the Defoe-mercantile tradition of empire is in its moral geography and ethnography, which vividly express the driving force of the modern world-system as a cultural centrifuge in which WASPS show themselves morally more weighty than all people from the semiperiphery of Europe (the south and, above all in this case, Spain) and (more self-evidently and so more serenely) those from the outer arena. Dana tells us that Californians (being Mexican Spanish) are idle and thriftless, can make nothing for themselves, and buy things from others at four times their Boston prices. California women ruin themselves by their fondness for dress: "Nothing is more common than to see a woman living in a house of only two rooms, with the ground for a floor, dressed in spangled satin shoes, silk gown, high comb, and gilt, if not gold, earrings and necklace. If their husbands do not dress them well enough, they will soon receive presents from others." (65).

This passage notes many of the criteria that distinguished WASPs from non-WASPs ranging from marital morality, measures of economic self-respect, and conflicts between luxury and display and solid comfort to characteristic textiles and colors. Predictably, Californians have aesthetic compensations for their moral and practical feebleness. They have beautiful voices, and speak a beautiful Spanish; a common bullock driver speaks like an ambassador at a royal audience. Americans allow them these advantages in art, in compensation for their defeat in life.

Of course, the English and the Americans have engrossed all the trade, "having more industry, frugality, and enterprise than the natives" (68). And, when it comes to fighting, "Forty Kentucky hunters, with their rifles, and a dozen of Yankees and Englishmen, were a match for a whole regiment of hungry, drawling, lazy half-breeds" (13). These adjectives (note that their hunger too is held against them) indicate, by negation, the WASP qualities of self-control, competence, and energy. Later Dana describes a young Spaniard as "a good representation of a decayed gentleman. He reminded me much of some of the characters in *Gil Blas* . . . He had a slight and elegant figure, moved gracefully, danced and waltzed beautifully, spoke good Castilian, with a pleasant and refined voice and accent, and had, throughout, the bearing of a man of birth and figure" (199–200). Dana puts beside this aristocrat a "fat, coarse, vulgar, pretentious fellow of a Yankee trader" (199–200). But the trader will dispossess the aristocrat; for the latter, all charm and no power, belongs to literature and the past.

The political and moral philosophy behind such a passage derives, of course, from caste thinking. Dana's position is Scott's; his liveliest sympathies are with the aristocrat, but that is *because* his deeper judgment is for the trader. The latter represents the reality principle, and *therefore* the former is associated with pleasure, with the aesthetic, the erotic, the play principle.

By the same token, Dana displays, *vis-à-vis* the Sandwich Island laborers he works with in California, a tenderness comparable with Melville's for the Others he met on Nukheva: "They were the most interesting, intelligent, and kind-hearted people that I ever fell in with. I felt a positive attachment for almost all of them" (121). They shared everything with each other and bound themselves in absolute loyalty each to his particular friend. Dana's particular friend among them was called Hope. "I felt a strong affection for him, and preferred him to any of my own countrymen there; and I believe there was nothing which he would not have done for me" (208). These men came from the outer arena, beyond the modern system; consequently, they presented no challenge, even of the trivial nature presented by the Spaniards. Dana's fondness for them is a form of cultural sentimentality—but one we cannot afford to despise.

The 1859 appendix to the book, "Twenty-Four Years Later," is very inferior to the rest of the book in quality but not in interest. The falling off shows how closely and completely adventure is tied to its function as the energizing myth of the modern system. The chapter is inferior in imaginative quality because Dana's celebration of the progress California has made under United States rule is as vulgar in its logic and rhetoric as Mark Twain was to be on similar topics. He boasts of the brilliant saloons of the steamboat he arrives on, of the lighthouse that is one of the most costly and effective in the world, of the hundred thousand inhabitants of booming San Francisco ("the sole emporium of the awakened Pacific"), and so on. He says it was all so glorious he could scarcely keep his hold on reality. We reply, *sotto voce,* that he *did* lose his hold on taste and truth.

In San Francisco he met a man he had known, fifteen years before in New England, as a strict and formal Congregational deacon; a symbol of old New England seriousness. Now the man is quite changed: "Gone was the downcast eye, the bated breath, the solemn, non-natural voice, the watchful gait, stepping as though he felt himself responsible for the balance of the moral universe. He walked with a stride, an uplifted, open countenance, his face covered with beard, whiskers, and moustache, his voice strong and natural—and, in short, he had put off the New England deacon and become a human being" (314). Manliness here triumphs over godliness with a complacency disastrous even to the aesthetic sense. Of course, this is an example of the "geographical" social thinking that Americans so often applied to their experience. The free land of the West transforms the New England temperament; nature triumphs over the old forms of culture, in this man as in the nation at large. His face now sprouts hair as the prairies will sprout corn, because everything is expanding. Dana assures us that the former deacon was

as devoted to religion and good works as he had been formerly—
"the same internally, but externally, what a change!" But the
reader returns the phrase upon Dana, with the terms transposed
and the approving tone reversed.

Still, such critical indignation at Dana is beside the point, and
unfair. The adventure, as he lived it and wrote it in the 1830s, was
of course, preliminary to the commercial and political expansion
of the U.S.A. in the 1850s. Adventure *was* the energizing myth
of expansion; its glamor at its most genuine—and it was never
more genuine than in *Two Years Before the Mast*—was a lure
with a limited function and thus had to fade when that function
was fulfilled. Dana's narrative was as much in the service of the
United States' acquisition of California as was Captain Thomson's commercial enterprise—and a thousand other ventures—as
innocently and as undeniably at work for political ends.

Being an adventurer was not pure romance but one step in a
practical career, for many men. The fabled mountain men, and
even the frontiersmen Judge Hall saw, were mythic adventurers
for a few years only, spending the rest of their careers as entrepreneurs. William Goetzmann demonstrates this point in *Exploration and Empire.* Even in fiction, we remember, Robinson
Crusoe did not remain on his island forever; he went home to
England, there to live like a rich man on the proceeds of his
adventure. An adventurer lived out a myth for a few years only;
a nation believed in a given myth only as long as a certain political situation lasted. (See, for example, England's sudden shift in
response to Kipling, once the empire was clearly doomed.)
Cooper's Natty Bumppo, we are told, moved out of the clearing,
out of comfort and civilization, off toward more myth,
whenever the sound of settlement, commerce, and prosperity
came close. But Cooper wrote romances, and one cannot blame
Dana for not behaving like a romantic hero. Cooper himself did
not. (He wrote his romances in Paris.) Dana knew that his adventure had been launched in the name of profits, of American
hegemony, of commercial prosperity. However, he had moralized
and spiritualized it. And when commercial prosperity followed
from such adventures, he did his best to rejoice.

Chapter 6	MELVILLE'S *TYPEE* (1846)

Melville's story tells how he, like Dana, served as a sailor but deserted when his ship stopped at a South Sea island. He and a friend made their way to a hidden valley where they were adopted by the Typee. The culture of the island seems as paradisiacal as its climate, and all is play and pleasure until the sailors realize that they are prisoners, as well as guests, and that their hosts are cannibals. From this point on, the story concerns Melville's desperate efforts to escape.

Typee appeared in 1846, within the same decade as *Nick of the Woods* and *Two Years Before the Mast*. It may be seen as standing halfway between those two, in terms of the variables of the adventure form; superficially it is an autobiographical narrative, like Dana's, but more genuinely a piece of fiction, like Bird's.

Literary scholars have proved that Melville invented or stole from earlier books many of the events and descriptions presented in *Typee* as personal experience. He did not, however, invent an adventure plot like Cooper's—one involving the inheritance of land and a young man's apprenticeship to an old guide. Instead he wrote the ostensibly autobiographical story of a young writer exposing himself to danger and low life. In the 1840s many American writers were producing similar adventure narratives.

Seen in terms of social function, however, *Typee* is unlike both kinds of adventure, being to an important degree an antiadventure rather than an energizing myth of the modern world-system; in fact, to an important degree, it is deenergizing. This reversal of the meaning of adventure is perhaps Melville's most important contribution to the development of the genre. For in spite of appearances to the contrary, *Typee* does belong to the adventure genre. It has many features that place it in the series that began with *Robinson Crusoe.* The hero's horror of cannibalism, for instance, is the mainspring of the plot, which has, like the Leatherstocking novels and *Nick of the Woods,* a basic structure of captivity and escape. It has, in Mehevi, the Typee nobleman, a version of that romantic native hero found in Defoe (in *Captain Singleton*) and Cooper (in Chingachgook) and in many other adventures. It has a white man who has gone native and had himself tattooed—another figure found in adventure tales from Defoe's *Captain Singleton* on. It has an episode in which the hero is identified as—because he is a white man—an expert in guns. And so on. It was as an adventure that *Typee* was recognized and welcomed, by critics and ordinary readers, when it appeared, and as such that it was offered by Melville. Indeed, throughout his lifetime, it remained his most popular book.

From the start its reception was international. Like *Two Years Before the Mast* and *Nick of the Woods, Typee* was published almost simultaneously in England and America (in fact, it appeared first in England). So this (to some degree mistaken) recognition is another proof of the shaping powers of the adventure genre, which could assimilate material of quite a different character with no symptoms of indigestion. For as a function of an expanding society, adventure in those days exerted power over both writer and reader, acting not merely to relax and divert readers, but also to concentrate their nerve and muscle for the task of expanding the modern system all over the globe. It could even make use of Melville's ambiguous imaginings as material for this propaganda.

Melville was long known as "the author of *Typee,*" which was not to his liking in later years. He complained, in the middle of writing *Moby Dick,* that he would go down to posterity only as "the man who lived among the cannibals." Defining posterity as the babies who would be born about the time he died, he predicted that *Typee* would be given to them along with their gingerbread. (It was, of course, the demeaning fate of most adventures to be written for adults, but handed over to the children of the next generation. Everything designed for immediate use as a stimulus to practical action suffers that fate; it has too many associations, goes out of style quickly, looks used, and makes people self-conscious. However, critics believe that Melville rebelled against the fate of being an adventure writer for other reasons that were more important and more specific to him. Melville was very much the man of letters, the creator and creature of literature; he was remarkably gifted with words and rather ungifted in other ways. Thus the underprivileged position of adventure writer within the greater world of literature must have been painful to him. He wanted to be a "great writer," like Shakespeare (the Romantic Shakespeare), and he knew he could never achieve that status by writing adventures.

The underprivileged position of the genre was not, of course, something formally assigned by an academy or recognized by Melville from outward stigma. It was something he felt, independently even of thinking it, by virtue of his own incorporation of the values of that literary system. Where, after all, was such a system to be found if not in the minds of men like Melville? Take, for example, the matter of the close dependence on factual truth assumed for the adventure. This was an uncongenial constraint for Melville (as it was not for Dana), and he took considerable liberties with the truth in *Typee*. For instance, he claimed to have spent four months in Nukuheva, when in truth he had only been there three or four weeks; he invented the lake on which Fayaway and the narrator go sailing. Moreover, he claimed not to have read the books from which he in fact borrowed many descriptions.

As a writer of adventures, Melville was under pressure from publishers, and in danger from critics, in this matter of truth. Harper Brothers rejected his manuscript on the grounds that it could not be true and, therefore, "could have no real value." John Murray of London accepted it for his Home and Colonial Library but was still worried about its veracity; he had Melville introduce more general factual information about the island and the natives to strengthen its credibility. Adventures, then, had to be factually true in order to be mythically true. (They *could* be fiction, as long as it was fiction-based-on-fact, as *Robinson Crusoe* shows. Even so, any element of fiction pulled the narrative away from adventure and toward romance.) Murray's Home and Colonial Library advertised its volumes as being "compact enough to be carried into the Backwoods of America" and "the remotest cantonments" of India. They were the energizing myth of empire, the reading matter of adventurers; they could not afford to be "mere fiction."

Melville, of course, rebelled against such constraints on imaginative truth. He wanted his book to be seen as literature, and in the present century it is taken as literature. As George Woodcock says in introducing his 1972 edition of *Typee:* "Today we are inclined to see Melville as the explorer of the realm of darkness within the human mind rather than of the golden islands where the crucial time of his youth was spent" (7).[1] But to see Melville exclusively in these terms is to exalt literature at the expense of history, to scorn the broad cultural function of books in the name of their high-cultural function. *Typee* is, in fact, an important achievement as an adventure, and to ignore that character would be as crass as to ignore *Moby Dick*'s character as metaphysical tragedy. If we are to do adventure—and Melville—justice we must temporarily suspend our mental tug-of-war between pure and impure literature.

Adventure had, in those days, a literary tradition; and, as one would expect, Melville shows himself very sensitive to it in his own writing. He cites the English sea writers Smollett, Marryatt, and Dibdin, and refers often to "the illustrious Cook," as well as to the accounts of the voyages of Carteret, Anson, Kotzebue, and Vancouver. The latter were true accounts, written by the men who had made the voyages, but even Smollett and Marryatt, who wrote fiction, knew the sea well. Adventure, then, was written by adventurers, rather than men of letters: only adventurers had the right to write such books. When Melville himself first went to sea, he may have intended to use the experience as literary material. But he almost certainly went to sea primarily because he *had read* adventures rather than *in order to* write them. If there was a priority within the interdependence of life and letters in adventure, it belonged to the former.* But it was gentlemen-adventurers who wrote books; and if Melville made himself into an adventurer, and so presented himself to his readers, he also defined himself very assertively in caste terms—as a gentleman and man of letters.

---

*Melville himself would have agreed to this proposition, but Melvilleans, being critics and men of letters, probably would not; it is notable how often critical treatments of adventure fail in tact because critics can believe only in the priority of literature. The weakness of, for instance, structuralism is that it looks first for "the literariness of literature," and so denies the substance of the truly substantial books of our culture, which belong to genres that mix literariness with something else.

As we saw in Cooper's novels, in *Nick of the Woods* and in *Two Years Before the Mast*, caste thinking had already played an important part in adventure in America. But because *Typee* is an autobiographical narrative, Melville may be said not to have forced a caste hero upon his readers as egregiously as Bird and Cooper did. True, his narrator is rather notably a cultivated gentleman, but he *was* after all Herman Melville, who was one; and because *Typee*'s other characters are men of another race rather than another class, our sense of the gap separating him from them is not a class or caste difference. (In *Omoo* and *Redburn*, on the other hand, we do find a difference of that kind separating the narrator from the others, and it is much insisted on.)

Nevertheless, there is a marked caste character to *Typee*, and it is to be located in the discourse itself. The reader is engaged, by the sentences, in playing the role of gentleman. Take, for instance, the following passage, which describes the advantages of life in Polynesia:

> There were none of those thousand sources of irritation that the ingenuity of civilized man has created to mar his own felicity. There were no foreclosures of mortgages, no protested notes, no bills payable, no debts of honour in Typee; no unreasonable tailors and shoe-makers, perversely bent on being paid; no duns of any description; no assault and battery attorneys, to foment discord, backing their clients up to a quarrel, and then knocking their heads together; no poor relations, ever-lastingly occupying the spare bed-chamber, and diminishing the elbow-room at the family dinner-table; no destitute widows with their children starving on the cold charities of the world; no beggars; no debtors' prisons; no proud and hardhearted nabobs in Typee; or, to sum it up all in one word—no Money! . . . In this secluded abode of happiness there were no cross old women, no cruel step-dames, no withered spinsters, no love-sick maidens (181–82).[1]

What is striking here is that the point of view the reader is invited to share (which is not autobiographically "Melville," but generically "the author") is clearly that of a man-about-town; a man, a bachelor, and one devoted to pleasure. This becomes even clearer when the passage is set beside another, from Book IV of

Gulliver's Travels, which Woodcock suggests as its source: "here was neither physician to destroy my body, nor lawyer to ruin my fortune; no informer to watch my words and actions, or forge accusations against me for hire; here were no gibers, censurers, backbiters, pickpockets, highwaymen, housebreakers, attorneys, bawds, buffoons, gamesters, politicians, wits, splenetics, tedious talkers, controversists, ravishers, murderers, robbers, virtuosos; . . . no encouragers to vice, by seducement or example; no dungeon, axes, gibbets, whipping-posts or pillories."[2] Swift's point of view is *not* limitedly masculine, well-to-do, and idle; it is that of a Londoner subject to life in a modern city and to the trials that afflict men and women, old and young, rich and poor. By Melville's time, however, in America, at least for writers like him, the author-figure was identified with the clubman, which points up one of the difficulties the adventure genre encountered in America. When the adventurer doubles as clubman, he loses his capacity to be more the common man than other people. As late as Twain, American authors can be seen wrestling with the problem of combining all these roles—author, adventurer, and clubman.

The clubman point of view intrudes very blatantly into, for instance, Melville's account of the Ti, the men's house of the Typee: "The Ti was a right jovial place. It did my heart, as well as my body, good to visit it. Secure from female intrusion, there was no restraint upon the hilarity of the warriors, who, like the gentlemen of Europe after the cloth is drawn and the ladies retire, freely indulged their mirth" (213). This tone of voice—with its natural complement of roguish intimations of erotic naughtiness—is, of course, not much help in understanding either the Typee or Melville. It is false in every sense.

Luckily the gentleman persona also influences the author in better ways. It leads him to a humanist-*philosophe* attitude toward native life and Western imperialism that Melville uses to remarkable effect. *Typee* takes a position, vis-à-vis European traders and the "civilization" they brought to "uncivilized" lands, like that of *Gulliver's Travels.* The Marquesans, he says, cordially hated the French: "but the impulses of their resentment were neutralized by their dread of the floating batteries, which lay with their fatal tubes ostentatiously pointed, not at fortifications and redoubts, but at a handful of bamboo sheds, sheltered in a grove of cocoanuts! A valiant warrior doubtless, but a prudent one too, was this same Rear-Admiral De Petit-Thouars. Four heavy, double-banked frigates and three corvettes to frighten a parcel of naked heathen into subjection! Sixty eight pounders to demolish huts of cocoanut boughs, and Congreve rockets to set on fire a few canoesheds!" (51).

To build this anti-imperialist and antimodernist slant into an adventure was, of course, to give the latter a very different meaning from that found in Defoe, Scott, or even Cooper. Melville is here to be compared with Swift, not with adventure writers. *Gulliver's Travels* was, in fact, read as an adventure, but against its author's intentions, which are clear enough to us now. Such misreading of *Typee* also occurred; in determining readers' responses, the adventure genre overrode the author's intentions.

Melville's sponsors are not, however, Swift so much as the French Encyclopedists. For *Typee* is directed against throne and altar, especially the latter. Melville praises the islanders for instituting so little difference between their chiefs and other people and makes fun of the high priest, Kokory, the "Lord Primate of Typee," for his "sleek and complacent appearance," and for the "funny little image" he consults. Melville commends the Typee religion on the grounds that "the festival had been nothing more than a jovial mingling of the tribe; the idols were quite as harmless as any other logs of wood; and the priests were the merriest dogs in the valley" (240). This is not a Christian satire on paganism, as it may appear, but rather the reverse, for the main targets of Melville's religious animus are Christian missionaries. He paints some corrosive images of missionaries and even worse ones of their wives: for instance, one "robust, red-faced, and very lady-like personage, a missionary's spouse, who day after day for months together took her regular airings in a little go-cart drawn by two of the islanders, one an old grey-headed man, and the other a roguish stripling, both being, with the exception of the fig-leaf, as naked as when they were born" (267). The cart got stuck; this lady, Melville tells us, "used to think nothing of driving the cows to pasture on the old farm in New England; but times have changed since then. So she retains her seat and bawls out, 'Hookee! Hookee!' (pull, pull)" (268). This event happened on Honolulu, which Melville satirically describes as "a community of disinterested merchants and devoted self-exiled heralds of the Cross" (267). And it is worth noting that Melville assigns the lady a New England origin. New England was the source of missionaries and merchants and of the animating spirit of the modern world, which Melville opposed. His loyalties went to New York, the home of relaxed epicurean men of letters. Morally speaking, New Englanders were the energizers of the modern system, while New Yorkers were skeptical onlookers.

This irreverence reminds us of the anticlerical satire the French *philosophes* employed as part of their criticism of the *ancien régime.* Melville makes just as unrestrained a criticism of modern imperialism: "It may be asserted without fear of contradiction, that in all the cases of outrages committed by Polynesians, Europeans have at some time or other been the aggressors, and that the cruel and bloodthirsty disposition of some of the islanders is mainly to be ascribed to the influence of such examples" (64).

He describes a confrontation between an old and tattooed chief and a polished and splendid French admiral:

> At what an immeasurable distance, thought I, are these two beings removed from each other. In the one is shown the result of long centuries of progressive civilization and refinement, which have gradually converted the mere creature into the semblance of all that is elevated and grand; while the other, after the lapse of the same period, has not advanced one step in the career of improvement. "Yet, after all," quoth I to myself, "insensible as he is to a thousand wants, and removed from harassing cares, may not the savage be the happier man of the two?" (66).

This reference to happiness suggests that, of all the *philosophes*, it is to Rousseau that Melville was most indebted, and many other passages confirm that impression. It is, after all, in Rousseau that we find the satiric criticism of European civilization married, as it is in Melville, to a romantic appreciation of other modes of being. Of whom but Rousseau can we think when we read: "Civilization does not engross all the virtues of humanity: she has not even her full share of them. They flourish in greater abundance and attain greater strength among many barbarous people. The hospitality of the wild Arab, the courage of the North American Indian, and the faithful friendship of some of the Polynesian nations, far surpass anything of a similar kind among the polished communities of Europe" (274). And Melville answers the charge of cannibalism by citing the fiendish skill of our death-dealing engines, which make the white man "the most ferocious animal on the face of the earth" (180).

Rousseau has been claimed as the progenitor of all modern anthropology—as the first to take the modern anthropologist's attitude toward both primitive peoples and his own, European, society—and this too is a clue to what makes *Typee* unlike other adventures. It is Lévi-Strauss who makes that association—and indeed there is some similarity of attitude between his *Tristes Tropiques* and *Typee*, as there is between both works and certain writings of Rousseau.

One way of naming all the features that make *Typee* different from earlier WASP adventures is to say that the book is an anthropologist's reminiscence. Its narrator's energies do not go into making things, or growing things—like Robinson Crusoe's—or into fighting or falling in love—like Waverley's—but into observing the Typees' economy, marital customs, and eating habits, speculating about their myths, and, above all, appreciating their way of life and its unlikeness to his own. As an adventure hero, the narrator is egregiously passive; as an observing intelligence, he is strikingly active. He is that mutilated man (Lévi-Strauss's phrase for the anthropologist) who goes out of his own society to heal himself; at the same time, he embodies his civilization's remorse and self-accusation.*

More strikingly, perhaps, Melville is ready to go nearly as far as Lévi-Strauss in recommending "nondifferentiation," which the latter says would be necessary in order to achieve the social harmony both men desire. Lévi-Strauss prefers the repetitive clockwork dynamism of traditional societies to the ever-changing and expanding thermodynamic kinetics of our own. The latter works by building up contrasting states of, for example, heat and cold, to generate explosive forces as materials change from one state to the other—as water becomes steam and drives pistons. Thus Western society is explosively forceful in

---

*The narrator's mysterious lameness is a floating signifier in *Typee*, which can attach itself legitimately enough to the idea of the mutilated anthropologist.

ways that other societies are not, because they do not incorporate such differences[3] (e.g., Melville's Nukuheva). Lévi-Strauss even recommends the sexual nondifferentiation of Buddhist monks and nuns. In a similar vein, Melville recommends the loose freedom of Typee polyandry, and the slack agreement and agreeableness of Typee thought: "There was one admirable trait in the general character of the Typees which, more than anything else, secured my admiration: it was the unanimity of feeling they displayed on every occasion . . . I do not conceive that they could support a debating society for a single night" (274). They were unimaginable as citizens of a modern democracy, as inert as the sixth-century Englishmen the Connecticut Yankee would later try to stir up.

As we have said, *Typee* is an adventure. But the central character does not become a hero because he does not really act. *Typee* is, in fact, also an antiadventure, for many of the ideological determinants of the genre are reversed here. For instance, traders, the mercantile caste, are among the villains of *Typee*: "But there is, nevertheless, many a petty trader [Americans are not excluded] that has navigated the Pacific whose course from island to island might be traced by a series of cold-blooded robberies, kidnappings, and murders, the iniquity of which might be considered almost sufficient to sink her guilty timbers to the bottom of the sea." (63). The idea of "the trader" includes more than trading; it includes, as we noted, both "evangelical" (missionary) and "New England," for of all American types it has always been the New Englander who has been the trader, who has demonstrated the Robinson Crusoe qualities. (In *Omoo*, the one American expatriate who is doing something commercial and purposeful on Tahiti, is a New Englander.) And in the appendix to *Typee* we read of Dr. Jull, "a sanctimonious apothecary-adventurer" who stirred up trouble against the English on the Sandwich Islands, with his "junto of ignorant and designing Methodist elders" (334–35). Melville's sympathies in that affair were with Jull's opponent, Lord George Paulet, the English captain—that is, with the aristo-military caste.

The mercantile caste was, of course, the dominant one in nineteenth-century America, especially in matters of public opinion, and Melville was willing to ally himself temporarily with any enemy of that caste. His permanent allegiance, however, went, as we have seen, to Rousseauist romanticism, understanding that as one strand in the radical humanist tradition of cultural criticism. Melville constantly translates features of Typee culture into WASP (Yankee) terms, with generally and jocosely satiric effect. He constantly praises it for its unprogressive character, unchangingness, and lack of "bustle" and "go."

Above all, he subjects America to criticism—most effective when it is least explicit—by erotic and hedonist criteria. When his ship first enters the harbor of Nukuheva a flock of young girls swims out to meet it: "and I watched the rising and falling of their forms, and beheld the uplifted right arm bearing above the water the girdle of tappa, and their long hair trailing beside them as they swam. I almost fancied they could be nothing else than so many mermaids . . . All of them at length succeeded in getting up the ship's side, where they clung dripping with the brine and glowing from their bath, their jet-black tresses streaming over their shoulders, and half enveloping their otherwise naked forms" (48). These swimming nymphs, as Melville calls them, wound up their hair, dried themselves, oiled their bodies, and "were quickly frolicking about the decks." How unimaginable in Boston, the reader reflects (and how unfortunate that that is true)!

In the valley of the Typee, the whole world is eroticized: "All around [the lake's] banks waved luxuriant masses of tropical foliage, soaring high above which were seen, here and there, the symmetrical shaft of the cocoanut tree, surmounted by its tufts of graceful branches, drooping in the air like so many waving ostrich plumes" (188). It is typical of the differences between Defoe's and Melville's visions of the island and the native that in *Robinson Crusoe* the word *naked* is always preceded by the modifier or intensifier *stark*, whereas in *Typee* nakedness is not shocking but alluring—although relaxingly rather than arousingly so.

This eroticism permeates the serious thinking of the book. For instance, the criticism of the missionaries is often associated with their wives and thus, indirectly with their marriages and their sexuality. Besides the coarse, robust, red-faced lady mentioned before, there is a story of quite a beautiful missionary's wife whom her husband brought to the island, "believing much in the efficacy of female influence." The islanders at first gazed at this strangely dressed figure in mute admiration but then "sought to pierce the sacred veil of calico" she wore; "her sex once ascertained, their idolatry was changed into contempt . . . To the horror of her affectionate spouse, she was stripped of her garments, and given to understand that she could no longer carry on her deceits with impunity" (39). She was not "evangelical" or meek enough to accept this incident, and the couple left the island. These two are contrasted, implicitly and unfavorably, with Melville himself, who follows the islanders' ways, is at ease with them, and grows fond of them. It is notable how confidently Melville affronts the more "serious" part of his reading audience and allies himself with the men of erotic sophistication and religious skepticism.

The sharpest criticism Melville makes of European intrusion into the islands—although his criticism is veiled out of propriety—is that it brought venereal disease. It is erotic damage the Europeans did to this erotic culture, and it is an erotic criticism Melville levels at them. His hedonism is a natural extension. The islanders, we are often told, do not spoil their lives with work (as we do). In fact, Melville seems to have exaggerated this aspect of Typee culture, denying that they practiced agriculture (which they did) and attributing to earlier races the Typees' engineering feats with blocks of stone. He wished to see only "the perpetual hilarity reigning through the whole extent of the vale . . . [the natives] . . . reclining beneath the shadows of one of the beautiful groves . . . employed in weaving chaplets and necklaces" (181–82).

This eroticism and hedonism is certainly an expansive movement of the mind, but it seems necessary—at least within the space of this argument—not to describe it as expanding and intensifying the self in the way that the earlier adventure writers do. Melville is not interested here in the self, with its powers of action, responsibility, and will; what stirs to life under his influence is the imagination, with its faculties of appreciation, speculation, and detachment—all passive from the point of view of the self. It may be better in his case to speak of escape rather than expansion, if we can exorcise the deprecatory connotations of "escapism." What Melville is escaping from, at his best, are deforming constraints and compulsions that have been forced upon the citizens of the modern system; to escape from them can be the way to more life. Nonetheless, to escape is not self-expansion.

Thus if *Typee* is, like *Nick of the Woods* and *Two Years Before the Mast*, a Jacksonian romance historically (in that it belongs to the period in which Jacksonian politics were practiced), it is not Jacksonian in its essential spirit. Often enough Melville talks as if it were—his hero is, ultimately, desperate to escape from his island paradise—for he had a genius for catching any idea that was in the air and rephrasing it eloquently, without feeling much responsibility to shape his behavior or his other thoughts in conformity with it. His own movement of the mind, however, that which is authentic and original in him, is away from empire and the modern system, and toward any alternative.

The action, or relaxation, on Nukuheva is the very opposite of the action on Robinson Crusoe's island, and it is decidedly different from anything in Scott's or Cooper's novels. *Typee* is an adventure-antiadventure. This may sound like one of scholarship's factitious fictions, but in fact the genre can be found in many other places; in the story of The Mutiny of the *Bounty;* in Mark Twain's and Henry Adams's accounts of the South Sea islands; and in Eugene O'Neill's mythical polarity, which opposes those islands to New England. (America has found many more uses for this myth than England.) Even in the mid-twentieth century, the sarong, the lei, the aloha, and Dorothy Lamour and her attendant troupe of Wahinis were still meaningful signs in popular culture, still promising total relaxation as the proper reward (indeed, the natural result) of extra effort.

The adventure-antiadventure is thus a real enough phenomenon, while the paradoxical structure attributed to it by that label—the mutual opposition of its two main elements—surely finds some confirmation in its aptitude for debased or satiric uses. In *Typee*'s own day, the antiadventure was coopted by the adventure, and the book was read against some of its writer's meanings. Now it is in danger of the opposite fate. In the nineteenth century the genre imposed itself upon the author, because WASP culture was expansive, confident, imperial, and sent out commands that constrained even serious writers and critical minds. Melville's whole career is testimony to the ineffectuality of his struggle against them. In the twentieth century, on the other hand, we are more likely to impose the writer's meaning (just because it is subversive) upon the genre and to see the book as an antiadventure. But to read *Typee* that way also means losing something—the most interesting feature of the book, its ambiguity.

Chapter 7   PARKMAN'S
            THE OREGON
            TRAIL
            (1849)

F rancis Parkman's *The Oregon Trail*
is an adventure written (after it had been lived) by a brilliant
American intellectual; which is not quite how one would describe our earlier writers. In it we see the old traditions of American philosophy, the tradition of New England Christian piety,
summarily dismissed in favor of an almost opposite tendency
toward militarism and *Machtpolitik*. This short book contains
the seeds or the crystals of enormous changes, which were soon
realized in areas remote from both "adventure" and "literature"
in any ordinary sense.

The career of American adventure was more successful in the
realm of history-writing than in that of pure literature. The main
effort of American historians in the nineteenth century was to
turn world history into an adventure tale—the adventures of the
nations as they broke free of empire. At least that was true of the
four, closely interconnected New England historians—Prescott,
Bancroft, Motley, and Parkman[1]—David Levin treats in his *History as Romantic Art*.

They wrote history as adventure, in the sense that they put a
hero at the center of their narratives (someone like George Washington or Montcalm or Ferdinand and Isabella) and that the
shape of their stories was determined by his or her fate; the story
reached its climax with the triumph or tragedy of the hero. One
could say also that, like Cooper and Bird, they were always
concerned with the provenance and destiny of the land and that
their heroes had to learn from the forest or the sea or from
solitude lessons not to be found in books or schools. (It is no
accident that Cooper and Irving wrote histories themselves—as

did Scott in England—for there was a deep similarity between their kind of adventure writing and nineteenth-century history.) But the essential likeness was that they wrote history not as the success story of an individual—but of a group-individual, the American people, or the Anglo-Saxon race.

In his *The Pioneers of France in the New World* (1865), Parkman described his subject as

> The attempt of Feudalism, Monarchy, and Rome to master a continent [these three can be taken to represent old-style imperialism] . . . Feudalism still strong in life, though enveloped and overborne by new-born Centralization; Monarchy in the flush of triumphant power; Rome, nerved by disaster, springing with renewed vitality from ashes and corruption, and ranging the earth to reconquer abroad what she had lost at home . . . [It was a contest between] Liberty and Absolutism, New England and New France. The one was the offspring of a triumphant government; the other of an oppressed and fugitive people; the one an unflinching champion of the Roman Catholic reaction; the other, a vanguard of the Reform [England and Reform represent the. new, anti-imperialist empire].[2]

The character of nineteenth-century history (in its difference from the history written by Hume and Gibbon) reflects, of course, the triumphant world career of the Anglo-Saxons and the self-confidence that success bred in them. But it also reflects something almost opposite—something we have already met in Dana. It is the anxiety the ruling class felt when it faced the classes it ruled; the anxiety was especially strong in America, where all the traditions of the establishment were confronted and tested by new forces. Were the men of those privileged classes strong enough, American enough, to rule in America? The single narrative that shows this anxiety most vividly, and illustrates the heroic therapy by which it was cured, was Parkman's *The Oregon Trail;* in it we see a truly brilliant intellectual shaping his creed, and his character as a historian, in the crucible of adventure.

The adventure itself took place in 1846 when Parkman, then twenty-three, set off with his friend, Quincy Adams Shaw, to follow the westward trail used by immigrants heading for Oregon, but what Parkman most wanted to see was the camps of the Pawnee and the Sioux, and he wanted to see those tribes at war.

He was in considerable danger at times, partly because he fell very sick when he was alone; and he developed the skills, of shooting and riding, and the qualities, of courage and command, that make a hero of adventure. He kept a notebook on the spot and wrote this account three years later, when he was in considerable pain.

This narrative is autobiographical, like Dana's and Irving's, but it also introduces features that were familiar to readers of fictional American adventures. Most strikingly, Parkman presents a man of the wilderness (recognized by contemporary readers as another Natty Bumppo) from whom the young Parkman learned how to hunt and track and how to be a man. He also portrays Indians in much greater detail and vividness than Cooper and Bird achieved. Finally, he describes the act of killing with a frankness no autobiographical writer had yet dared—the killing of animals directly—but there are also many anecdotes of war and hand-to-hand combat between men. Thus, Parkman's narrative is, on several counts, an *American* adventure, aristocratic as it is.

The incongruity lies in the fact that Parkman's father was a Unitarian minister, a pupil and associate of William Ellery Channing, the great saint and hero of the Boston Unitarians and all American peace lovers. The father too was a notable preacher, and we read that his voice was praised as being of "a sweet, mild, unctuous smoothness"; such a voice was an advantage that must have counted as a liability with many—think what such an attribute would tell us about its owner in a Dickens novel. And young Parkman was one of those who counted it a liability: "For his high-mettled son, in turn, the ministerial calling, the 'decorum of the cloth,' and much else his father personified were to be lifelong irritants and subjects of incisive sallies."[3] The saintly Channing was the son's *bête noire;* the boy's early drawings of Revolutionary war veterans show him constructing a model of masculinity quite unlike his father or the Brahmin Channing.

In *The Oregon Trail,* Parkman's language for praising his friends is aristo-military—"my gallant and high-minded companion and our noble-hearted guide"—and it is significant that his favorite author seems to have been Byron (213–14).[4] On his first trip to Europe, Parkman had traveled from Gibraltar to Malta aboard a British troopship, and he preferred Anglicanism to Boston/Unitarianism with all the zest of Cooper.

Here in this old world, I seem, thank heaven, to be carried about half a century backwards in time . . . A becoming horror of dissenters, especially Unitarians, prevails everywhere. No one cants here of temperance reform, or of systems of diet—eat, drink, and be merry is the motto everywhere, and a stronger and hardier race of men than those around me now never laughed at the doctors. Above all there is no canting of peace. A wholesome system of coercion is manifest in all directions . . . and the honest prayer that success should crown all these warlike preparations, yesterday responded to by fifty voices. There was none of the new-fangled suspicion that such belligerent petitions might be averse to the spirit of a religion that inculcates peace as its foundation.[5]

But even though he rejected so much of his heritage, Parkman remained in some sense a Puritan. In this narrative he is self-consciously engaged in conquering himself, or rather in conquering the forces of sickness within his body. (He referred to his diseases collectively as "The Enemy.") He notes on page 95 that "a violent pain awoke me, and I found myself attacked by the same disorder that occasioned such heavy losses to the army on the Rio Grande." (The military allusion—rather comical in this case, where he is talking about diarrhea—is characteristic of Parkman.) Later, "I was so reduced by illness that I could seldom walk without reeling like a drunken man, and when I rose from my seat upon the ground, the landscape suddenly grew dim before my eyes" (124). And there comes a moment when he confronts and accepts the probability that he may die out there.

Through sickness, and other means, his virtue is continually being tested, and he demonstrates it in quasi-religious fashion. One cannot fail to recognize the shaping force of the Puritan imagination in passages like this: "Having left my horse in Raymond's keeping, I began to climb the mountain. I was weak and weary, and made slow progress, often pausing to rest, but after an hour, I gained a height whence the little valley out of which I had climbed seemed like a deep, dark gulf, though the inaccessible peak of the mountain was still towering to a much greater distance above" (192). This is obviously a moral as well as a natural landscape. Parkman is renewing the images of Bunyan's *Pilgrim's Progress,* although with a difference: his landscape is real in origin, and he *makes it* allegorical.

The lives of the other three New England historians were ordered by similar images of struggle, sickness, journeying on, and eventual triumph. But what Parkman makes especially clear is the way this Carlylean heroism could accompany and support a shift in caste persona from the mercantile to the aristo-military. Parkman was the son of a Unitarian minister and grandson of a Boston merchant, but he referred to the clergy as "vermin," and his respect went all to warriors, white and Indian. As an undergraduate at Harvard, he took private lessons in boxing, shooting, and riding and applied himself to whiskey punch, woodcraft, and Indian war whoops. He declared pretty girls and horses "the first-ratest things in nature."

The aristo-military caste usually asserts itself as more masculine than others, and Parkman asserted that the Anglo-Saxon race was peculiarly masculine: "peculiarly fitted for self-government . . . An uncommon vigor, joined to the hardy virtues of a masculine race, marked the New England type. The sinews, it is true, were hardened at the expense of blood and flesh—and this literally as well as figuratively; but the staple of character was a sturdy conscientiousness, an undespairing courage, patriotism, public spirit, sagacity, and a strong good sense."[6] This emphasis on sturdiness and strength is also found in the other New England historians, and they also reinterpreted the history of their people in terms more appropriate to an adventure tale than a religious mission. Although they were less radical than Parkman, they all redesigned the character, the caste character, of their group.

The most striking thing about Parkman's narrative, considered as a New England document, is its overt enthusiasm for war, especially for a primitive war between Indian tribes. "Here their warlike rites were to be celebrated with more than ordinary solemnity, and a thousand warriors, as it was said, were to set out for the enemies' country . . . I was greatly rejoiced to hear it. I had come into the country chiefly with a view of observing the Indian character" (94). And later he tells us that "I was vexed at the possibility that after all I might lose the rare opportunity of seeing the Indian under his most fearful and characteristic aspect" (105–106).

He declares a general belief in war: "for, from minnows to men, life is incessant war" (208). He has a corresponding enthusiasm for armies; in the twelfth chapter, "Ill-luck," he describes the march of an Indian army, and the gallop of warriors thrice around a village, with a vividness equal to Scott's in *Waverley.*

Predictably, the virtue he makes most of is that of chivalric courage, and he tells frontier dueling anecdotes that celebrate it: "But when Bordeaux, looking from his door, saw the Canadian, gun in hand, standing in the area and calling on him to come out and fight, his heart failed him; he chose to remain where he was" (104). A few pages farther on, an Indian hero calls out his enemy in vain, and, "striding to the entrance of the lodge, stabbed the chief's best horse, which was picketed there" (110). Moreover, he often reminds us of the dangerousness of these men he lives with and likes: "I would not have encamped along with him without watching his movements with a suspicious eye," for he knew the man needed a scalp (199).

But perhaps an even clearer caste mark than courage is the touch of brutality he flaunts: "A smart cut of the whip restored his cheerfulness" (34), or "he [Parkman's Boston companion] seized upon a red-hot brand from the fire, and clapped it against the forehead of the old squaw, who set up an unearthly howl, at which the rest of the family broke into a laugh" (92). Such remarks affront the Brahmin conventions governing first-person narratives and assert a different caste identity. Parkman is not a mere writer; he is an aristocrat.

He feels himself very unlike the American emigrants—the "Kentucky fellows," as he calls them—and to cross the plains he joins forces with an English captain instead. This is clearly a matter of caste sensibility. What he objects to most in the emigrants (the "off-scourings of the frontier") is their curiosity. He was "tormented by the intrusive questioning of the men who thronged among us. Yankee curiosity was nothing to theirs. They demanded our names, whence we came, whither we were going, and what was our business" (75). At the end of the narrative another such group "came crowding round by scores, pushing between our first visitors, and staring at us with unabashed faces" (269). The message is clear: dignity and reserve are the prime virtues of good breeding, of pure race.

The idea of "going native" receives a corresponding scorn: "They were a mongrel race; yet the French blood seemed to predominate; in a few, indeed, might be seen the snaky black eye of the Indian half-breed, and, one and all, they seemed to aim at assimilating themselves to their red associates" (62). At Fort Laramie, the Indians are all morally mongrels or half-breeds and so are their animals: they "had tied their wretched, neglected little ponies by dozens along the fences and out-houses . . . [their village] sufficiently illustrated the condition of its unfortunate and self-abandoned occupants . . . [its houses] in utter ruin and neglect . . . narrow, obstructed paths . . . a stray calf, pig, or a pony" (28). The Anglo-Saxon, on the other hand, is a moral thoroughbred: "The trader was a blue-eyed, open-faced man . . . a neat, well-furnished room . . . neatly carpeted . . . a well-filled bookcase" (29).

There are passages in which national types are listed seemingly at random but actually ranging upward from the decadent and ill-bred to the Anglo-Saxon hero. He sees a group of

> thirty or forty dark slavish-looking Spaniards, gazing stupidly out from beneath their broad hats . . . crouching over a smouldering fire was a group of Indians . . . one or two French hunters from the mountains, with their long hair and buckskin dresses . . . and finally three men, obviously Anglo-Saxons, with rifles lying across their knees . . . The foremost of these, a tall, strong figure, with a clear blue eye and an open, intelligent face, might very well represent that race of restless and intrepid pioneers whose axes and rifles have opened a path from the Alleghanies to the western prairies (15).

These images of breeding illustrate Parkman's racism (which was prevalent in the other historians too) but they also signal the caste thinking that interests me here. The greatest hero of Parkman's idea of breeding is the guide, Henry Châtillon, and it is clear that his breeding has nothing to do with noble birth or genetic heritage or social advantages; for Châtillon, a democratic hero, is a natural American hero. Nonetheless, he is in sympathy with, and a promoter of, aristocracy. He tells Parkman that gentlemen of the right sort can stand hardship better than the average man. Châtillon himself is described as a tall, well-dressed man, with a frank and open face: "His age was about thirty, he was six feet high, and very powerfully and gracefully moulded. The prairies had been his school; he could neither read nor write, but he had a natural refinement and delicacy of mind, such as is rare even in women. His manly face was a mirror of uprightness, simplicity, and kindness of heart; he had, moreover, a keen perception of character, and a tact that would preserve him from flagrant error in any society" (21).

He is, of course, another Natty Bumppo. All Parkman has added to Cooper's image is a more erotic feeling for the hero's physique. Châtillon appears in the book's last paragraph, dressed to great advantage, for "he had a native good taste which always led him to pay great attention to his personal appearance. His tall athletic figure with its easy flexible motions appeared to advantage in his present dress; and his fine face, though roughened by a thousand storms, was not at all out of keeping with it" (286). Parkman described the guide to Frederick Remington, when the latter illustrated the book in the 1890s, as "the most striking combination of strength and symmetry I have ever seen . . . a figure so well-knit and well-moulded that awkwardness was impossible to it."[7] Unlike Natty, Châtillon is essentially graceful.

Such heroes, hunters, were equally democratic and chivalrous; Parkman remarks of trappers in general: "I defy the annals of chivalry to furnish the record of a life more wild and perilous than that of a Rocky Mountain trapper" (111). But the language used about Châtillon is a little fashionable, moral, and sentimental—indeed a little foolish. He is Cooper's hero, rather than Parkman's—the young Natty of the late novels, the genteel hero. Parkman's own sensibility is significantly wilder and more savage, as we see when he writes about the Indians.

The sensibility ordering this narrative exerts a strong pressure toward heroism, and not a moral heroism; or at least the morality is not Brahmin. This becomes clearest in the central episodes in which Parkman leaves his Boston comrade and Châtillon and is alone with the Indians. But before we turn to that topic, it is worth noting another result of that pressure, the type-casting of the other people, the nonheroes, as either eccentrics (like the Captain) or enemies (like the man called R—) or clowns (like Tête Rouge). It is clear that these social roles are all alternatives to heroism, subordinate roles that surround and support that major option. About the last we are told, "Tête Rouge rather enjoyed being laughed at, for he was an odd compound of weakness, eccentricity, and good nature . . . he served the purpose of a jester in a feudal castle; our camp would have been lifeless without him" (240, 262). Parkman's comment is not ungenerous; but, of course, he took great care not to become a jester himself. He was determined to be one of the knights of the castle.

The war Parkman went in search of did not take place, but in its stead he took part in several magnificent hunts; hunts are, of course, second-best to war for the military sensibility and were to figure prominently in later American adventures. In Chapter 7, "The Buffalo," we get the first hunt description (although earlier there is a caricature hunt in which the Captain shoots a cow). There are, in fact, several variations on the hunt theme, and they are structured significantly. In the first half of the book, the emphasis is on the chase, whereas in the second half it is on the kill. Perhaps Parkman's most striking case description is of the "grim old warrior" buffalo: "He was miserably emaciated; his mane was all in tatters; his hide was bare and rough as an elephant's, and covered with dried patches of the mud in which he had been wallowing. He showed all his ribs whenever he moved. He looked like some grizzly old ruffian grown gray in blood and violence, and scowling on all the world from his misanthropic seclusion. The old savage looked up when I first approached, and gave me a fierce stare. Then he fell to grazing again with an air of contemptuous indifference" (276). It is surely clear that what Parkman feels for the object of this long description is love; he is identifying, as Hemingway and Faulkner were to do later—with a caste hero: "I had full opportunity of studying his countenance . . . It seemed to me that he stood there motionless for a full quarter of an hour staring at me through the tangled locks of his mane. For my part, I remained as quiet as he, and looked quite as hard . . . 'My friend,' thought I, 'if you'll let me off, I'll let you off'" (276). But, of course, letting him off is against the rules of the hunt, of the caste game, and in the end Parkman kills the bull.

Later he describes his greatest historical hero, La Salle, in terms (of hard grim misanthropy) that recall the buffalo: "He was a tower of adamant, against whose impregnable front hardship and danger, the rage of many of the elements, the southern sun, the northern blast, fatigue, famine, disease, delay, disappointment, and deferred hope emptied their quivers in vain . . .

Coriolanus-like . . . a heart of intrepid mettle . . . America owes him an enduring memory; for in this masculine figure she sees the pioneer who guided her to the possession of her richest heritage."[8] Parkman has before sufficiently stressed the solitary friendlessness of La Salle's fate for us to recognize in both this peroration and in the buffalo passage the same paradoxical sympathy and admiration—which is implicitly self-referential. Parkman sees himself, wants to see himself, as another such solitary hero, hunter, or explorer.

Although hunting is an activity of the aristo-military caste, being a hunter in the American sense is in some ways not a caste activity, in that it takes a place in a nonsocial space, outside the frontier of society. It faces away from other social and caste activities. Just for that reason, however, it represents more vividly the "sacramental" function of the man of violence of the military caste: he who kills, violates the taboo against violence on behalf of the rest of society. Thus, if the hunter fails to represent the social aspect of caste, he nonetheless represents its religious aspect vividly.

Early on in the narrative, Parkman tells with enthusiasm the story of a Dahcotah warrior who "performed a notable exploit" in a Pawnee village. He climbed the roof of a lodge by night, dropped in through the smoke hole, drew his knife, stirred the fire to see by, and stabbed and scalped several victims. Then he rushed outside, yelled a Sioux war cry, shouted his name in triumph and defiance, and "darted out upon the dark prairie" (55). Parkman presents this anecdote with a notable absence of disapproval or distance and, in effect, commends it to us. It is in such Indian exploits, and in the rituals of war and hunting, that he finds the models and sanctions for the caste change he is undergoing—which, by his example, he is inducting his people into. The high-cultural traditions of New England were very different in these matters, but nature and the Indians constituted an area of myth in which a new cult could be established. Thus, after an account of a hunt, Parkman describes the cutting up of the animals, conveying the feeling that the Indians were taking part in a sacrament of blood: "The twisted sinews were cut apart, the ponderous bones fell asunder as if by magic, and in a moment the vast carcase was reduced to a heap of bloody ruins . . . Some were cracking the huge thigh-bones and devouring the marrow within; others were cutting away pieces of liver, and other approved morsels, and swallowing them on the spot with the appetite of wolves. The faces of most of them, besmeared with blood from ear to ear, looked grim and horrible enough" (161). These scenes also subserve a sense of plenitude, of overflowing Edenic nature: "The face of the country was dotted far and wide with countless hundreds of buffalo. They trooped along in files and columns, bulls, cows, and calves, on the green faces of the declivities in front. They scrambled away over the hills to the right and left; and far off, the pale blue swells in the extreme distance were dotted with innumerable specks" (67). And later, this is a hunter's Paradise: "The grove bloomed with myriads of wild roses, with their sweet perfume fraught with recollections of home. As we emerged from the trees, a rattlesnake, as large as a man's arm, and more than four feet long, lay coiled on a rock, fiercely rattling and hissing at us; a gray hare, twice as large as those of New England, leaped up from the tall ferns; curlew flew screaming over our heads, and a host of little prairie dogs sat yelping at us at the mouths of their burrows on the dry plain beyond" (96). Thus everything is larger than life (larger than reality, larger than in civilized New England), and the hunter is the priest of the cult of nature.

At the center of Parkman's narrative, and of the cult of nature, stands the Indian. He portrays three main types: the warrior, who is also the hero, the figure of splendid naked virility; the hag, the embodiment of all that is odious and ridiculous in Indian culture, all that reminds the white man that he is glad to be white; and the adolescent boy who is about to become a warrior and so is the most beautiful of all.

The first warrior we meet is nearly six feet tall, "lithely and gracefully, yet strongly proportioned; and with a skin singularly clear and delicate." He is naked to the waist, and "from the back of his head descended a line of glittering brass plates, tapering from the size of a doubloon to that of a half-dime" (76). Another warrior displays his war equipment to Parkman: "Among the rest was a superb head-dress of feathers. Taking this from its case, he put it on and stood before me, perfectly conscious of the gallant air which it gave to his dark face and his vigorous graceful figure" (187). And another, Mahto-Tonka, "never arrayed himself in gaudy blankets and glittering necklaces, but left his statue-like

form, limbed like an Apollo of bronze, to win its way to favour
. . . gorgeous as a champion in panoply, he rides round and
round within the great circle of lodges, balancing with a graceful
buoyancy to the free movements of his war-horse, while with
sedate brow he sings his song to the Great Spirit. Young rival
warriors look askance at him; vermilion-cheeked girls gaze in
admiration; boys whoop and scream in a thrill of delight, and old
women yell forth his name and proclaim his praises from lodge
to lodge" (120). The language of chivalry ("champion in
panoply") was standard literary ornament in the nineteenth century after Scott; but Parkman saves it from mere romanticism
and gives it its original aristo-military meaning, allying medieval
terms with observations of savage warriors.

He consistently stresses the nakedness of the men, but the
effect is quite different from both the shocked disapproval of
Defoe and the gentle paneroticism of Melville. In Parkman's
narrative, nakedness is an enhancement of the virile. The naked
warrior is the living phallus, to be which or to have which constitutes the desire of everyone in the community: "Others again
stood carelessly among the throng, with nothing to conceal the
matchless symmetry of their forms. There was one in particular,
a ferocious fellow named the Mad Wolf, who, with the bow in
his hand and the quiver at his back, might have seemed, but for
his face, the Pythian Apollo himself" (23). It is part of the
glamour of such figures that they do no work; as Veblen points
out, in such cultures, work is something that women do, while
the men perform exploits—notably hunting and war.

It is clear that the images of Indian life that Parkman constructs
are powerfully erotic for us, especially that of the young warrior.
But the image of "the Indian" also includes many elements that
are marked as repellent, such as the old women, physically ugly,
shrill, abusive, and domineering. Indeed, Parkman calls many
Indian types squalid or degenerate, and the disorganization of an
Indian village on the move clearly disturbs him by its pell-mell
rush: "Behind followed a wild procession, hurrying in haste and
disorder down the hill and over the plain below; horses, mules,
and dogs; heavily burdened traineaux; mounted warriors,
squaws walking amid the throng, and a host of children" (114).

His image of the Indian boy is more lyrical. Parkman picks
one called the Hail Storm and depicts him as a "light graceful

figure reclining on the ground in an easy attitude" while "his handsome face had all the tranquility of Indian self-control" (198). In action we see him "riding without stirrups or saddle, and leading his eager little horse to full speed" after a gigantic buffalo (161). When the latter turns upon him, the Hail Storm fled, clinging "in his seat like a leech, and secure in the speed of his little pony, looked round towards us and laughed." Parkman records the Hail Storm's transition from boyhood to manhood in detail and in delight, safeguarding that delight with an insistence that the boy was dangerous even to him, Parkman: "I have no doubt that the handsome, smooth-faced boy burned with desire to flesh his maiden scalping-knife, and I would not have encamped alone with him without watching his movements with a suspicious eye" (199).

These different images of the Indian cohere because the Indians are felt to be as a whole a version of nature. The heart of nature, for Parkman, is savagery, in the sense in which Emerson used the term in his essay on Power: "In history the great moment is when the savage is just ceasing to be savage . . . Everything good in nature and the world is in that moment of transition, when the swarthy juices still flow plentifully from Nature, but their astringency or acidity is got out by ethics and humanity."⁹ This idea of nature is what Cooper never grasped, and what no one before Parkman was able to embrace so wholeheartedly. Thoreau said, "I love the wild not less than the good," but it was Parkman who made it true. He turned away from a moral-contemplative static nature toward a bloody, disordered, and, in many ways, horrifying jungle out of which beauty and splendor blossom unpredictably.

The form of this vision of nature can be represented as a threefold concentric system. First of all, nature is wild, in a sense that merges, quite explicitly, with squalor. The natural lacks the shapes and forms that men expect and need to find in life. At the beginning we see a prairie brook, "twisting from side to side through a hollow; now forming holes of stagnant water, and now gliding over the mud in a scarcely perceptible current, among a growth of sickly bushes, and great clumps of tall rank grass" (35). The Pawnees' dogs, we are told, "have not acquired the civilized accomplishment of barking, but howl like their wild cousins of the prairie" (18). Squaws are too natural to smile—

they can only laugh; among the Indians, only the warriors have form. Nature, therefore, is formlessness, or inadequate form.

Then, more essentially, for those who penetrate through that outer manifestation, nature is splendid fierceness and force: "We were leading a pair of mules to Kanzas when the storm broke. Such sharp and incessant flashes of lightning, such stunning and continuous thunder I had never heard before. The woods were completely obscured by the diagonal sheets of rain that fell with a heavy roar, and rose in spray from the ground, and the streams swelled so rapidly that we could hardly ford them" (18). And in another storm: "The thunder here is not like the tame thunder of the Atlantic coast. Bursting with a terrific crash above our heads, it roared around the boundless waste of prairie, seeming to roll around the whole circle of the firmament with a peculiar and awful reverberation" (45). Yet for those who have endured both the squalidness of nature and her fearful dangers, for those who have kept faith and penetrated further inward, nature is beauty: "The storm clearing away at about sunset opened a noble prospect . . . The sun streamed from the breaking clouds upon the swift and angry Missouri and on the vast expanse of forest that stretched from its banks to the distant bluffs . . . Looking over an intervening belt of bushes, we saw the green, ocean-like expanse of prairie, stretching swell beyond swell to the horizon . . . All the trees and saplings were in flower, or budding into fresh leaf; the red clusters of the maple blossoms and the rich flowers of the Indian apple were there in profusion" (18–19).

This is the serene and effulgent moment of reward known by those who have truly served nature. As Parkman understands that service, it is only the hunter, the member of the aristo-military caste, who has done so. Since there are no such storms in civilized New England, the Brahmin and the mercantile castes into which he was born stand remote and averted from this nature. And so does all New England, all Anglo-Saxonry, unless it will rededicate itself to the cult. It is thus a very subversive manifesto that lies beneath the narrative surface of *The Oregon Trail.* This adventure carries a different message from those of Melville, Dana, Bird, or indeed Scott and Defoe. But the message was not unique, even then; which must explain why the book did not arouse more protest. Although Parkman's histories are necessarily more objective and scholarly than his adventure, and though the other American historians were of less fiery and strenuous temperament than he, still all New England history-writing of the nineteenth century carried something of this subversive message of adventure.

Given his aristo-military aspirations, it is natural that Parkman should have grown conservative and antidemocratic as time passed. When the Civil War broke out, he was at first dismayed—as was Dana—by the election of Lincoln as national leader, finding the Midwesterner "feeble and ungainly." He even had some temporary sympathy with the South in the Civil War, recognizing it as a military and chivalric society. But (again like Dana) he played a patriot's part in the war and actively promoted the North's cause.

Happier and more active in his old age than Dana, he seems to have quite enjoyed his dislike for modern liberal developments. In the late seventies he wrote, for example, against women's suffrage, but the zest of his own performance seems to have made him buoyant. On January 1, 1882, he wrote to a French friend: "I am sitting in my own study, a caribou rug under my feet, beaver skins on the sofa, and portraits of Montcalm, Amherst, and Wolfe over the fire along with a large red stone pipe which a Sioux chief gave me, and the sword of my younger brother, an officer in the war of 1861–5, who, after surviving a thousand dangers, was killed by an accidental fall in California."[10] He had successfully transferred the caste-loyalties of the Boston Brahmins from the clergy to the aristo-military caste.

Part Three

THREE ANOMALIES

Carson's *Autobiography* (1856)
Twain's *Roughing It* (1872)
Roosevelt's *Autobiography* (1913)

A frontiersman who wrote his own life-story, a man of letters who lived the life of the frontier, and a gentleman who became president by virtue of his adventures.

In the second half of this book, and particularly in this section, the focus on one particular book of each writer grows less sharp and exclusive. Instead the chapters focus on whole oeuvres or lives and pay more attention to contemporary movements of thought. In the context of modern literary ideas we need more persuading to take adventure seriously.

Chapter 8

CARSON'S *AUTOBIOGRAPHY* (1856)

The next three authors, Carson, Twain, and Roosevelt, are anomalies from a formal point of view, as I explained in Chapter 1. They also correspond to an anomalous period in the history of adventure. The reader will notice a gap in the publishing dates of my texts—for nearly 65 years separate *Roughing It* (1872) from *The Green Hills of Africa* (1935)—and may wonder if there was in those years a falling-off in the number of adventures written or published. But the case was more nearly the opposite. There were so many adventures published in that period, and they are of such varied interest, that it was hard for me to choose one to represent the others. Moreover, the quality of the individual tale is less interesting than the quantity and the character of the total product. Above all, the form had become so stylized that new examples merely reproduced the old features. Thus the literary genre failed in authenticity and ceased to be an appropriate lens through which to see history. We begin to find adventure everywhere *except* in genuinely literary terms.

This general and vulgar efflorescence of the cult of adventure is presumably explained by the triumph of capitalist industry in America and, then, by the emergence of conscious imperialism, first in England and then here. The Anglo-Saxon adventure was having its happy ending in world domination; this was the time of Cecil Rhodes, of Victoria's assumption of the imperial style, of Alfred Thayer Mahan's call for a big navy, and of the Spanish-American War. But, as in other stories, the happy ending, the wealth and power awarded to the central character, did not satisfy, did not sustain the scrutiny of the critical reader. It was an unhappy time for the citizen of sensitive conscience: the age of colonial wars, machine guns, battleships, and gunboat diplomacy. It was the Gilded Age; when America glittered as never before, but with a veneer under which lay black iron.

And to this imperialization of patriotic feeling there corresponded the obvious vulgarization of the literary genre, adventure. For this was also the period of the dime novel, the mass fiction that escaped from all high-culture discipline and spread across American publishing, starting from the Boston publishers, Beadle and Adams. The original Beadle title *(Malaeska: the Indian Wife of the White Hunter)* appeared in the summer of 1860. Altogether Beadle published 33 series, amounting to 5,000 titles (although this figure includes many partial or total duplications). During the Civil War, dime novels were shipped to the Union troops by the freight car load, for they were thought suitable to inspire the soldiers to perform their part in the national adventure. After the war, they were read on the frontier by men whose lives they represented in fictional form. As we shall see in the cases of Kit Carson and Bill Cody, such stories in fact reflected back into their heroes' lives—and interfered with those lives.

Carson was a figure like Parkman's hero Châtillon, and his life and adventures were notable examples of the legend that inspired so many young Americans in the nineteenth century. The message readers took from his autobiography was just the same as that they took from *The Oregon Trail,* although the literary character of the two books is entirely different, for Carson was neither a writer nor a thinker, but an adventurer, pure and simple.

His autobiography gives us the adventurer's adventure but not in his own language; for Carson was illiterate. This account was written by someone else (most likely a family friend called Turly), who gave the narrative a meager and dull correctness of style. It is a far cry from both the high-culture eloquence of historians like Parkman and the low-culture vitality of adventurers like Mike Fink ("I'm a Salt River roarer and I love the wimming and I'm chockfull of fight"). In living speech Carson was probably closer to Fink than this narrative lets appear; once when the official mask slips we hear him telling another man that he will rip his guts.

Still, the official mask is not so gross an imposture in Carson's case—on Carson's face—as it would be on other frontier heroes. He was ready to be coopted by the government, as Indian agent and other things, and he apparently always wore a manner of taciturn (but authoritative) calm that was perhaps not unlike the literary style Turly devised for him. He was easily translated to the purposes of ruling-class hero worship. Whereas Mike Fink was described as being of Herculean proportions, naked to the waist, perfectly symmetrical, colored like an Indian, and so on, apparently no one ever saw Carson with his clothes off; certainly no biographers presented him as an erotic figure or a troublemaker. Moreover the meagerness of diction and dullness of detail of this narrative have, in some cases, the effect of authenticating his heroism and substantiating his anecdotes. The modern equivalents are the laconic speech and expressionless faces of John Wayne and Gary Cooper.

Carson's narrative conforms to the pattern and spirit of the classical modern adventure. He served two years of apprenticeship, but in 1826, at seventeen, decided that "the business did not suit me and, having heard so many tales of life in the mountains of the West, I concluded to leave him. He was a good man, and I often recall the kind treatment I received at his hand" (4).[1] This is exactly the starting point (in tone as well as event) of *Robinson Crusoe;* and, like Crusoe, Carson sincerely deplores the foolish wastefulness of other trappers/sailors, who risk their lives for money and then spend it like water. The great adventure of his life is thus said to be only an episode, an escapade, an act of conscious naughtiness. The real values he proclaims are those of the middle class and are predominantly moral.

But, of course, the reader does not believe this disclaimer while reading *Robinson Crusoe* or *Kit Carson.* The feelings both evoke are all on the side of adventure; morality—at least in its Golden Rule or distributive aspect, of treating others as you would wish to be treated—gets short shrift. A few pages after the passage quoted, Carson describes how he persuaded his comrades to kill some Indians, because he wanted "satisfaction for the trouble and hardships they had gone through" (26). "Satisfaction" is a key term in this book, with its debased-chivalric connotation of a code of honor. (It was, incidentally, the motive alleged for one of the most striking deeds of slaughter in *Captain Singleton.*) Besides Defoe's heroes, those of other adventures are called to mind. Like Natty Bumppo, Carson grew tired of the settlements after only a few days in St. Louis (65); and like Parkman's Châtillon, he is particularly good friends with his only serious rival as a trapper, Leroux. Indeed, Melville, when he reviewed *The Oregon Trail,* remarked that Châtillon was another Kit Carson. Both conform to the traditional pattern of the adventure hero.

Most strikingly, Carson, like Natty and Châtillon (and Nathan and Beatte), was first presented to the American public (at least the reading public) through his encounters with a handsome and romantic young hero, John C. Frémont, behind whom stood his wife, Jessie Benton, and her father, Senator Thomas Hart Benton of Missouri. The configuration Carson–Frémont–Jessie Benton Frémont–Senator Benton strikingly resembles one found in many novels by Cooper; for instance, Natty–Edwards–Elizabeth Temple Edwards–Judge Temple in *The Pioneers.* An impoverished young aristocrat inherits actual power from his father-in-law and mythic prestige from a scout. In Carson's case federal policies and international politics were at stake.

In *The Dictionary of American Biography,* we read that "Frémont was precocious, handsome, and daring, and quickly showed an aptitude for obtaining protectors."[2] Like Cooper's Edwards, he was of romantic, mysterious/scandalous, origins and an adventurer in more than one sense.

He began his career by joining the Topographical Corps of the Army, and on surveying expeditions made friends with the mountain men of John Jacob Astor's American Fur Company. Having met Senator Benton, chief supporter of Jackson and national spokesman for the frontier and expansion, he eloped with the senator's 16-year-old daughter, Jessie. When Benton got over his anger, he became Frémont's ally and political protector, as Judge Temple was Edwards's; and Jessie Benton Frémont largely wrote the reports on her husband's expeditions that made him a popular, indeed a national, hero. They were something new in the way of Government Reports, being written as adventures, with events given a skillful slant toward the romantic and heroic. The Frémonts' model, we are told, was Irving's *Captain Bonneville;* they also made use of the form devised by novelists like Cooper.

On the first of these expeditions, which was inspired by the United States' hope of annexing Oregon, Frémont picked up Kit

Carson in St. Louis and made him his guide. The report of the expedition, published in 1843, made much of the link between the two men and was a great popular success, with many reprints. The report of the second expedition, in 1844–10,000 copies were printed—showed the Oregon Trail to be feasible for emigrants and so promoted the movement chronicled by Parkman. The third expedition was inspired by hopes of military intervention in California, and Frémont and Carson played prominent parts in the war that broke out there. Because of his habit of dashing insubordination, Frémont was court-martialed and left the army; but he struck gold in California, and settled down there as a rich man. He was nominated for the presidency by the Republicans in 1856, and again in 1864, as the hero of the radicals dissatisfied with Lincoln. His 1928 biography by Allan Nevins was entitled *Frémont, the West's Greatest Adventurer.* Thus he had a political career that reminds us as much of Theodore Roosevelt as of Cooper's romantic young heroes and that shows clearly the way literature and politics were interwoven in America. Carson was presented as the "old" guide from whom Frémont learned his skill in adventure, and thus inherited his Americanness. (In fact, Carson was only four years older than Frémont.)

We get some of this information from footnotes to the Lakeside Classics edition of Carson's autobiography, which also gives modern readers the necessary background to appreciate (as Carson's contemporary readers may have done without footnotes) all that he modestly was not saying.[3] Thus, on page 80, he tells us only that "Frémont, with myself and five or six other men, went ahead to Sutter's Fort for provision"; the footnote tells us that the trip was a two-month ordeal from which the explorers emerged as a woeful procession of skeleton men leading skeleton horses. And the introduction contrasts four sentences by Carson with a six-page account by another witness to the same events, the latter full of the most hectic adventures and heroic exploits by Carson.

His taciturnity extended into straightforward illiteracy, of course; and the illiteracy merged, on its other side, into nature—Carson's style is natural, in its hard and simple outlines, and is entirely free from the softness and sophistication of culture. He is more authentic as an adventurer than either Dana or Parkman, not only because of the greater magnitude of his deeds but also because of the lesser fluency of his tongue. "Don't talk about it or you will lose it," said Hemingway much later, and that is obviously a major truth within the manly code these writers are celebrating. Yet one is bound to notice that Hemingway did an awful lot of talking about it, and so did Dana and Parkman and all of the others. The only one who really shuts up in print, who makes an authentic impression of talking without saying much, who does not deploy the subtleties and paradoxes of the professional orator praising silence, is Kit Carson.

Of course, a different aspect of this silence emerges in the casual attitude Carson takes up toward the killing he has committed. Perhaps "casual" is too definite a word; what is most striking is the lack of feeling or emphasis, the absence of reflection and responsibility. Of one engagement he remarks that though he does not know how many Indians they killed, "it was a perfect butchery" (*LC*95). At first reading, it seems possible to put the stress on "butchery" and take "perfect" as a rather effete intensifier expressing moral shock. But the next sentence says that they had accomplished their purpose of giving "the Indians such a chastisement that it would be long before they would again think of attacking the settlements." One soon realizes that "chastisement" is a word used repeatedly in this context and is the most significant word in the book. On second reading, then, one puts the stress on "perfect" to express satisfaction (in both senses), taking "butchery" as a value-neutral description. Carson's attitude toward native Americans, and to the battles in which he killed them, is that of the pedagogic administrator; that is, he erases both the emotional facts of slaughter and the practical facts of his own position as adventurer. His declared motive could plausibly explain only another kind of action—an administrator disciplining those committed to his charge.

In his dealings with whites, Carson seems to display a certain vindictiveness, although only faint traces of this motive appear in the narrative. For example, in an account of a duel with a Frenchman called Shunar, Carson says that he "taught him a lesson"; a footnote indicates that he had killed the man (giving a grim ring to his "we had no more bother with this French bully") and that for the rest of his life he "retained a feeling of lively resentment" against Shunar's memory (*LC*44). In his account of Colonel Summer, who failed to send Carson aid when he needed it, there seems to be a powerful anger expressed by heavy irony—"the gallant old Colonel"—and by tight-lipped understatement—"I do not consider myself under any obligation to him" (145). Given the dull, smooth surface of the narrative, these small wrinkles signal something boiling beneath.

The Lakeside Classic edition is not ready to make that sort of point about Carson, for its main argument is that he was "gentle, generous, honest and courageous—a veritable Chevalier Bayard of the western wilderness" (*LC*xxxii). (This was written in 1935, toward the end of the period when that sort of comment was still possible.) But it does note occasions when Carson claimed that the Americans had only two cannons, although in reality they had six;* and it points out that a Mexican general whom Carson calls very impertinent "was not without excuse in ordering such a body of armed men to leave the country" (*LC*93). Finally, after Carson has described the shooting of "the bravest Indian I ever saw," a footnote adds that "the bravery he had displayed did not deter Carson from crushing his head with a hatchet, or one of Frémont's Delaware followers from scalping him" (*LC*98).

But on the whole it is left to the reader to discover and (as best he can) swallow the killing and the moral casualness of comments like "in the success of recovering our horses and sending many a redskin to his long home, our sufferings were soon forgotten" (*LC*28). This casualness is likely to leave a powerful impression on the mind of the modern reader, an impression that bears upon the history of the adventure genre as a whole. For in this autobiography the casualness is linked to deceit, and the adventure is linked to imperialism, more transparently than in other narratives of this kind. The reader finds himself present at the masking or veiling of the unpleasant facts of empire. A footnote on page 137 tells us that, when five Indians were killed, their scalps were taken by an American sergeant as "a voucher," but that, "in transmitting this report to his superiors at Washington, Major Grier thought it desirable to explain that the scalps were taken

---

*Whether or not Carson made an honest mistake, we need not regard this as personal boasting. It was a necessary convention of adventure that the whites should be at a disadvantage, should be struggling against odds. The reader could not respond with the right feelings if the whites had a material advantage. This was one of the differences between the facts of imperialism and the myth of adventure.

'by two or three Mexican herdsmen who came up after the fight was over.' "

Again, at the end of one of his longest descriptions of fighting, Carson says, "I wished to do them as much damage as I could, and directed their houses to be set on fire. The flag being dry, the fire was a beautiful sight. The Indians had commenced the war with us without cause. I thought they should be chastized in a summary manner, and they were severely punished. Frémont saw the fire at a distance, and knowing that we were engaged, hurried forward to join us, but he arrived too late to join in the sport" (100). We notice, of course, the words *beautiful* and *sport;* but the tone of the voice is too dull, its inflections are too stiff to let us read those words as betraying a heartless aestheticism; it may be that Carson just chose the wrong words for what he meant to say. On the other hand, we may suppose that he had no lively feelings about the burning and the battle to contradict the implications of those words—no feelings to be outraged by them.

What the literary reader has to resist is the temptation to judge Carson no hero because of his moral lapses. There seems no reason to doubt that he was, in fact, the great adventurer his contemporaries acclaimed him; nor to ascribe to other adventurers the moral delicacy, generosity, or passion that he lacked. We should not be deceived by Cooper and Bird and their romanticism. Carson was a real hero of adventure, and heroes are not notable for such qualities. On the other hand, real adventurers remain figures with power over other people's imaginations.

After 1842 Frémont was Carson's link to Washington, the government, and the ruling class. His senator father-in-law considered himself the heir to both Andrew Jackson and Thomas Jefferson and the trustee of the cause of United States expansion across the continent. Moreover, Frémont's marital and parental links were far from merely sentimental or static. By the 1840s, Jessie Benton Frémont worked hard to make her husband famous and, because Carson was a part of his own political cause, her father exerted all his influence in the same direction. With Frémont, Carson rose to national eminence; he was a valuable political property. When summoned to Washington (where he was interviewed by President Polk and given a military commission), he stayed in the Bentons' home. He was their adventurer and the hero of their cause—which they were making the nation's. This cause was a political embodiment of adventure. The United States was to be different from Europe precisely because it was—in several senses—"the place of adventures."

Frémont's expeditions were geographical surveys, and so carried all the prestige of science, and all the innocence of exploration. This was the age of explorers—they were the nineteenth century's most highly approved adventurers—like David Livingstone and Henry Stanley in Africa. But Frémont's expeditions also were on occasion quasi-military expeditions looking for trouble; in Mexican California, for example, they supported American settlers who wanted to separate from Spain and join the United States. Between 1846 and 1848, as we have seen, Carson, acting in concert with American soldiers, helped inflict a serious defeat on the Mexican forces. Thus he made the historically crucial transition from frontiersman to Army man, from adventurer to imperialist. The change seems to have been entirely to his taste. At about that time, he was just beginning to turn himself into a farmer in New Mexico. But when he heard that Frémont was leading a second expedition, he sold his land immediately (at a considerable financial loss); exploration, surveying, and military action were much more his style than agriculture and commerce.

Even before joining Frémont and the army, Carson had had contact with large organizations and official enterprises through commercial fur trading companies that sent men into the mountains (for years at a time) to trap and hunt. (In 1822 Mike Fink answered an advertisement in a St. Louis paper for a hundred young men to ascend the Missouri to its source and remain in the wilderness for two or three years.) In 1827 Carson served as a cook to Ewing Young, who organized trapping parties in the Mexican Southwest, and in 1824 led a colonizing group to Oregon where he eventually acquired an enormous estate in the Willamette Valley. Later he served with the enormous Hudson's Bay Company.

But Carson was not so much proto-merchant as proto-administrator and soldier; after fighting alongside Frémont in 1853, he became an Indian agent in Taos. His attitude toward the Indians there was what one might have predicted: "If the chastisement of the Indians of this country were left to the citizens, I have no doubt that in a short period they would subdue them. As matters stand at present, the Indians are the masters of the country, and commit depredations whenever they please . . . The Apaches are now committing depredations daily, which go unpunished, and in my opinion, they may again commence hostilities ere long" (163, 168). These are some of the last remarks in the autobiography. In later life Carson did in fact fight the Apaches, the Utahs (1855–56), and the Navajo, who finally surrendered in April 1864. He used cannon against them—artillery was the great weapon the whites had, and the natives, in most parts of the world, did not—and it is said that Carson's sleep was haunted ever after by dreams of dying Navajo women and children. He was made a brigadier-general in 1865 and helped General Sherman conclude the peace treaties with the Indians in 1867.

His autobiography, written in 1856, was not published until 1926, but it was a source for several biographies that appeared soon after it was written. DeWitt C. Peters's *The Life and Adventures of Kit Carson* (1858), as its subtitle ("The Nestor of the Rocky Mountains") suggests, made Carson into a classical statue of wisdom, probity, and Victorian correctness. (Since Carson was only 49 in 1858, to call him a Nestor was clearly to force him into the role of old guide, fit to instruct the young hero, Frémont.) Another such biography was published in 1862 and another in 1873, Henry Nash Smith tells us in *Virgin Land.* The third of these, for instance, asks its readers to "think of such a man as Kit Carson, with his native delicacy of mind; a delicacy which never allowed him to use a profane word, to indulge in intoxicating drinks, to be guilty of an impure action, a man who enjoyed, above all things else, the communing of his own spirit with the silence, the solitude, the grandeur with which God has invested the illimitable wilderness."[4] This is, of course, the mountain man disguised as Brahmin hero, a climax to that long process of disguising that began with Natty Bumppo.

At the same time there was, at the popular, culturally irresponsible level, a different image of Carson as a rip-roaring slayer of bears and Indians. This was to be found in Emerson Bennet's *The Prairie Flower,* of 1849, and Charles Averill's *Kit Carson: The Prince of the Gold-Hunters,* also of 1849. Such "biographies" were published, from the 1840s on, in such weekly story-papers as *The Flag of Our Union* and *The New York Ledger.* This literature served the purposes of Benton's political group, but we should not suppose it to be their creation; it had its own natural momentum, and answered a widespread appetite for news about frontiersmen.

Carson's fame was a part of his personality, and his own self-consciousness. If he was only 49 when he was named the Nestor of the Rockies, he was only 40 when he came upon a book (probably, according to Smith, Averill's) that portrayed him as an infallible slayer of Indians and savior of whites. His discovery of this book is described in the autobiography, and it is especially meaningful because Carson came upon it in the wreckage of a wagon in which American prisoners had been abducted by Indians. Carson had come to their rescue and driven off their captors, only to find the woman he had hoped to save recently dead, with this book beside her. He surmises that she must have been reading it and drawing hope from the image it gave of his invincibility. Carson naturally turns this incident toward pathos, but from our point of view it conveys strikingly the extraordinary potency of the adventurer image. Picking up that book, Carson was in effect picking up a mythic mirror in which his own features were glorified and from which came the voice of America saying, "This is my beloved son."

The myth of the frontiersman was spread all over the West, not only by such biographies but also by place names. Carson himself grew up in the Boone's Lick country, because his father admired and followed Daniel Boone; and Mark Twain spent his first years on the frontier in Carson City, one of the many places named after Carson during his lifetime. There were also Fort Davy Crockett, Bent's Fort, and so on. The rivers and mountains, the fords and the forts all resounded to the heroes' names.

But the writers about these heroes, especially with serious or genteel pretensions, faced the difficult problem of relating the frontier legends to the categories of high-culture sensibility. It is clearly absurd to compare Kit Carson with Nestor or with the Chevalier Bayard, or to compare Mike Fink (as writers did) with Richard Coeur de Lion or Rob Roy: absurd because those names signify romance and literature rather than epic and legend. The American figures clearly *were* mythical, in a different way; they did not fit into "literary" or "classical" myths. They were, in fact, the antithesis of the official culture mythology; they were culture heroes, and yet they were also anticulture and antiheroes. This was one of the paradoxes Mark Twain exploited as a humorist (but which in some sense destroyed him as a serious writer). When America turned its imagination westward, as it did after the battle of New Orleans in 1815 (of course, the turning was not accomplished all at once, or completely), the American man of letters was presented with an insoluble problem: he had to create a literary culture out of anticultural material.

But these purely literary phenomena are less important, and less interesting, than the larger cultural ones represented by the mountain men. These can best be appreciated by taking a wider historical perspective. If we view the mountain men as part of the larger group of frontiersmen, we can compare them with their counterparts, the Cossacks of Czarist Russia. Both groups were the major instruments and mechanisms whereby the European civilization extended itself (in one case eastward, in the other westward) across whole continents between 1600 and 1900. This expansion is the significant history of those centuries, involving as it did vast numbers of miles and migrants, major increases in population among the colonizing peoples, and the decimation of the colonized. Moreover, there was the same ambivalence in the relation between the Cossacks and Russian city society as there was between the American frontiersmen and the cities in the settled lands. On the one hand, the frontiersmen were, in both countries, the citizens' defenders (or, more exactly, the carriers of their aggression) and imposed the disciplines of European civilization upon tribal nations who had never known them and on areas hitherto untouched by them. On the other hand, mountain men and Cossacks alike were profoundly hostile to cities and their civilization; they were in flight from it and were the major exemplars of social anarchy. The Cossacks were originally men who resisted the bonding of the Russian peasant to his soil. Moreover, both groups took from the tribes they fought many words, bits of costume (the buckskins), and behavior (the warwhoop, the scalping) in defiance of the city men. They mated often with women of the tribes; which meant, to some degree, that they repudiated marriage. Carson himself had two Cheyenne wives. When he stayed with the Bentons in Washington, he was uneasy with the ladies of the household until he had confessed to this crime against all they stood for, and had received their forgiveness.

I believe this global perspective is important, for it reveals something to Americans to say that frontiersmen were a kind of Cossacks; and it tells Russians something to say that the Cossacks were a kind of frontiersmen. And Englishmen need to realize that their disguised adventure heroes, from Crusoe on, belong to those same companies of pioneers and entrepreneurs of the wild. Adventure was the story told by, for, and about adventurers—frontiersmen and Cossacks. Even Robinson Crusoe, the shipwrecked sailor who makes an island grow, is only a bright simplification of that complex political truth, a myth.

We have already seen, in Dana's epilogue to *Two Years Before the Mast*, that the periodic indulgence in adventure was a pattern to be found in societies as well as individuals. Adventure was a myth. Being an adventurer was stepping into myth, and usually it was something a man did for a few years, hoping to find a fortune, and sustained always by the consciousness of being a figure in the collective dream. In the end he stepped back into "reality"—the way of life society designated as the norm—and received his reward. Even if he had not become rich he had made himself mythical. If he was lucky, like Carson, he reentered society as a hero in reality as well as in myth.

But Carson was not a hero of literature or of the reading class. And what his autobiography shows us, above all, is the importance of the literary aspect of the adventure genre. To read his book does not expand the reader's self; and this is not merely a matter of ineptitudes in the phrasing. It is a matter of what is not there. There is nothing in Carson's narrative to set the mind alight—quite apart from what there is to upset and dismay. And yet it is the story of a life that did set alight the minds of his contemporaries; to whom it came accompanied by oral legend. But lacking that accompaniment, such a book fails where the others we are examining succeed. Carson did become a hero (as Twain, for example, did not) because of the way he met the challenge of events; but he does not become one in this book, under our eyes, as we read. For the adventure tale is not just an account of adventurous deeds, any more than a poem is an account of a poetical subject. The adventure must be in the form and style too. An adventure is not an adventure unless it is exciting.

Carson's autobiography is, then, a manifestation of adventure in more than one sense: it is an authentic manifestation of how adventure really was and really was told by the men who lived it, and it is guaranteed authentic by the extraliterary criteria appropriate to the genre. But it also reveals the literary skills necessary for adventure to work as an energizing myth. Finally, it shows the seams of the connection between myth and reality—the points at which men like Carson passed from one to the other and back.

Chapter 9   TWAIN'S
                ROUGHING IT
                (1872)

Mark Twain wrote no adventures. The word occurs in many of his titles—*The Adventures of Huckleberry Finn, The Adventures of Tom Sawyer, The Adventures of A Connecticut Yankee in King Arthur's Court*—but these books are in fact only mock adventures; the author's eyes meet the reader's in amused complicity over the heads of the protagonists. The characters' adventures make them laughable rather than heroic.

In his preface to *Tom Sawyer,* Twain expresses the hope that adults read this "boys' book," to remind themselves "of what they once were themselves, and of how they felt and thought and talked, and what queer enterprises they sometimes engaged in." This view of adventure-reading makes the imaginative current run backward, in reminiscence, nostalgia, humor, and condescension. By contrast, when adventure is an energizing myth, the current flows forward, in aspiration, excitement, and unconscious self-preparation for one's own equally courageous and cunning deeds.

Twain's autobiographical books, *Roughing It* and *Life on the Mississippi,* although not entitled adventures, come nearer to the mark. In *Roughing It* he tells how he went west as a young man to Carson City, Nevada, then a frontier boomtown, and worked as a journalist and silver prospector. Later he went farther west, to California, and even farther, to the Sandwich Islands. He tells us of many adventures he had, but of the passive kind rather than the active, and he did not, by his own account, develop the skills of an adventurer. Instead his energy went into observing the adventure scene around him and, of course, into making jokes about it.

Twain thus did live adventures personally, and he was frequently on the edge of other people's exploits, for he was fascinated by adventurers. That is why a chapter of him belongs here, as much as does one on Kit Carson. But his books, like Carson's, are not adventures but accounts of adventurous events that actually occurred.

On the first page of *Roughing It* Twain tells us that his brother had been appointed secretary of the Nevada Territory where he would, of course, "see buffaloes and Indians, and prairie dogs, and antelopes, and have all kinds of adventures." Then he would come home and boast of what he had done: "What I suffered in contemplating his happiness, pen cannot describe" (1).[1] Thus the real emotions of adventure, for Twain, are exultance and envy, the emotions of the boaster and his audience.

The book's first action-joke is about—against—the guns that he and his companions carried on his trip west. The story is, in fact, a blasphemy against the adventure-ethos. But the crucial reason why *Roughing It* is no adventure is that the central character does not make himself a hero by his behavior in the events described, and so they do not constitute an energizing myth. Twain took no part in energizing myths; although he lived through the birth of the cowboy tale, he left it to Owen Wister, a Philadelphia gentleman, to write them. And yet he met, loved, read about, and wrote about heroes of the frontier who were real adventurers. He *lived* the myth of the frontier, which was adventure, but he did not write it. This paradox is to be explained, of course, by the fact that he was a humorist; but to solve the problem so quickly is to seal up what deserves to be unfolded and examined. There were social-historical reasons, as well as personal ones, why true adventures could not be written in his time.

In Twain's day the frontier myth, which had always had humorous aspects, even in *Nick of the Woods*, became preeminently a joke. Or perhaps one should say, more preliminarily and comprehensively, that it became a "show"; it became translatable into the terms of Buffalo Bill's Wild West. (Cody didn't want his exhibition called a "show" precisely because it *was* such a show!) Buffalo Bill's life was entwined with Twain's at several points, and the two men throw light on each other. Late in his life, for instance, Twain was delighted to be mistaken for the other man on Fifth Avenue.

Bill Cody was only 23 when, in 1869, "Ned Buntline" interviewed him and wrote a *New York Weekly* serial entitled "Buffalo Bill, the King of the Border Men—the Wildest and Truest Story I Ever Wrote." "Truest" may have been correct, for Buntline, himself an adventurer, was no truth teller. Nonetheless, this story too was larded with lies and exaggerations, and so were the later stories about Cody, including those he produced himself. He once wrote to his publisher about one of his narratives that "I have really gone a bit far this time." This inventiveness was well known about Cody and about the West in general; the West was "mythical" in the sense of being untrue.

As a result of this publicity, notables from England and Russia and the East Coast came to hunt on the prairie with Cody as their guide. One such group consisted of the friends of General Sheridan, the Civil War hero, and included James Gordon Bennett, the proprietor of the *New York Herald* and the founder of yellow journalism. They admired the picturesque Cody (a handsome youngster who wore his hair down on his shoulders); and in 1892, on their invitation, he went East where he attended Buntline's play about him. It was not many steps, or many months, to his actual appearance on the stage, playing himself. In 1882 he devised his own Wild West Show, a kind of circus on a very large scale that presented the living history of the West.

It is important to see the difference between his story and Kit Carson's. Cody was indeed a frontier hero and Indian killer; but instead of being the old guide to the young Easterner (Frémont) he was the young darling of General Sheridan and editor Bennett. He dressed up for them, and for the rest of his audience, in fringed buckskins, embroidered crimson shirts, custom-made Stetsons and sombreros that curved around his striking profile like a showgirl's hat. He got himself up as an Adonis and was photographed innumerable times. It was appropriate that, even before he went on the stage, he had turned the prairie into a theater, offering his hunting clients the thrills of Indian war dances, and even attacks, by persuading Indians to play themselves.

The extraordinary thing about his show was that not only did it stage Custer's Last Stand (still fresh in memory) but it also featured a hundred Indians who had "distinguished themselves" in that event or other Indian wars. Sitting Bull, the leader of the tribes who fought Custer, was employed in the show in 1885.

The mixture of history and theater was complex. Cody himself—dressed in his circus costume—had scalped a Cheyenne chief in 1876 and waved the scalp aloft, crying, "The first scalp for Custer." (The scalp was thereafter exhibited outside the show tent.) In 1890, when Sitting Bull was killed resisting arrest for his part in the Ghost Dancer disturbances, his circus-trained horse mistook the shot for a cue and bowed to the audience. Cody took the horse back into the show.

Thus the show included a lot of reality but absorbed it into unreality—into illusion and theater. (It is no wonder that Twain wrote Cody an enthusiastic letter, urging him to take it to England.) The West had become a national illusion: an adventure of the past that might in certain circumstances become real again, for certain individuals, but which—since the Indians were clearly doomed—could not stay real for long. In literature, too, a myth of the West was still powerful, but it was more and more consciously a myth; and it demanded more and more to be expressed as a joke. The land was suddenly full of frontier humorists, traveling, lecturing, writing, being written about, and invading the realm of literature. Even in New England, that quasi-Brahmin sanctum, the *Atlantic Monthly*, custodian of the nation's conscience, seriousness, values, and taste, was invaded by the jokesters and pranksters. Twain went to live in Connecticut, became a great friend of William Dean Howells, and joined the company of Emerson, Whittier, and Holmes, becoming the great American literary celebrity. And the material he exploited to make his career was the frontier myth—including the all-important persona of himself, the frontier humorist.

Roughing It is Twain's closest approach to adventure in style and substance. In it he recounts his years in Nevada and California in the 1860s, working as a silver miner, investing in stocks, being several times on the edge of a fortune, living in boomtowns, risking his life, and breathing the general fever. But, in fact, the book is literary tourism rather than adventure. A good deal of the book was first written for newspapers and describes natural curiosities of the West and the Sandwich Islands. When it was rewritten in book form, the proportion of human and historical curiosities increased.

In his attitude, Twain stands halfway between his adventure material and the literary reader. Thus he begins Chapter 10, "In order that the Eastern reader may have a clear conception of what a Rocky Mountain desperado is, in his highest stage of development . . ." He quotes whole chapters from other authorities and documents (about the Mormons, for instance) and easily passes over into unsignaled parody, even of a purely literary kind (e.g., his poem on the Erie Canal journey, and the sentimental novel serialized in the Virginia City newspaper). At the end, he describes how he became a humorous lecturer, analyzing the activity in very quantified and commercial terms. He tells jokes and then analyzes the technique of telling jokes; and then jokes about the techniques. We realize explicitly what had been implicit before, that Twain is a ruthless entertainer (somewhat parallel and related to the "ruthless entrepreneur") much of whose power derives from his aggression against and destruction of his own material. That material is adventure—situations of danger, exploits of courage, accumulations of property, manifestations of prudence, leadership, self-control, and all the talents and virtues of the adventurer. But Twain destroys it as adventure by making it a joke.

Nevertheless, adventure was Twain's life, or living space, as man and as writer. Of course, his ostensible literary identity is that of the antiadventurer, the cowardly boaster, the cheat and hoaxer, the lounger at life's banquet who mainly wants to drink and smoke and joke. But that does not mean that Twain wanted out of the adventurer's life. No doubt the real frontier contained as many men of that type as it contained of heroes. Indeed, that identity is a mirror image of the great adventurer and derives from it just as Tête Rouge derives from Parkman in *The Oregon Trail.* One might say that Twain is a mirror image of Kit Carson—loquacious where the other is taciturn, boastful where the other is modest, ineffectual, cowardly, lazy. (One could not say that of the contrast Twain makes with other styles of admirability—with John Adams, Jefferson, or Franklin. He is simply unrelated to them. But he is not simply unrelated to Carson because he is conscious every minute of *not* being such a man—such a *man.*) Thus being a humorist stands in no trivial or accidental relation to his not writing adventures. To be worthy to write adventures, you have to be an adventurer. Buffalo Bill Cody could be the star of a Wild West Show because he was an adventurer who had killed Indians. Twain was positively not an adventurer. His humorous essay on his unheroic exploits in the Civil War shows him capitalizing upon his failure, turning ignominy into a fund of material, deriving his identity as a humorist from his negation as a hero.

Twain's writing, and his life, was all about not writing adventure, even though even his statements are not simply negative messages. For instance, he manifests, in common with other adventure writers, a lively concern with caste. (The only adventure that does not express this concern is Carson's autobiography—no doubt because Carson was not a writer.) In part Twain is concerned to show himself a gentleman and a man of letters; although he is very uneasy in those roles and loudly disclaims those titles, his basic intent, like other writers', is to claim them. But he also declares his caste membership by describing a circle of frontier heroes. His way of belonging to that circle is parody—parody of them and of himself—but that fact does not affect the central issue—that his imagination is powerfully directed toward them. They are his superego.

This circle includes first of all the stage drivers. At one station, Twain's driver stretches and gapes complacently, then draws off his gloves with great deliberation and insufferable dignity,

> taking not the slightest notice of a dozen solicitous inquiries after his health, and humbly facetious and flattering accostings, and obsequious tenders of service . . . for in the eyes of a stage driver of that day, station keepers and hostlers were a sort of good enough low creatures, useful in their place, and helping to make up a world, but not the kind of beings which a person of distinction could afford to concern himself with . . . When they spoke to him they received his insolent silence meekly . . . when he opened his lips . . . he never honoured a particular individual with a remark, but addressed it with a broad generality to the horses, the stables, the surrounding country *and* the human underlings . . . the varlets roared and slapped their thighs, and swore it was the best thing they'd ever heard in all their lives . . . but they would instantly insult a passenger if he so far forgot himself as to crave a favor at their hands. (43).

This comes from a long and brilliant passage (there are several in the book) describing the power structure, the hierarchy, and the absoluteness of power of the frontier caste.

We can associate this with an overtly racist passage about the Goshute Indians, which expresses the frontiersmen's attitude to those they see as inferior to themselves.

A silent, sneaking, treacherous-looking race; taking note of everything, covertly, like all the other "Noble Red Men" that we (do not) read about, and betraying no sign in their countenances; indolent, everlastingly patient and tireless, like all other Indians; prideless beggars . . . a people whose only shelter is a rag cast on a bush to keep off a portion of the snow, and yet who inhabit one of the most rocky, wintry, repulsive wastes that our country, or any other can exhibit. The Bushmen and our Goshutes are manifestly descended from the self-same gorilla, or kangaroo, or Norway rat, whichever animal-Adam the Darwinians trace them to (118).

These two passages deserve to be put alongside the story told by Mahatma Gandhi, in *Satyagraha in South Africa,* of how he was thrown off a coach by the driver and beaten because he resisted. You see there exactly the same social types, locked into the same configuration; and you realize that Twain's humor depends upon seeing the world caste system from the top down—seeing the Native Americans as outcasts.

I am taking the liberty, here, to twist the term *caste* a little out of its ordinary function. I am defining the word geographically—or at least geography plays an important part in the definition, since I assign them to the frontier. But social geography is as important to Twain as physical; when he describes his apprenticeship to steamboat piloting in *Life on the Mississippi,* he presents Mr. Bixby and the other pilots as heroes of the same kind as the stage drivers. The apprentice admires them—and consequently hates them—as figures of power; and they treat him as an aspirant to share that power, an aspirant who must be trained and tempered to it, above all by humiliation. The most striking example of this training is described in Chapter 13 in which Bixby involves the captain and, apparently, the whole crew in a conspiracy to undermine his apprentice's confidence in his ability to run a certain crossing by himself. At the climax, when the boy has panicked and called out for help, "I heard the door close gently. I looked around, and there stood Mr. Bixby, smiling a bland, sweet smile. Then the audience on the hurricane deck sent up a thundergust of humiliating laughter. I saw it all, now, and I felt meaner than the meanest man in human history."[2]

It is worth noting that this subterfuge was arranged in the name of teaching the boy to have confidence in his own judgment; from now on he will remember not to panic, however much other people insinuate doubts of his capacity. Thus the gift of power is reversed as it is given, the point of the sword replaces the hilt, pride is interlaced with humiliation, and opposites are interwoven intimately. In this caste training, power exchange is the crux of every relationship. In *Roughing It*, Twain's part in this training system is—so far as it is explicitly stated—somewhat hidden, but *Life on the Mississippi* shows how large a part it had played in his own life.

Just after the incident mentioned, Twain begins a chapter (entitled "Rank and Dignity of Piloting") by defining the pilot's dignity in terms of freedom: "A pilot, in those days, was the only unfettered and entirely independent human being that lived in the earth."[3] He goes on to describe "a boy of eighteen taking a great steamer serenely into what seemed almost certain destruction, and the aged captain standing mutely by, filled with apprehension but powerless to interfere." But we notice the word "powerless"; the pilot's freedom is always a matter of having power over others; the question is always, who has the power? Later in the passage Twain goes on to speak of the pilot being a "great personage," who is spoken to "with great deference." Clearly "freedom" has turned into something else. He concludes: "By long habit, pilots came to put all their wishes in the form of commands. It 'gravels' me, to this day, to put my will in the weak form of a request, instead of launching it in the crisp language of an order."[4] Without believing his remark literally, we should, I think, take note of what it tells us about the importance of caste training in Twain's life.

The frontier caste felt itself to stand between the genteel upper classes and the outcasts (in Twain's America, the Native Americans). It both resented the latter and felt a jealous animus against the higher castes. In all his books Twain was the national spokesman for the "democratic" and "patriotic" feelings of this caste. Thus his Connecticut Yankee says, counting on his reader's complacent indignation, "In the remote England of my birth-time, the sheep-witted earl who could claim long descent from a king's leman, acquired at second hand from the slums of London, was a better man than I was . . ." (Twain and his reader congratulate themselves.) "Of course, that taint, that reverence for rank and title, had been in our American blood, too—I know that; but when I left America it had disappeared, at least to all intents and purposes."[5] The only rank and title the Yankee will take from King Arthur is "Boss," which we can take to be a frontier title, full of the lust for power and status, but feeling itself to be rebellious and self-made. Lower-caste power is cruder, less sanctified and legitimized by cultural forms than that of priests and nobles.

Roughing It gives us some particularly startling and challenging examples of Twain's power worship; it describes Slade, the division agent who killed 26 men. (Slade, in fact, employed the young Bill Cody.) He is first introduced to us as "a man who awfully avenged all injuries, affronts, insults or slights, of whatever kind—on the spot if he could, years afterwards if lack of opportunity compelled it; a man whose hate tortured him day and night till vengeance appeased it—and not an ordinary vengeance either, but his enemy's absolute death—nothing less; a man whose face would light up with a terrible joy when he surprised a foe and had him at a disadvantage" (70). This is a Gothic-novel portrait, of a Byronic hero-villain. But Twain develops it into something different, by later calling Slade "a high and efficient servant of the Overland," locating him in his vocation, and showing him as the agent of order: "Slade took up his residence sweetly and peacefully in the midst of this hive of horse-thieves and assassins, and the very first time one of them aired his insolent swaggering in his presence he shot him dead! . . . they respected him, admired him, feared him, and obeyed him!" (72). By this point, Slade is a figure as admirable as Mr. Bixby in *Life on the Mississippi.*

Twain's feelings about Slade's moral status remain ambivalent and responsive above all to the power he embodied and the freedom he had carved out for himself on the frontier. He tells a truly horrible tale of Slade's shooting a man at his own front door, pushing his corpse inside the house with his foot, setting the house on fire, and burning up the man's widow and three children. (Later he describes Slade's whining and begging for mercy when his turn to face death comes.) Yet Twain's comment as he sat at breakfast with the man is: "Here was romance, and I was sitting face to face with it" (75). There is no evidence of any firm rejection, or clear criticism, of this romance. Twain had committed his loyalties to the frontier caste, with its cult of power, and he could not withdraw them, even in a book, where they were so out of place.

Although several other figures who belong to Twain's circle of heroes are described in *Roughing It*, I will mention only two more. One of them, Captain Blakely, arrested a man and hung him on his own authority, after (but only in response to the persuasions of his friends) summarily trying him. Twain admires Blakely more wholeheartedly than he does Slade and presents him as a warm-hearted lover of rough justice; but in putting the man and his anecdote into a book, the moral plausibility of his performance evaporates, and the reader is left very uneasy. Twain's account of the Admiral presents no such moral challenge to the reader's sympathies but is written in equally ambiguous language; he is described as "a roaring, terrific combination of wind and lightning and thunder, and earnest whole-souled profanity" (331). He tells lies and forces other people to pretend to believe them, by the terrorism of his social style. The central anecdote concerns his defeat and humiliation, to the joy of all who have suffered under him; its interest is that it brings out the ambivalence of Twain's own feelings. This is an anecdote of humiliation, revenge, and triumph, and yet we are told that the Admiral is loved by all and is as tender-hearted as a girl. The rationale seems to be that *everyone* grabs power and oppresses others with it; everyone else hates whoever has it; and there is no right or wrong to the matter.

Finally there is a famous passage about the young frontiersmen who founded the state of California. This story can be regarded as a climax to the cult of young men as adventurers that began in *Robinson Crusoe*. Defoe, and later writers, excused adventure as an imprudence characteristic of young men; they mitigated its moral challenge by chronological parentheses which inserted it as a dependent clause into a predominantly prudential moral scheme. Twain, however, presents young manhood and adventure as the supreme moment of life.

It was the only population of the kind that the world has ever seen gathered together, and it is not likely that the world will ever see its like again. For, observe, it was an assemblage of two hundred thousand young men—not simpering, dainty, kid-gloved weaklings, but stalwart, muscular, dauntless young braves, brimful of push and energy, and royally endowed with every attribute that goes to make up a peerless and magnificent manhood—the very pick and choice of the world's glorious ones. No women, no children, no gray and stooping veterans—none but erect, bright-eyed, quick-moving, strong-handed young giants—the strangest population, the finest population, the most gallant host that ever trooped down the startled solitudes of an unpeopled land (309).

Here, for once, the pantheon of the frontier religion is evoked with none of Twain's usual ambivalence. This manly assembly embodies the cult implicit in all adventure, and Twain is its high priest.

On the other hand, when this frontier caste looks at the heroes of other social groups—medieval knights or genteel Brahmins—it satirizes them unmercifully, in *Life on the Mississippi* and *Connecticut Yankee*. The frontiersmen make a counterinsistence on reality—unpleasant and disconcerting reality of both the moral and physical kind. Notable cases of both kinds of satire are found in Twain's attack on Scott in *Life on the Mississippi* and his hostility to Cooper, which finds brief expression twice in *Roughing It;* in the latter he sneers at Cooper's idea of the Noble Red Man and is led into his shocking racist virulence against the Goshute Indians.

When the frontier mind wants to make affirmations that will win the assent of the reading nation as a whole, they are of the (low) order of sentimental patriotism (the passage about the flag on Mount Davidson, lit up by the sun on the day of Gettysburg) (303); anecdotes of social or moral pathos (the poor man who procures for a poorer one a sumptuous meal, on credit, and goes off to eat for a dime himself) (322); passages of nature poetry (New England's meadow expanses and cathedral-windowed elms) (305); or attempts at the sublime (the volcanoes of the Sandwich Islands) (397, 409). Twain is not even a good writer of this rather bad sort of thing. He falls into easily avoided bathos, cliché, vulgarity, or, at best, commonplace, no doubt because of his deep ambivalence and irritability. The latter serves him well as a humorist but disqualifies him as a moralist. He could question but not affirm values; if he could have affirmed any such, they would have been those of adventure and he would have been an adventure writer.

His relations with the Brahmin writers were always a bit uneasy. There is a famous anecdote of the parody lecture he gave about Emerson, Holmes, and Whittier, in their presence; it caused most people present deep embarrassment. Twain had miscalculated his effect and was very unhappy to be thought to have insulted the great Brahmins; but, of course, he had intended to *seem* to insult them. The incident is matched by the story of his successful congratulatory address to General Grant, the hero of the Civil War, at a great gathering of Grant worshippers. Following a series of speakers praising the great man, Twain described Grant as he had been as a baby, trying to get his toe in his mouth. The guests were at first inhibited by embarrassment but then proportionately enthusiastic in their response, as was Grant himself. Twain wrote to his wife, exulting that he had "broken up that man of iron"—had *made* Grant laugh. His letter is full of triumphant, playful aggression; the humorous lecturer had shown himself to be a man of action, in that setting, while the soldier-politician was reduced to passivity.

Twain's relations to his adventure heroes were almost equally uneasy. He was their jester. In *The Oregon Trail* Parkman described one of his companions, Tête Rouge, as selfish and cowardly: "Yet we would not have lost him on any account; he served the purpose of a jester in a feudal castle; our camp would have been lifeless without him."[6] This was the purpose Twain served, too; *Roughing It* was written by a Tête Rouge of genius. Parkman was himself determined to be a hero, but he acknowledged a kinship to Tête Rouge—the kinship of superior to inferior within the adventure circle. Twain also was akin to his heroes, as inferior to superior. Both Parkman's narrative and Twain's show the pressures of the frontier situation and the adventure ethos, the pressure to make men into either heroes of virility (the writer's comrades or rivals) or something radically alternative—jesters, counselors, or enemies. Men like Twain, the

Tête Rouge of first the frontier and then finance capitalism, belonged to the ethos of adventure even as they betrayed it, mocked it, and, in a sense, opposed it.

The main news *Roughing It* has to give us about adventure is that, at least in America, in the 1860s it changed from being a source of strength for society to one of weakness. From being an origin of substantiality and health, it became an origin of corruption and fever. Of course, many other events were occurring in America besides those Twain describes (it is notable that he completely omits the Civil War); thus we cannot reinterpret history in general on the evidence of this book. But we can say what it tells us—that the profit gained by adventure ceased to be, as *Robinson Crusoe* had said it was, moral money. Crusoe went home to England, a man of substance because of his profitable adventures. The fortunes Twain describes being accumulated in Nevada and California were all fairy gold; they withered away overnight or brought their owners unhappiness. What else could happen when they were derived at best from mere chance (and more likely from fraud or trick) and cost sickness, starvation, robbery, and murder?

Something similar was to be true of Twain's later financial speculations and the fortune Buffalo Bill made. The later domestic life of both men was also unhappy, and their self-respect was eroded in ways that clearly paralleled the erosion of the moral myth of the West, which they had exploited. Cody's show passed out of his control in later years, and his part in it became more and more ignominious, partly because he became an alcoholic. Twain became more and more an entertainer of rich men and a creature of the footlights. By the time *Roughing It* came out as a book he had lost all power to represent the heroic West.

There are, of course, many adventure situations described in *Roughing It*, sequences of action that ought to have been adventure. There is, for instance, the time Twain and his companions were lost in the snow (described in Chapter 32). In this case it is particularly clear that Twain is not writing adventure, for the men pass the night in a snowdrift, having made up their minds to death and repented of all their sins and bad habits. But in the morning they find themselves only 15 steps from a comfortable inn; and immediately, though separately, each man resumes his bad habits. Here Twain mocks both the substance of adventure (the danger they were in) and the spirit of adventure (the moral self-discipline it brought).

The adventure writer Twain most resembles is Melville, in *Typee.* This becomes especially clear in the Sandwich Islands section of *Roughing It,* where Twain makes the same points as Melville about the sensuality and general eroticism of the islands (the near-nakedness of the girls) and where he stresses (and half-approves) their cult of relaxation. This approval of the relaxed Polynesian life-style is linked to the skepticism both men share, about many western values, but above all about missionary Christianity. Chapter 72 ends: "The nation was without a religion. The missionary ship arrived in safety shortly afterward, timed by providential exactness to meet the emergency, and the Gospel was planted as in virgin soil." And, on page 356, we are told that the missionaries have taught the women "a profound respect for chastity—in other people. Perhaps that is enough to say on that head. The national sin will die out when the race does, but perhaps not earlier. But doubtless this purifying is not far off, when we reflect that contact with civilization and the whites has reduced the native population from *four hundred thousand* [Captain Cook's estimate] to *fifty-five thousand* in something over eighty years." The to and fro of those sentences—each phrase reversing the tendency of the preceding one—vividly conveys the habitual skepticism of Twain's mind.

If Twain reminds us of Melville, it is no doubt also because *Typee,* like *Roughing It,* is an antiadventure. Indeed Twain goes further in that direction, as we see in his reflections on Captain Cook, the explorer-hero whom Melville revered. Standing on the spot where Cook was killed (a story familiar to every schoolboy in the wide world, Twain says), he tries to work up a tribute to the man and a pathos about the event but declares that he cannot. (This is one of his book's moments of truth.) On the contrary, Twain says, Cook *deserved* his death at the natives' hands because he accepted their gifts, encouraged the delusion that he was a god, and inflicted injury and death upon the natives. "Plain unvarnished history takes the romance out of Captain Cook's assassination, and renders a deliberate verdict of justifiable homicide" (385). It was nearly a hundred years after the event when Twain rebelled against commemorating it; clearly that rebellion marks an epoch in the history of adventure. (In fact, we can see in his comments on Cook a foreshadowing of Conrad's treatment of Kurtz in *Heart of Darkness.*)

But Cook was English, and so his adventure was avowedly imperialist. The more challenging kind of adventure was American and popular, and the truth about it emerges raggedly and involuntarily in Twain's narrative, expressed in his own values— chaos, and the social chaos he describes. For instance, Chapter 26, entitled "The Silver Fever—State of the Market—Silver Bricks—Tales Told—Off for the Humboldt Mines," begins: "By and by I was smitten with the silver fever . . . day in and day out the talk pelted our ears and the excitement waxed hotter and hotter. I would have been more or less than human if I had not gone mad like the rest . . . I succumbed and grew as frenzied as the craziest" (151–52). This is the point Twain drives home over and over again: the silver mining in Nevada, the gold mining in California, the business of registering claims, assaying ore, buying and trading stock, all the social and political life of Carson City and Virginia City. Twain reports the palpable inadequacy of every attempt made—by no matter what agency of culture—to make moral sense of this life, out of everyone's underlying conviction that the determining forces are blind chance, personal luck, or ruthless cunning and violence. The frontier, which had meant wide open spaces and Nature—God's great self-manifestation—now meant boomtowns and ghost towns, abandoned mines, scarred hillsides, and deserts. Fever/boom/burst/bubble/crash/ghost/craze—all Twain's images of finance capitalism deny it either substance or health.

This was a general, an international phenomenon, as the Anglo-Saxon nations turned to empires. The changes in the West stood for changes in the world in general, as could be seen in Buffalo Bill's Wild West. Cody hired a hundred Zulus to represent the Zulu war when that made the headlines; he did a Charge of the Light Brigade when he was in England; and in 1898, even before the United States declared war on Spain, he had Cuban campaigners and did military drills. After the Spanish-American War, the Battle of San Juan Hill replaced Custer's Last Stand, and he even employed some of the real Rough Riders. In 1901 he dramatized the Boxer Rebellion in China. (In many of these episodes, his Indians represented all the antagonists of the white race, whether Chinese or African.) The pageant he began to present in 1886 was called "The Drama of Civilization," and after 1893 he had a "Congress of the Rough Riders of the World" that included Russian Cossacks and South American gauchos. (Roosevelt seems to have taken the term Rough Riders from Cody.) Thus the conquest of the West represented the worldwide triumph of the white race; and the corruption of the myth of the West represented the corruption of that larger myth.

Moreover, the power adventurers had found in nature, and had appropriated by worship (whether the moral sublimity of Cooper's forest or the splendid savagery of Parkman's warriors), had turned to excitement, had fermented. There had always been some ambiguity about the frontier experience; in *Nick of the Woods*, Ralph Stackpole's exultation in the Salt River might have been called excitement as much as power. But in *Two Years Before the Mast*, for instance, Dana makes a convincing case that he found power in the sea. In *Roughing It*, however, I think there is no sense of nature as powerful. Even in *Life on the Mississippi*, the famous passages about the river, beautiful as they are, do not manifest power of this sort—the sort a man could appropriate and grow stronger for. The river is magnificent in its indifference, its quantitative massiveness; men can approach it only by submitting to it—most typically, by letting it carry them. In *Life on the Mississippi* and *Huckleberry Finn*, Twain loves the river because it lets him drift, lets him relax.

By contrast, in *Roughing It* we find a Disneyesque attitude toward nature, that is, a Southwest-humor attitude. The anecdote of the coyote and the dog in Chapter 5 is a vivid example. The coyote looks spiritless and cowardly and runs away from the dog, "smiling" over its shoulder in a timid way that fills the dog "entirely full of encouragement and worldly ambition" (50). But then suddenly the coyote seems to say, " 'Well, I shall have to tear myself away from you, bub—business is business, and it will not do for me to be fooling along this way all day, and forthwith there is a rushing sound, and the sudden splitting of a long crack through the atmosphere, and behold that dog is solitary and alone in the midst of a vast solitude" (51). This is a caricature version of animal life, which gives it excitement but denies it power. Its anthropomorphism is disrespectful and, as such, it is consonant with Twain's versions of social life, human nature, and the moral law.

In *Roughing It,* adventure takes place *in society.* It is a social act, involving numbers of people, and closely linked to the stock exchange, the day's price of silver and gold, the law courts and the prisons, to newspapers and books and lectures. The moral adventurer like Natty Bumppo is replaced by Slade, and nature is replaced by the boomtown. Above all, instead of Robinson Crusoe, who returned to England with money to buy himself an estate and become a gentleman—in other words, to add substance to the home society—we see men who are losing their substance (fortune and health) in the quest for easy money. And we see a whole structure of values and culture shuddering and collapsing.

We see this most intimately and convincingly in Twain's own mind and language, in his identity as a writer, in his humor. It is not only a matter of value ambivalence but of the whole enterprise of hoax journalism, of parody and lying (Twain gives many examples of journalism as lying). It is a matter of irritability, for Twain's humor is essentially a series of swerves away from value affirmations or denials. Anyone he loves he necessarily hates, like the Admiral; or, like Slade, he hates and so loves. Anything he admires he necessarily begins to parody, and anything he is merely comfortable with he begins to despise. It is a matter of his love for speed and violence, which are denials in image form of stability and affirmation. That is what gives pungency to the coyote anecdote, and to Dick Barker's story of his cat, who is blown up while he is blasting.

> All of a sudden it began to rain rocks and rubbage, an' directly he came down ker-whop about ten feet off I'm where we stood. Well, I reckon he was p'haps the orneriest-looking beast you ever see. One ear was set back on his neck, 'n' his tail was stove up, 'n' his eye-whiskers was swinged off, 'n' he was all blacked up with powder an' smoke, 'n' all sloppy with mud 'n' slush f'm one end to the other (329).

This very film-cartoon image is of course pure humor, a mere sign of Twain's sensibility. But what it tells us about that sensibility is that it is triggered to respond to violence and to desecrate even the fondest images of affection and trust.

At its best, in some of the tall tales, or the adaptation of tall tales, like the one told on page 65, this humor is a matter of fantasy, of pure free gaiety of spirit defying reality. But most of the time, the strain of resentful irritability and reactive exasperation can be felt even in the techniques of lexical, imagistic, and narrative distortion that are the mechanisms of his humor. Twain embodies in his very prose style, as well as in his choice of topics and in the statements that slide through the defensive grill of his irony, the corruptive ferment of his time.

In Twain, the adventures which had seemed to take place always in the mythic no-man's-land beyond reality's frontier now took place in society under the glare of arc lamps. The filtering process of Crusoe's long, slow return to England (a process paralleled in the writing process by the simplifying and filtering conventions of adventure) could no longer operate. The eruptive flow was breaking out right under everyone's feet. This was the moment, in America in the 1860s, that Twain was there to record and, even more, to live through and embody. It was a crucial moment in the fate of adventure.

Chapter 10 ROOSEVELT'S *AUTOBIOGRAPHY* (1913)

Theodore Roosevelt brought adventure into national and international politics as an official symbol. In his "splendid little war" against Spain and the regiment of Rough Riders he raised for it he gave the soldier-adventurer a prominent role in the national destiny. The mustering places for those troops were the frontier lands of New Mexico, Arizona, Oklahoma, and Indian territory, and most of the soldiers were frontiersmen—minor and would-be Kit Carsons. In his account of the regiment Roosevelt makes play with names like Cherokee Bill and Happy Jack of Arizona; he tells us that many of the men had committed crimes, and many were professional gamblers, and so on. Like Parkman, he recommends the thrill of making friends with someone who may try to murder you. Above all, he stresses the social mix. There were college athletes from Harvard and Yale, New York clubmen, New York policemen, Indians and half-breeds, and English gentlemen. What did such various types have in common? "They were to a man born adventurers, in the old sense of the word" (*RR*28).[1]

The most striking figures in his narrative are in fact aristocrats. Allyn Capron was the fifth generation of his family to serve in the U.S. Army: "Tall and lithe, a remarkable boxer and walker, a first class rider and shot, with yellow hair and piercing blue eyes, he looked what he was, the archetype of the fighting man" (*RR*27). The implicit moral of Roosevelt's narrative is that aristocrats are needed to give discipline to raw fighting men. In other places, he made this point explicit. Left to themselves, even frontiersmen could not form an army or a nation; social bodies need to combine social classes; frontiersmen need Roosevelts, Caprons, and men like Hamilton Fish.

The latter served as a sergeant with the Rough Riders, although his watch bore the heraldic arms of the Fishes and the Stuyvesants.

> A huge fellow, of enormous strength and endurance, and dauntless courage, he took naturally to a soldier's life . . . As we stood around the flickering blaze that night, I caught myself admiring the splendid bodily vigor of Capron and Fish—the captain and the sergeant. Their frames seemed of steel, to withstand all fatigue; they were flushed with health; in their eyes shone high resolve and fiery desire. Two finer types of the fighting man, two better representatives of the American soldier, there were not in the whole army . . . Within twelve hours, they both were dead (*RR*90).

This atavistic rhetoric, celebrating the "enormous strength" of the "fighting man" and his death in battle, is implicitly nationalist or imperialist. It is a way for the man of letters and politics to fuse his own ideals with those of the frontiersman. It unites Dana's readers with Bird's, Parkman's with Twain's. It gives Carson's readers what they were looking for in his autobiography.

Rough Riders is clearly an adventure that belongs in this section, at least as much as Carson's autobiography and Twain's *Roughing It*. What distinguishes it from them, of course, is its overtly national scope—it is about a war, about national politics. Roosevelt tells us that he and General Wood, his superior officer, "both felt very strongly that such a war would be as righteous as it would be advantageous to the honor and the interests of the nation" (*RR*13). The vocabulary of honor and righteousness makes it as much an adventure or a romance as a political event. About Wood he says: "It was a pleasure to deal with a man of high ideals, who scorned everything mean and base, and who also possessed those robust and hardy qualities of body and mind, for the lack of which no merely negative virtues can ever atone. He was by nature a soldier of the highest type, and, like most natural soldiers, he was, of course, born with a keen longing for adventure" (12).

The language of the narrative comes from the chivalric adventure.

Once a strange ship steamed up too close, and instantly the nearest torpedo-boat was slipped like a greyhound from the leash, and sped across the water toward it; but the stranger proved harmless, and the swift, delicate, death-fraught craft returned again . . . It was very pleasant, sailing southward through the tropic seas toward the unknown . . . The men on the ship were young and strong, eager to face what lay hidden before them, eager for adventure where risk was the price of gain . . . [And when a dead man is buried at sea, it is] in the ooze that holds the timbers of so many gallant ships, and the bones of so many fearless adventurers (74, 75, 233).

However, I have chosen Roosevelt's *Autobiography* rather than *Rough Riders* to represent him here, because it is his life as a whole which is most important to our argument. Theodore Roosevelt was the son of a well-to-do Dutch merchant who had turned from business to philanthropy and social action in his later years. Among his ancestry he names a Pennsylvania Quaker and some "peace-loving Germans," but he shows a preference for his other, Scotch-Irish forebears, whom he describes as "*not a peaceful people.*" (We recall Cooper's preferences among national types.)

His father was a big man with a striking beard and a buoyant manner, and Theodore admired him passionately, in a way that seems to have set a pattern for his future relationships, and his admiration of the manliness of other men. He describes his father as the embodiment of genial power: "I never knew anyone who got greater joy out of living than did my father, or anyone who more whole-heartedly performed every duty . . . He was a big, powerful man, with a leonine face, and his heart filled with gentleness for those who needed help or protection" (*A*9). The Roosevelts led a rich, warm family life, which the son reproduced in his turn, and which formed the background to his personal and political style. It was a ruling-class family life, in which family fun was combined with competitiveness, training for power, and social responsibility. When someone criticized his own sons' competitive zeal at football, Theodore said, "I would rather one should die than have them grow up weaklings" (WH142).

Theodore was also, in an almost literal way, a self-made man.

Asthmatic from birth, he went to many doctors as a child, without finding a cure. At 12 he told his father (throwing back his head), "I'll make my body." And he did. Later he made himself into a cowboy, a reforming politician, a military man, and so on. "I never won anything without hard labor and the exercise of my best judgment and careful planning and working long in advance. Having been a rather sickly and awkward boy, I was as a young man at first both nervous and distrustful of my own prowess" (WH32). He tells us about being bullied by other boys on a stagecoach ride. But he believed that, as Captain Marryatt said, you must act as if you were not afraid; and then, if you have the right stuff in you, your will will grow stronger.

As a young man he was not prepossessing. When he first went to the New York State Assembly in 1881, an upstate journalist wrote about him, "What will New York send us next?" A *Pittsburgh Dispatch* reporter who met him in April 1885 called him a typical New York dude, dyspeptic, lisping, and piping-voiced. Thus he had to learn manhood. When he went to live in the Dakota Badlands in 1884, he was again laughed at and called a dude and "four eyes" (because of his eyeglasses). But he proved himself. Two years later the same *Dispatch* reporter said that he was as brown as a berry, 30 pounds heavier, and had a voice hearty enough to drive oxen.[2]

This was the kind of transformation nineteenth-century reporters were well qualified to appreciate, for it was the inner drama of adventure. He became a splendid animal. In 1886 the *Sioux Falls Press* wrote that Roosevelt was "one of the finest thoroughbreds you ever met—a whole-souled, clear-headed, high-minded gentleman" (WH34). Another characteristic object of praise (from the *Washington Post*) was his "passionate hatred of meanness, humbug, and cowardice" (WH93). The idea implicit behind all this praise is that key romantic ideal, "manliness." Roosevelt was "manly" (that is, generous and warm); he showed "manhood" (firmness, endurance, leadership, chivalry); he *was a man* (which is to say, divine, although of course no "man" could be caught thinking such a thing). Such manliness was achieved, above all, through adventure.

One could of course describe Roosevelt's personality in less sympathetic terms, but he does seem to have been in some ways innocent in his heartiness. His sexual attitudes, for instance, were completely Victorian; his father taught him, he said, that men should be as pure as women. He disliked the schoolboy stories of his friend Kipling in *Stalky and Co.* because he could not like boys who behaved as Kipling's heroes did. He had himself stepped out of *Tom Brown's Schooldays*, a boys' book of an earlier type.

In general, Roosevelt made a sharp distinction between those inside and those outside any group he belonged to; he believed quite fervently in the values that united those inside. In consequence he was class conscious and class limited, although he was not, in any sense, a snob. He was rather a great enthusiast for his own family, his own class, his own schools. In July 1901 he held seminars for Harvard and Yale men, arguing the need for "men of character" to enter politics in order to promote loyalty to the party and the Union.

He made a cult of physical fitness—he performed daily workouts in the gym throughout his life—which he saw as the means to moral and spiritual fitness. And he made a cult of nature, conceiving it as something to be wrestled with and something to be investigated, as an extension of his own physical prowess, and as a sparring partner. He was a naturalist and a camper from childhood and exulted in hunting.

American political leaders, he claimed, were all of stalwart frame and health and "when they sprang from the frontier folk, as did Lincoln and Andrew Jackson, they usually hunted much in their youth."[3] When he described to his sister his own first bear-kill, about 1885, we hear the note of innocent self-praise, the sign of successful self-formation: "doubtless my face was pretty white, but the blue barrel was as steady as a rock as I glanced along it until I could see the top of the beard fairly between his two sinister looking eyes; [we hear also of course the innocent heroics of a fight between good and evil] . . . the great brute was struggling in a death agony" (WH55). He wrote about such subjects for the general public, too, and his trilogy of books about hunting, ranching, and nature observation, published between 1885 and 1893, set a new style. His chapter on the habits of the grizzly bear in *Wilderness Hunter* was the most comprehensive work on the subject at that time.

Roosevelt's interests also extended to history and biography, and he wrote the life stories of Thomas Hart Benton and

Gouverneur Morris. He praised Benton's "abounding vitality, rugged intellect, and indomitable will . . . deeply imbued with the masterful, overbearing spirit of the West . . . [where] each man was impelled mainly by sheer love of adventure . . . the fundamental virtues of hardihood and manliness."[4] The description illustrates how fundamental to his sense of history, both of the individual and of the group, were the ideas of adventure and manliness.

The two interests, political biography and man's struggle with nature, came together in his four-volume *The Winning of the West,* which won praise from professional historians. Frederick Jackson Turner was pleased by Roosevelt's enthusiasm for the pioneers and his dismissal of "the Indian question" (the moral criticism of white imperialism), which had been raised by New England Brahmins.

As a historian, Roosevelt was of the school of Parkman and Motley, praising the pioneers in fullsome terms: "They were doing their share of a work which began with the conquest of Britain, that entered on its second and wider period after the defeat of the Spanish Armada, that culminated in the marvelous growth of the United States" (WH62). He conveyed the excitement of settling the frontier, employing the sort of eloquent propaganda prose we associate with his heir, Winston Churchill: "a stern race of freemen who toiled hard, endured greatly, and fronted adversity bravely . . . they acted under orders from neither king nor congress; they were not carrying out the plans of any farsighted leader. In obedience to their instincts working half-blindly within their breasts, spurred ever onward by the fierce desires of their eager hearts . . . They warred and settled from the high hill valleys of the French Broad . . . to where the Golden Gate lets through the long-heaving waters of the Pacific" (WH 64, 62).

He was unsympathetic to labor as an organized political movement. He was hostile toward the Haymarket anarchists of Chicago and furious when Governor Altgeld of Illinois—styled "another Robespierre" by Roosevelt—pardoned three of them in 1893. Similarly, he disliked Robert La Follette of Wisconsin, an isolationist and intellectual, and was an enemy of William Jennings Bryan, the populist who represented the farmers and small townsmen of the West. Agrarians, intellectuals, labor supporters—all were out of Roosevelt's ken for they belonged to other castes. Such men were politically serious in a way that was alien to Roosevelt's own kind of seriousness.

The men in politics to whom he related easily and fruitfully were usually men of the ruling caste, graduates of Ivy League colleges. They were like Roosevelt in social background but their temperaments were in sharp contrast to his own. Typical were Henry Cabot Lodge, John Hay, and Elihu Root—all older and colder men. The reciprocity between them and him is suggested by Roosevelt's remarks about Hay after the latter's death and the subsequent publication of his letters in 1909: "His close intimacy with Henry James and Henry Adams—charming men, but exceedingly undesirable companions for any man not of strong nature—and the tone of satirical cynicism which they admired . . . impaired his usefulness as a public man" (WH273). Roosevelt himself was the opposite of satirical and cynical; one might almost compare his relationship to Hay to that of d'Artagnan confronting Athos (and even more Richelieu) in Dumas's *The Three Musketeers*. Kipling too treated this pattern, that of the ardent young man protestingly submitting to older, colder, somewhat sinister potentates while implicitly claiming superiority to them (admitting naiveté but claiming the preference of onlookers).[5] It is indeed one of the master myths of adventure and can be seen in all the "old guide" figures of Western stories, from Natty Bumppo on, who prepare ardent young heroes to be their heirs.

No matter what his age Roosevelt was always the young man, the adventurer. He had a strong sense of responsibility but an equally strong streak of what one might call irresponsibility. The former took various forms as personal, caste, and state responsibility. He was one of the great reformers of American politics, in local and federal civil service reform and in the conservation of natural resources like the Grand Canyon and Niagara Falls. "Of all Roosevelt's constructive endeavors, the movement for conservation was most marked by sustained intelligence and administrative force" (WH304). As president, with the help of such devoted administrators as Gifford Pinchot and Frederick H. Newell, he set up the Inland Waterways Commission, added vast tracts to the National Forests, and improved the National Park system.

In 1912, he founded the Progressive Party, an innovation in radical politics in America. It was the party of doctors, lawyers, teachers, civic leaders, even settlement workers—the educated and reforming class. "Our prize exhibit was Jane Addams" said William Allen White, and she in fact seconded Roosevelt's nomination (WH412). It was also the party of youth—the delegates were 10 to 15 years younger than the Republicans he had left to the Taft conservatives. Their rhetoric was radical, righteous, even religious. They sang "Onward, Christian Soldiers" and "The Battle Hymn of the Republic," and Roosevelt's acceptance address was entitled "Confession of Faith." In it he said, "We stand at Armageddon and we battle for the Lord." This religious rhetoric came naturally to Roosevelt; his attack on the muckrakers in 1906 had been couched in the language of *Pilgrim's Progress,* and when he died his friends praised him in similar terms. Kipling's memorial to him was entitled "Great-Heart," and Lodge's Senate eulogy ended, "So Valiant-for-Truth passed over and all the trumpets sounded for him on the other side."

Although the foregoing suggests social responsibility, or at least a moral inspiration in social politics, Roosevelt was also committed to a kind of irrationalism and adventurism and militarism that most people would call irresponsible. In 1886 he proposed to raise, in his own words, "as utterly reckless a set of desperadoes as ever sat in the saddle" to fight against Mexico (WH99). He was always eager for war, as were his friends Lodge, Hays, Holmes, and Brooks Adams. When he reviewed the latter's *Law of Civilization and Decay,* he shared its regret at the passing away of military men. He said that he would have gone to fight in Cuba, even if it had meant leaving his wife's deathbed, because it was "my chance to cut my little notch on the stick that stands as a measuring rod in every family" (WH105).

His love of war was allied naturally to an expansionist and imperialist policy. During the presidential campaign of 1900, he said: "We cannot avoid facing the fact that we occupy a new place among the people of the world . . . Greatness means strife for nation and man alike . . . We must dare to be great" (WH113). This was a decisive change from earlier American policies. The Democratic candidate, Bryan, was still preaching that "imperialism finds no warrant in the Bible," a belief that echoed earlier political rhetoric in America. In effect, Roosevelt was joining hands with English imperialists like Kipling. In London he spoke in justification of England's suzerainty over Egypt, which was then much criticized: "Now either you have the right to be in Egypt or you have not; either it is or it is not your duty to establish and keep order" (WH358). He was thanked for his support by English imperialists, many of whom were his personal friends.

Roosevelt's declarations attracted worldwide attention and even disturbed the Russian novelist Leo Tolstoy, who was a religious and social radical. The latter wrote a letter to the *North American Review* denouncing the new American imperialism and, in effect, supporting Bryan; Roosevelt responded by launching an attack on Tolstoy's "complete inability to face facts . . . his readiness to turn aside from the truth in the pursuit of any phantom, however foolish." Roosevelt doubted whether Tolstoy's "influence has really been very extensive among men of action; of course it has a certain weight among men who live only in the closet, in the library, and among the high minded" (*LE*320). In his autobiography he says that the peace-at-any-price man is thoroughly mischievous (*A*204). He was always ready to defend militarism, or at least to attack antimilitarism. He longed for an American Kipling to celebrate the American soldier and America's Indian Scouts: "Many of our people who know well enough by name the Sikh and Goorkha auxiliaries of the British army would be puzzled by a reference to Major North's Pawnee scouts or the Apaches of Captain Crawford" (*LE*262). He believed in peace, he said, but as things are now, "the nation that cannot fight, the people that have lost the fighting edge, that have lost the virile virtues, occupy a position as dangerous as it is ignoble" (*LE*253).

Roosevelt was also a man of letters, and all his life he reached a large audience of readers with his historical, naturalist, and adventure narratives. He forged a new alliance between literature and adventure: "The love of books and the love of outdoors have gone together amongst the men I have known" (*A*318). In *African Game Trails* (1910) he tells readers about his pigskin library. These were the books he had bound in pigskin for when he went hunting, because "often my reading would be done while resting under a tree at noon, perhaps beside the carcase of a beast I had killed, or else while waiting for camp to be pitched; and in either case it might be impossible to get water for washing. In consequence the books were stained with blood, sweat, gun-oil, dust, and ashes" (339). These excreta are the chrism of adventure, by which his books were ennobled.

His library included five books by Borrow and five by Scott, three by Macaulay, three by Harte, two by Twain, and two by Cooper. As we might expect, he read Austen but reread Scott. Also as we might have supposed, he was a great admirer of Parkman, who was "not one of those hysterical beings who feel that this continent ought to have been left to the Indians because it was wholly impossible to take it from them without inflicting and suffering a myriad of wrongs" (*LE*250). He was also a great admirer of Captain Alfred Thayer Mahan, the theorist of sea power and advocate of American imperialism. Reviewing Mahan's *Life of Nelson* in 1897, Roosevelt wrote:

> The victories of peace are great, but the victories of war are greater. No merchant, no banker, no railroad magnate, no inventor of improved industrial processes, can do for any nation what can be done for it by its great fighting men. No triumph of peace can equal the armed triumph over malice domestic or foreign levy. No qualities called out by a purely peaceful life stand on a level with those stern and virile virtues which move the man of stout heart and strong hand who upholds the honor of their flag in battle (*LE*283–84).

This is a clear declaration of aristo-military loyalty.

After his term as President, Roosevelt returned to adventure, spending ten months in East Africa, where he shot 9 lions, 8 elephants, 13 rhinoceroses, etc., and described it all in *Scribner's Magazine*, articles later published as *African Game Trails*. In the foreword he speaks of "the joy of wandering through lonely lands; the joy of hunting the mighty and terrible lords of the wilderness, the cunning, the wary, and the grim. In these greatest of the world's great hunting grounds there are mountain peaks whose snows are dazzling under the equatorial sun; swamps where the slime oozes and bubbles and festers in the steaming heat . . . forests of gorgeous beauty, where death broods in the dark and silent depths" (*AT*vii).

Later he went to Brazil, and explored—at the risk of his life— a part of the country Lévi-Strauss described for a later generation. Senator Henry Cabot Lodge said the whole American people participated in Roosevelt's adventures, watched him set off for Africa with the absorbed attention of a boy reading *Robinson Crusoe* (WH356).

His opinions about literature were naturally on the side of adventure and against the "realistic" novel in the contemporary sense of realism, which implied both urban subjects and a pessimistic-sardonic philosophy. He called Zola's characters hideous human swine and Tolstoy's *Kreutzer Sonata* morally perverse. On one occasion he referred to Henry James as a miserable little snob. What he wanted in literature is represented by Owen Wister's *The Virginian* and Wister's other stories and essays about cowboys, with illustrations by Frederick Remington. The cowboy myth was a fairly conscious adaptation of popular legends to ruling-class purposes and drew on the model of English imperialism; Wister consciously set out to be the Kipling of the sagebrush, and Roosevelt promoted that myth. He declared that Wister and Remington were doing great work for their country and invited them to the White House to meet Kipling.

Wister was attempting again what Cooper had attempted 50 years before: he wanted to shanghai a popular-culture hero and set him to work for the ruling class. In this case, the popular hero was the cowboy, a semi-Mexican roughneck recently written about in the dime novels. Wister transformed him into a college man on vacation, an upper-class adventurer. Roosevelt was naturally delighted to promote this cultural hijacking.

Artist Remington eagerly joined Roosevelt's volunteers in the Spanish-American War, but he was appalled by the battleships and by the impersonality of modern war. Nevertheless, when the Rough Riders held their last meeting before disbanding, they presented Remington's bronze sculpture "The Bronco Buster" to Roosevelt. The latter also commissioned Remington to paint the official picture of their famous charge up San Juan Hill.

There were thus several links between the three of them, links that made them representative of many others of their class and era. By about this time something like an aristocratic class had developed in the East and had even laid claim to the West. E. Digby Baltzell says that by 1901 "a class of Protestant patricians . . . led the nation and dominated its traditions . . . held the vast majority of positions at the very heart of the national power, and set the styles in art and letters, in the universities, in sports, and in the more popular culture which governs the aspirations and values of the masses."[6] This was the class Roosevelt represented. In a defensive response to the new business plutocracy (or perhaps in a mobilizing of resources to give that new class its proper ethos) new social patterns established themselves very quickly after 1870. For example, in the next 30 years, three-quarters of the students at Exeter Academy went on to Harvard University, while three-quarters at Andover Academy attended Yale. By the time Roosevelt went to Harvard, social clubs at both universities were becoming very important.

As for the link with the West, according to White, it was financial as well as sentimental. Ivy League graduates went out West as stockbreeders—cattle barons—as Roosevelt himself did. Wister first went out to Cheyenne as the guest of the Teschemachev and de Billier Company which was founded in 1879 by two Harvard men and managed by another. The company was a powerful force in developing the cattle business in that part of the West. But it was a sentimental and imaginative link too. No one identified the West with "the commonplace domesticated area within the agricultural frontier . . . [but always with] . . . the exhilarating region of adventure and comradeship in the open air."[7] All of these images were the concepts of a semiofficial cult maintained at the highest national level by Roosevelt.

As literary tastemaker, too, Roosevelt was influential. He recommended W. H. Hudson's writings by saying: "To cultivated men who love life in the open, and possess a taste for the adventurous and picturesque, they stand in a place by themselves."[8] He praised Richard Harding Davis by calling him "as good an American as ever lived . . . [whose] heart flamed against cruelty and injustice. His writings form a textbook of Americanism which all our people would do well to read at the present time."[9]

A connection was generally drawn—by the responsible and gentlemanly class—between adventure literature and cultural, or national, health. It was the readers of that class who praised the adventurers; to do so was implicitly to attack more modern and "unhealthy" writers. Amongst the latter they, including Roosevelt, would no doubt have included D. H. Lawrence and James Joyce. (Both *Sons and Lovers* and *A Portrait of the Artist as a Young Man* were in print when Roosevelt wrote his *Literary Essays*). Eager for the approbation of the literary class, Hemingway placed himself decisively among the modern novelists, even though he had more in common with the adventure writers.

Thus in the period beginning around 1900, adventure received the support of powerful readers, but only at the cost of the writers' allegiance. Kipling was the only major exception to that rule; and by 1918 it was clear that even he had lost his readership among literary people. Despite a continuing demand from general readers and publishers, the adventure writer with artistic ambitions was in a cruel dilemma, especially in England after 1918. In America some major writers escaped from the dilemma, and may even be said to have made a certain kind of aestheticized adventure the dominant mode in fiction.

Part Four

THREE AESTHETES

Hemingway's *The Green Hills of
Africa* (1935)
Faulkner's "The Bear" (1942)
Mailer's *Why Are We in Vietnam?*
(1967)

In the twentieth century adventure becomes a kind of art (for
Hemingway), a myth and ritual (for Faulkner), and an existential
metaphor (for Mailer).

Chapter 11   HEMINGWAY'S
               THE GREEN HILLS
               OF AFRICA
               (1935)

Ⅰf, during Theodore Roosevelt's lifetime, adventure ceased to interest ambitious writers, or at least men of letters, what happened to the cult of adventure in the early twentieth century? By and large, it transferred itself from books to films. Of course, popular writers like Zane Grey and William Rice Burroughs continued to write best-sellers, but it was in the movies that the old images we have studied were newly minted. From Cody's Wild West Show and the stage-melodrama tradition of *Nick of the Woods* was born the Western; and, starting with John Ford's *Iron Horse* (1924) and William S. Hart's *Tumbleweeds* (1926), Hollywood made it the dominant genre. In *Red River* (1948) Montgomery Clift renews the character of the young man (like Oliver Edwards in *The Pioneers*) who inherits his manhood from the rougher and gruffer hero (John Wayne) who embodies the old America; in *High Noon* (1952) Grace Kelly replays the ineffectual struggle of Quakers against the demands of action; and in *The Searchers* John Ford retells the revenge story of *Nick of the Woods*. As late as 1958, 54 feature Westerns were being shown on American screens, and eight out of the top ten television shows (and 10 percent of the fiction) were Westerns.[1]

Moreover, the tradition of nineteenth-century adventure was enshrined in the Hollywood of the 1920s in other film genres (pirate and costume dramas) and in certain stars. Douglas Fairbanks has been described as "an incarnation of the spirit of Theodore Roosevelt and his Rough Riders . . . apostle of the active life."[2] He authored books with such Rooseveltian titles as *Laugh and Live, Initiative and Self-Reliance,* and *Making Life Worth-*

While and was famous for Rooseveltian sayings like "One of the best things in this little old world is enthusiasm." Fairbanks began making films in 1918 but at first appeared in contemporary comedies (a typical title is *His Majesty the American*). In 1920 he made *The Mark of Zorro* and began the career of laughing gymnastics for which he is now famous; his most popular films included *Robin Hood, The Thief of Baghdad,* and *The Iron Mask.* His career ended when sound came in in 1929, but he was replaced by Errol Flynn. The latter too played Robin Hood, Captain Blood, Sea Hawk, and Don Juan, and he went on to play contemporary military heroes, as John Wayne did. Thus the star system preserved and transmitted the old American myth of adventure in a form largely exempt from the controls of criticism.

Literature, however, took itself seriously and was bound to respond to contemporary events, and to critical ideas about them, in ways that inhibited such optimistic enthusiasm. The First World War shocked young writers like Hemingway into "signing a separate peace" and rejecting the chivalric language of honor and glory associated with the romance-adventure. Nevertheless, the war left some writers—again Hemingway is a prime example—imprinted with the image of a more tragic, modern adventure.

One sees that imprint most easily in some of Hemingway's early Nick Adams stories, but it is a constant strain throughout his work. *The Green Hills of Africa*, published in 1935, is the story of Hemingway's safari, of the hunting country, the forests, the plains, the dawns, the natives, the animals he trekked and shot (or lost), and the rules (about weapons and comforts) imposed by the ethos of the hunt. He took some risks and suffered much discomfort (from heat, insects, exhaustion) and was totally submerged in the hunt experience. But though fully engaged in grappling with the moment, Hemingway was always aware of that other experience—of cities, and politics, and literature—from which he had turned away. His adventure is a highly formalized one which he "plays against" the lives of his fellow writers and the lives of his readers.

It was, in fact, disillusioned writers like Hemingway who, in this century, were to make the most serious literary use of adventure, to marry that genre to the literary criteria that seemed so hostile to it. By engaging deliberately in real-life adventures (typically hunting), Hemingway, Faulkner, and Mailer renewed their faith in such traditional concepts as honor and made art the appanage of men of action. In the middle of the century, when America was at the height of its power, they did what Kipling had done in England 50 years earlier, when England was at the corresponding height of imperial greatness. But Kipling's moment was so brief and his achievement so limited (he wrote no book-length adventures for adults) that we can say that he only attempted the dignifying of adventure which the American novelists achieved.

The American writers learned from Kipling, but they also learned from compatriots like Stephen Crane, Frank Norris, and Jack London. Crane invented the persona of the war correspondent for the novelist; Norris developed the adventure form so that it could accommodate women as central characters; and London, in his best books, brought adventure together with a revolutionary political consciousness. All three were important models for the later writers, especially Hemingway and Mailer.

In twentieth-century America, unlike the nineteenth century, it was necessary to approach adventure through myth and symbol before it could be made into literature. That, at least, is what the example of Faulkner and Mailer suggests. Hemingway's stories, too, although he offers only the bare facts of adventure, are always legends, and, in such later works as *The Old Man and the Sea*, the legendary deepens into myth. What, in fact, the twentieth century bestowed on its serious writers, upon those who aspired to be great, was on the one hand myth and symbol and, on the other, the Symbolist techniques of deflection and diffraction. These techniques which seemed at first glance resistant to exciting narrative, proved, particularly in Faulkner's hands, to be more flexible than they looked.

In terms of content, the twentieth century demanded of its writers a display of realism in erotics and politics. Adventure had to be both resexualized and repoliticized in order to seem modern and intellectually serious. Hemingway's literary hegemony in the middle of the century was largely the result of his success at doing both. His heroes seem worlds away from those of nineteenth-century adventurers, for they carry with them a detailed sexual history and a political past. In both areas of experience, however, they have made a defiant disengagement, a declaration of future noncommitment—in this consists Hemingway's "realism," his modernism. Nevertheless, they seem to promise future engagement, both in love and in political action, and it is up to the women and the politicians to show the Hemingway hero reason why he should commit himself again.

Much of this sensibility, and its objective correlatives in form, had been worked out by Kipling; he is, in fact, the missing link in American literary history. His own starting point had been the American rather than the English frontier (his literary master was Mark Twain), but he had escaped the limits of frontier humor and worked out the frontier sensibility's *serious* relations with the metropolis. He had accepted the responsibility for an imperial literature to serve the purposes of the empire's ruling class. This made him a powerful, but also a sinister, master for twentieth-century American writers. To seem relevant in modern terms, Kipling's praise of the empire's rulers had to be combined with something that seemed to be the opposite—a cynical rejection of both the rhetoric of officialdom and the complacency of middle-class moralism combined with a defiant self-identification with the victims of imperialism. We find this combination in Hemingway, Faulkner, and Mailer.

All three write about men who take responsibility for the lives and deaths of others, but they stress the immoralism of such work, not its official glamour. They write about the adventures and misadventures of men of war, men of power (sometimes on a small scale), and men on the frontier (of a literal country or of social respectability). Because their subject matter is adventure, their values are male chauvinist and *machtpolitikal.* To liberal-reforming readers—and to radical feminists or war resisters—they seem crudely reactionary. The idea of American literature they represent is one that is very generally disliked today because it exalts the adventure tradition in American literature.

It will be easy to show how directly the modern history of America stands behind Faulkner's *The Bear* and Mailer's *Why Are We in Vietnam?* Indeed, it would not be hard to do the same with other books by Hemingway, like *Across the River and into the Trees. The Green Hills of Africa,* however, is a more intricate and interesting case. Strictly speaking, one cannot say that this book "represents" American empire in any sense. But it does represent the ethos of the hunt, and it implies an "imperial" worldview on his part—a worldview that, for instance, honors warriors and hunters over elected politicians, shrewd businessmen, prudent householders, and other heroes of modern democracy. The figure Hemingway made of himself in this book, and maintained for the rest of his life, was that of the great artist-hunter, who traveled the world with his entourage and lived by an ethos that outraged modern moralism. It was an aristo-military, an imperial hunt that Hemingway engaged in; hunting was important to him just because it *was* imperial in that sense. The hunt was an alternative to revolution and war, an avocation for a writer, and Hemingway, as hunter-writer, represented in Africa and Cuba and elsewhere the great American empire. Only Americans were rich enough, relaxed enough, big enough (physically and morally) to live such a life.

But to be taken seriously as a writer, Hemingway had to persuade the critics to accept this composite identity of the artist-hunter. Certainly it was an idea that went against modern literary tradition, and it had links to intellectually discredited figures like Theodore Roosevelt. In fact, *The Green Hills of Africa* is very like *African Game Trails*, which was written just a generation earlier.

But with remarkable skill, Hemingway managed to impose himself on the world of letters as a modernist writer—he associated his work with that of Gertrude Stein rather than with Roosevelt—and in so doing he redeemed adventure for American literature. How did he do it? We take Hemingway's own answer, in the first chapter of *The Green Hills of Africa*, as a starting point. When Kandinsky asks him who the good American writers are, he replies, "The good writers are Henry James, Stephen Crane, and Mark Twain" (22).[3] The first name looks odd in that list, especially when we add Hemingway himself to it. But it is the sign that Hemingway is offering himself to us as a high-brow writer, as the heir of James as well as of Twain. He also has Kandinsky recognize him as a poet whose work he had read in the highbrow German magazine *Querschnitt.* Thus Hemingway's essential identity as a serious modernist writer is established, and his love of hunting can now be added to that identity.

He continues: "All modern American literature comes from one book by Mark Twain called *Huckleberry Finn.* If you read it you must stop where the Nigger Jim is stolen from the boys.

That is the real end. The rest is just cheating. But it's the best book we've had. All American writing comes from that." The Crane stories he recommends are "The Open Boat" and "The Blue Hotel," both adventures, one set at sea, the other on the frontier. In the former the narrator is called the "correspondent," the form of the adventure-writer identity that Crane bequeathed to Hemingway, and that made adventure writing in the twentieth century different from what it had been in Twain's time.

Even in *The Red Badge of Courage*, which was purely a product of his historical imagination, Crane writes out of that identity, for the authorial eye is clearly scanning the battlefield like a correspondent's, and "Henry Fleming" is a transparent fiction. Hemingway wrote about the Italian campaign of 1916 and the Spanish Civil War in the same way. Clearly Crane taught Hemingway a lot about adventure writing. The vision of the war correspondent shapes things in quite a different way from that of Twain's humorous tourist guide (which Hemingway employs in *The Green Hills of Africa* and *Death in the Afternoon*).

Probably, however, the most important literary precursor for Hemingway was no American writer, but Kipling, even though he was largely a silent and suppressed sponsor, like Roosevelt. Kipling was also a war correspondent; it was Kipling, after all, who found in British aristo-military idioms of behavior and speech an effective way for the adventure hero to style himself socially. Those idioms were perfectly adapted to self-parody of a kind that disengaged the parodist from serious social intercourse and left him innocent of all claims to personality, sensibility, and soul while reinforcing his claims to virility, action, and command. One example of this is the figure of Pop in *The Green Hills of Africa.*

Hemingway is less famous for his command of the aristo-military idiom than for the "translated speech" of Spanish bullfighters or African trackers, and of Americans talking to the latter across a language gap. But even here Kipling was his precursor, and the objective is the same in both cases—to rescue speech from the evil it does in the novel of manners and in the world of social intercourse, where it spins the substance of a man's virtue out into brittle structures of thought and feeling that shiver into nothingness. In "A Conference of the Powers" we are told about one of Kipling's heroic young subalterns that "he had

done the work; he could not speak; the two don't go together."
"Doesn't do to talk too much about all this. Talk the whole thing away," as Wilson says in "The Short Happy Life of Francis Macomber."[4] In Kipling and Hemingway, speech is as much the refusal of expression and communication as it is their assertion; it becomes a gag or plug or stanching bandage to stop virtue from bleeding away.

Hemingway followed Kipling in this use of the English aristo-military style, and he chose for himself a caste very like Kipling's. He wanted to be a hunter (fisherman, boxer, and so forth)—the sort of hunter who might mix with captains of war, captains of industry, and captains courageous but also with great artists, captains of another kind. In the 1920s he could not publicly associate himself with Kipling, the discredited spokesman for an empire so evidently in decline. Hemingway, moreover, had begun to write as a spokesman for the disillusioned; he had "signed a separate peace." But once he got over the shock of his war experience, his view of adventure became more affirmative—not unlike Kipling's or Parkman's.

In *The Green Hills of Africa* he moves adventure back to the geographical frontiers, away from the squalor and indignity in which Twain had left it. Like Parkman, he admires and respects old bulls: "a big, old, thick-necked, dark-maned, wonder-horned, tawny-hided, beer-horse built bugler of a bull-elk" (138). He also describes an ignoble animal, the hyena (who eats his own intestines), an important addition to the hunter's bestiary. The whole adventure takes place in a hunter's paradise very like Parkman's:

Then the plain was behind us and ahead there were big trees and we were entering a country the loveliest that I had seen in Africa. The grass was green and smooth, short as a meadow that has been mown and is newly grown, and the trees were big, high-trunked, and old with no undergrowth but only the smooth green of the turf like a deer park and we drove on through shade and patches of sunlight following a faint path the Wanderobo pointed out. I could not believe we had suddenly come to any such wonderful country . . . there, standing in an open space between the trees, his head up, staring at us, the bristles on his back erect, long, thick, white tusks upcurving, his eyes showing bright, was a very large wart-hog boar, watching us from less than twenty yards . . . None of us had ever seen a wart hog that would not bolt off, fast-trotting, tail in air. This was a virgin country (217–18).

And if it is Parkman's country, it is also Kipling's. One of the characters says, " 'Then, too, in reality I am a king here. It is very pleasant. Waking in the morning I extend one foot and the boy places the sock on it. When I am ready I extend the other foot and he adjusts the other sock. I step from under the mosquito bar into my drawers which are held for me. Don't you think that is very marvellous?' " (31). And Hemingway replies, "It's marvellous."

In other books, however, Hemingway, like Twain, presented adventures that occur within society—stories of boxers, gamblers, gangsters, and whores. But they are less disturbing than Twain's because they occur on a social frontier that is well known and classical, one that does not threaten to change the whole society. Such motifs, moreover, were most notable in his early work of the 1920s, and in short forms; they reached a major expression in *To Have and Have Not* (1937), in which Harry Morgan belongs to society's frontier on land, although at sea he is on nature's frontier.

In *The Green Hills of Africa*, Hemingway's love of adventure is linked to the concern for manners and manliness, for the style of a great gentleman. For example, he tells us that the Masai "had that attitude that makes brothers, that unexpressed but instant and complete acceptance that you must be Masai wherever it is you come from. That attitude you only get from the best of the English, the best of the Hungarians and the very best Spaniards; the thing that used to be the most clear distinction of nobility when there was nobility" (221). By this stage in Hemingway's development, the existential anxiety of his yearly work has faded away, and a Kipling-like concern with international caste has taken its place. But adventure is still an antidote to the poisons of civilization.

In *To Have and Have Not*, those poisons are depicted satirically, in portraits of rich American tourists and would-be writers. In *The Green Hills of Africa*, they are only alluded to, and they are associated with being a writer, which includes being read, being reviewed, being famous, being in competition with others. Adventure is an antidote to literature.

Early in the book, Hemingway compares the two activities: "The way to hunt is for as long as you live against as long as there is such and such an animal; just as the way to paint is as long as there is you and colors and canvas, and to write as long as you can live and there is pencil and paper or ink or any machine to do it with" (12). Yet a few pages later he distinguishes himself from other writers (the only one he names is James) by claiming that his real life is nonliterary: " 'I am interested in other things. I have a good life but I must write because if I do not write a certain amount I do not enjoy the rest of my life . . . I have my life which I enjoy and which is a damned good life' 'Hunting kudu?' 'Yes. Hunting kudu and many other things' " (24–25). Later he rejoices, while hunting, that he feels "no obligation and no compulsion to write" (55). (Kandinsky's question about hunting kudu reflects the latter's man-of-letters disapproval; he himself "kills nothing"; he is interested in native dances instead of hunting. Hemingway clearly intends to persuade the reader to see the hunter-writer image as the more authentic of the two.)

More than once, Hemingway claims that hunting and writing have the same character for him. This means that writing (his writing) is like hunting, antisocial, almost anticultural. In one such declaration he says, "I did not take my own life seriously any more, any one else's life, yes, but not mine. They all wanted something that I did not want and I would get it without wanting it, if I worked. To work was the only thing" (72). In another, justifying his disengagement from society as a whole and his hunting as a sign of it, he says:

I did nothing that had not been done to me. I had been shot and I had been crippled and gotten away. I expected, always, to be killed by one thing or another and I, truly, did not mind that any more . . . If you serve time for society, democracy, and the other things quite young, and declining any further enlistment make yourself responsible only to yourself, you exchange the pleasant, comforting stench of comrades for something you can never feel in any other way than by yourself.* That something I cannot yet define completely but the feeling comes when you write well and truly of something and know impersonally you have written in that way and those who are paid to read it and report on it do not like the subject so they say it is all a fake, yet you know its value absolutely (148–49).

At other moments, of course, he presents writing as a morally suspect occupation, the opposite of hunting and adventure. This, however, is writing as other people practice it, although he admits that sometimes it can infect his own attitude too. There is a dialectic between the two activities, which he resolves in a number of Kipling-like ways. For instance, he presents writing in terms of a muscular skill, like boxing, hunting, bullfighting, and other crafts and performance skills. Or he relates it to war. À propos of Tolstoy, Hemingway reflects, "What a great advantage an experience of war was to a writer"; and of Flaubert, who "had seen a revolution and the Commune and a revolution is much the best if you do not become bigoted because everyone speaks the same language"; while Stendhal had seen a war and "Napoleon taught him how to write" (70–71). Thus he sometimes comes close to making war and revolution seem ancillary to literature: "A country, finally, erodes . . . the people all die . . . except those who practiced the arts" (109). This "aesthetic" resolution is not very convincing, but the continued effort to resolve the problem is interesting, even impressive.

The hunting, like the writing, is presented in terms of manners and techniques, including social and moral techniques. Hemingway puts a heavy stress on the difference between modes of behavior that are acceptable (which build up the individual, the group, or the social occasion) and those that are not. The most completely contrasted characters, at opposite ends along this line of value, are Pop, the white hunter, and Garrick, a native tracker to whom they give that name because they find him theatrical.

---

*One might object that Hemingway devotes a lot of energy on his safari to arousing the "pleasant, comforting stench of comrades" and that he seeks a great deal of reassurance from them about his performance as a hunter. But that is a criticism of how well he lived up to his principles, not of the principles themselves, which concern us here.

Pop is, in one sense, the exemplary hero of the book; at the end, Hemingway says the whole thing was written to memorialize him. Pop knows how to help everyone behave well; he helps them avoid vanity and yet feel good about themselves. He knows just when to praise Hemingway—"That was a hell of a shot," Pop said. "A hell of a shot. Don't ever tell any one you made that one" (79)—and also when, immediately afterward, to mock him—"And you're a good tracker, and a fine bird-shot, too," Pop said. "Tell us the rest of that" (80). Garrick, on the other hand, talks too loud, makes too much of himself, and finally appears wearing "a large and very floppy, black and white ostrich-plume head-dress" (86). All the real men on the safari, native and white, are very curt with Garrick. Hemingway entertains fantasies of shooting him in the behind, "just to see the look on his face" (178), and finally sticks a shovel handle into his belly and shares the joke with M'Cola and Kamau. Garrick threatens to spoil everything because the others' pleasure in what they are doing depends on a shared dignity of style.

Karl is a shadowy but crucial figure in the story. He is shadowy (hard for the reader to grasp) because of the competition between him and Hemingway, which makes the latter uneasy in handling him as a character. He is crucial because he is someone learning to be a hunter, and he has, we gather, the gifts a hunter needs. (This is not quite clear, which is part of the shadowy effect; what is implied is not quite that he has them but that Hemingway and Pop are generously attributing them to him.) Even so, he is emotional and excitable in bad senses, prone to bitterness when disappointed and somewhat withdrawn. He is thin and sallow, his eyes tired-looking and "seemingly a little desperate." He always feels tricked or betrayed. He is confused, and needs to be sorted out, clarified into the proper hunter's form.

Hemingway himself is the character who behaves best, although he also behaves badly, almost very badly. He is the central character, the heart of the drama, in whom things are in flux. Other characters are fixed, but his fate is being decided before our eyes. What he nearly does badly is to talk too much and to compete bitterly and grudgingly against Karl in the hunt. "Talking too much" implies talking too seriously and excitedly, too egotistically—typically, talking about his writing. At one point he calls this "verbal dysentery," and it is a tendency that, if developed, would align him finally with Garrick as the butt for all "real men."

Discussing literature and his precursors, Hemingway implicitly defines himself as a "naturalist," like Roosevelt (he does not, of course, mention him. The real life hunter from whom Pop is drawn had known Roosevelt and thought Hemingway resembled him, but that is never mentioned in the book.) The only nineteenth-century American naturalist he recommends is Thoreau, even though he says he has not been able to read Thoreau himself: "Because I cannot read other naturalists unless they are being extremely accurate and not literary. Naturalists should all work alone and someone else should correlate their findings for them" (21). Both naturalism and adventure are, apparently, ways to insulate oneself from the world of writers.

Making adventure represent all literature is for Hemingway, as for Kipling, a way to escape the conflict between his two caste loyalties, to Brahmin-writers and to hunter-warriors. Adventure is, of course, aligned with hunting and the aristo-military caste, and the connection bears fruit in this book. Hemingway and Pop address each other as "Colonel"; he fondly remembers his old friend Chink—Captain Eric Edward Dorman-Smith, M.C., of his Majesty's Fifth Fusiliers, and evokes nostalgically the Italian regiments he had served with. In Chapter 1, Kandinsky is allowed to represent the point of view hostile to militarism and hunting, but his opinion is soon dismissed.

The main emphasis in *The Green Hills of Africa* is not on the adventures themselves, nor on the spiritual profit the adventurer draws from them, although both of these themes are carefully described and fully focused. The main stress is on the frame of mind in which adventure must be encountered if it is to be spiritually profitable and on the conduct of the adventure. This too is an emphasis Hemingway found in Kipling, but he found it in children's books like *The Jungle Book* (in the "law of the jungle") and *Stalky and Co.* (in the code imposed by Stalky on his friends). It was left to Hemingway to tell adult adventures with that focus and also to adapt modern sexuality to a function in adventure. (If he put the adventure back on the frontier, compared with his American precursors, he also took it away from boys and restored it to men, compared with his British precursors.)

Pop, the exemplar of conduct, is of course aristo-military. His real name is Colonel Jackson Phillip. We are told that he was Mrs. Hemingway's "ideal of how a man should be, brave, gentle, comic, never losing his temper, never bragging, never complaining except in joke, tolerant, understanding, intelligent, drinking a little too much as a good man should, and, to her eyes, very handsome" (64). This is a rather moralistic account, and perhaps needs to be supplemented by the description of Wilson, the white hunter in "The Short Happy Life of Francis Macomber,"—a story that is obviously close to *The Green Hills of Africa* in inspiration.

Wilson, who habitually sleeps with the wives of the men he takes on safari, is described as "about middle height with sandy hair, a stubby moustache, a very red face and extremely cold blue eyes with faint white wrinkles at the corners that grooved merrily when he smiled."[5] Both he and Pop speak the staccato dialect of the English public school and army (Pop refers to Mrs. Hemingway as "the little Memsahib"), but everything about them redounds to their moral credit and even to their romantic interest. Hemingway describes watching Pop asleep (when his soul is "close in his body") and suddenly seeing in him what Mrs. Hemingway saw: "His body no longer housed him fittingly . . . but inside he was young and lean and tall and hard as when he galloped lion on the plain below Wami" (73). (Karl, on the other hand, has "a being-dead look" when asleep.)

Pop is engaged in (discreetly, implicitly) training Karl. The training of an apprentice to join the ranks of master men—in this case, hunters—is a major topic of Twain's and Kipling's fiction. Implicitly, of course, this theme is a part of the action in all the adventures we have studied. In this book it is not fully focused, but it is a significant activity going on in the background and the shadows. When Karl comes back from an unsuccessful expedition to shoot kudu, "his mind bitterly revolving his failure," Pop says to Hemingway, "I thought he'd do well off by himself with no one to hurry him or rattle him. He'll be all right. He's a good lad . . . You're a little hard on him sometimes" (63). But it is implicit always that while Pop defends Karl to Hemingway, the reverse would not be true—because he does not talk about Hemingway with Karl and because Hemingway does not need defending or training; he is already a master man, and his problems are those of a master man. The primary alliances are between Hemingway and Pop, between Hemingway and Mrs. Hemingway, and between Hemingway and M'Cola. Karl is on the outside of this system of alliances. When Hemingway shoots a rhino and returns triumphant, he finds that Karl has just shot one much bigger; not only he but also Pop and Mrs. Hemingway are bitterly disappointed, and all three congratulate Karl unenthusiastically, "like people who were about to become seasick on a boat" (84).

Thus the story is full of "the pleasant, comforting stench of [Hemingway's] comrades," and it presents his need for that comfort (because of the competition between him and Karl) as a moral issue—the problem of how to prevent such competitiveness from corrupting the adventure and ruining the spiritual enterprise. Pop and Mrs. Hemingway are engaged in helping Hemingway to prevent this outcome. There is even a metaphysical dimension to the theme, although it is barely mentioned. Hemingway behaves better than Karl and so deserves better luck; but in fact Karl gets better luck. This breaks the laws of the adventure experience, for luck is of the greatest importance in hunting, and unless there is some connection between it and desert the adventure gestalt breaks apart. Hemingway has a right to be upset. If, as a writer, he sometimes spoils his own effects by writing too partisan an account of the events, he doesn't ruin the interest of his theme: "We had tried, in all the shoot, never to be competitive. Karl and I had each tried to give the other the better chance on everything that came up. I was, truly, very fond of him and he was entirely unselfish and altogether self-sacrificing. I knew I could outshoot him and I could always outwalk him and, steadily, he got trophies that made mine dwarfs in comparison" (86). There is the impressive theme, and there, in the naming of it, is the artistic failure; the disturbance of the authorial voice, the authorial authority, by grudge. "Altogether self-sacrificing" is an unreal virtue with which to credit a rival, and to follow that with "I knew I could outshoot him" is to betray the source of that inauthenticity. (The treatment of Mrs. Hemingway, referred to throughout as Poor Old Mama, is a worse failure in tone, although less relevant to my argument.)

Hemingway gets his ultimate endorsement, as a hunter and as a master man, from nature—that is, from the Africans. It comes, first of all, from M'Cola, the old hunter who teases him confidently; then from another old man who attaches himself to their party, and at the end of the day doesn't want money but runs after their car screaming, "B'wana! I want to go with B'wana!" (289). But, most strikingly, he is endorsed by some Africans he meets only on his final, successful shoot. After his climactic shot, they become excited, shout, embrace him, slap him on the shoulder, and then, "one after another they all shook hands in a strange way that I had never known in which they took your thumb in their fist and held it and shook it and pulled it and held it again, while they looked you in the eyes, fiercely" (231). Later Hemingway asks Pop what this means, and is told: " 'It's on the order of blood brotherhood but a little less formal. Who's been doing that to you?' 'Everybody but Kanau.' 'You're getting to be a hell of a fellow.' " Pop, of course, introduces the saving note of irony. Nonetheless, the scene of excitement is crucial—all those black hands grasping the white writer's, the hands of Nature herself blessing the man who has served Her, even though he also serves Culture. It is the supreme endorsement, which proves Hemingway to be a great hunter-writer and replaces the luck he was denied.

In this middle period of his writing career, Hemingway was even more famous for his bullfighting enthusiasm than for his love of hunting; *Death in the Afternoon* would have been the book to discuss here if it had been a narrative, for Hemingway connects the bullfight, even more clearly than the hunt, with art. In it adventure and art are fused. "Bullfighting is the only art in which the artist is in danger of death, and in which the degree of brilliance in the performance is left to the fighter's honour" (*DA*91). He shows again the connection between his own writing and his interest in this subject: "The only place where you could see life and death, i.e. violent death, now that the wars were over, was in the bull-ring, and I wanted very much to go to Spain to study it. I was trying to learn to write, commencing with the simplest things, and one of the simplest things of all and the most fundamental is violent death" (*DA*2).

He declares that this will be "a serious book on an unmoral subject" (*DA*4), and says on the very first page, "I suppose that from a modern moral point of view, that is, a Christian point of view, the whole bullfight is indefensible; there is certainly much cruelty, there is always danger, either sought or unlooked for, and there is always death." *His* morality is not modern but antique, not Christian but aesthetic; his adventure is fused with art perfectly: "I believe that the tragedy of the bullfight is so well ordered and so strongly disciplined by ritual" (*DA*8) that aestheticism merges into spirituality:

> The truly great killer must have a sense of honor and a sense of glory far beyond that of the ordinary bullfighter . . . he must have a spiritual enjoyment of the moment of killing. Killing cleanly and in a way which gives you aesthetic pleasure and pride has always been one of the greatest enjoyments of a part of the human race. Because the other part, which does not enjoy killing, has always been the more articulate and has furnished most of the good writers, we have had a very few statements of the true enjoyment of killing . . . the feeling of rebellion against death which comes from its administering. Once you accept the rule of death, thou shall not kill is an easily and a naturally obeyed commandment. But when a man is still in rebellion against death he has pleasure in taking to himself use of the Godlike attributes; that of giving it . . . These things are done in pride and pride, of course, is a Christian sin and a pagan virtue (232–33).

It is writing of this kind that spellbound so many writers between the wars, thinkers as well as storytellers, French as well as Americans. It is what he adds to Kipling, in the same way that Kipling added so much to Twain.

In fiction, Hemingway's best work is in *The Sun Also Rises,* where he might be said to be rewriting and redeeming Kipling's interesting botch of an autobiographical novel, *The Light That Failed.* Both novels have heroes who work for newspapers and live in a gang of beloved buddies, at times in a great city and at other times on its frontiers; both heroes suffer an incapacitating wound; both hopelessly love a perverse but beautiful woman (who admits that she is not good enough for him); and both books are about art. In Kipling's case, the hero is an artist, in Hemingway's he is an aficionado, and the artist is Romero the bullfighter; the two men are tied together by their love of art (and of Brett). This new concern with art makes a big difference to the adventure novel, even when the art in question involves killing and risking one's life. Romero is very unlike adventure heroes of the Crusoe kind. He risks death deliberately (whereas their adventure is partly accidental) and at fixed times, in fixed places, according to fixed rules, for money, and before an audience. He faces death in the afternoon. He works in entertainment, which he turns into art, and almost into religion. Like Kipling's Dick Heldar, he is a hero for men of the aristo-military caste, men who deal in death, not for merchants or Brahmins. But he appeals above all to the aesthetic sense. We might call such heroes aristo-aesthetic. They are suited to an empire's climactic phase, when it is consciously great, in risk of ending, and when adventure becomes a spectacle.

Chapter 12

FAULKNER'S "THE BEAR" (1942)

In the years after 1920, the canon and theory of American literature were rewritten under the covert and largely unconscious inspiration of imperialism—that is, of America's new world role as hegemonic ruler. Late-nineteenth-century literary taste was often seen as "genteel" or "feminine" (in the sense suggested in Ann Douglas's book *The Feminization of American Culture*). Its moral and social refinement were incompatible with adventure. But around 1917 this orthodoxy of taste in both writer and reader, embalmed in the Fireside Poets (a name applied to Emerson, Whittier, Lowell, and Holmes) was repudiated both by young novelists like Hemingway (in *Death in the Afternoon*) and by young theorists of taste like Van Wyck Brooks (in *America's Coming of Age*). Genteel culture was repudiated as narrow and provincial, afraid of tackling the really exciting themes of art.

This new taste, with its strongly masculine character, its attraction to violence, and its skepticism about refinement and piety, was in some ways similar to that embodied in the American adventure fiction of a hundred years earlier, with its nationalist polemic against radical Christianity. It was even more like Parkman's mid-nineteenth-century repudiation of his Unitarian heritage. When Theodore Roosevelt was elected president, Tolstoy, as a radical Christian, wrote a letter to the *North American Review* asking Americans to remain loyal to their mid-century New England writers and abolitionists. But, in effect, it was Roosevelt whom American writers followed in this controversy—although they did not publicly acknowledge him.

In terms of theory, this twentieth-century change of taste was ratified at a high-culture level of literary experiment and under the auspices of European Symbolism. It was a part, a leading part, of the general broadening of America's intellectual horizons in the years after the Great War, when so many young Americans "discovered" Europe, paganism, and modernism. Hemingway, as I have said, sought out Gertrude Stein's sponsorship as a young writer and, in effect, evaded that of Theodore Roosevelt. Edmund Wilson's *Axel's Castle* (1930) summed up the message of the Symbolist influence, announcing, for instance, the fashion for Eliot in poetry and Proust in fiction and the replacement of Shaw by Yeats as the era's most important Irish writer.

In American literature, the equivalent turned out to mean the demotion of Emerson and Thoreau, the Fireside Poets, and novelists like Theodore Dreiser and Sherwood Anderson. Promoted in their stead were Hawthorne and Melville, Emily Dickinson and Henry James, and other writers whose work communicated a sense of sin, of evil, of incommunicable depths and irresolvable complexities.

This shift in taste raised the prestige of some earlier American adventures—especially the more literary ones, such as *Moby Dick*—but at the price of reinterpreting them in Symbolist terms. Even *The Adventures of Huckleberry Finn* became a poem, a myth, an enigma; far from being a boys' book, it was a masterpiece so profound that undergraduates could scarcely be expected to understand it. Melville was rediscovered at the end of the 1920s as an American Dostoevsky. Hawthorne was revalued as an American Kafka.

The historical and geographical locus of this new literary sensibility was held to be the post-bellum South. The North was identified with the New England Fireside Poets in literary terms and in economic terms with industrialism, while socially the North was the modern world, with all its simplicities of understanding and its crudities of reforming zeal. The defeated South was the natural home of myth and tragedy, for it had seen through the modern myths; it had seen through nationalism itself and faced the facts of empire (that is, it had experienced slavery). It spoke the rhetoric of the eternal, the cyclical, the poetic truths. And its greatest spokesman was Faulkner.

In "The Bear," Ike McCaslin, as an old man, remembers how at the age of sixteen he helped to hunt and kill the famous bear, Old Ben. He remembers also the legend of the bear's long career, before he was born, and the respect for and awe of the bear felt by the men who hunt it down. He associates with that story his own experience of defeat in life and the experience of the defeated and guilty South. History, biography, and hunting tale fuse into one ritual and mythic tragedy.

"The Bear" is a good example of both the rhetoric and the adventure stories that formed the core of the new Southern literature. The bear-hunting anecdote around which it is built cannot but remind us of Parkman's buffalo killing, and there are ways in which the latter could be claimed as Faulkner's predecessor. Parkman said at the time of the Civil War, as Faulkner says in "The Bear," that the North owed the South a moral debt for being forced to fight: "The rebel cannon at Fort Sumter were the resurrection of our manhood"; and while the North could not train good officers, the South "compels a man to face wounds and death rather than incur the insupportable stigma of cowardice."[1] He admired the South more than the North just because the former was "essentially military." A hundred years later the Southern writers followed him, to general applause, under the stress (conscious or unconscious) of America's imperial destiny.

What was the connection between the imperial destiny felt by America and the intellectual fashion for complexity and elaboration, for irresolvable moral problems and a sense of man's original sin? It was a strong feeling for the great structures that shut man in from freedom, innocence, and spontaneity but that give him a splendid dwelling place. The nation, that ideal form of political innocence, had been displaced by the older and guiltier image of empire. In this period, the intellectually fashionable form of Christianity was the Roman Catholic Church, with its elaborately rationalist theology and hierarchical form. The Church seemed more authentic in this period because it was imperiality in religious terms; and imperiality was what men of letters were looking for everywhere.

"The Bear" was published only seven years after *The Green Hills of Africa,* and in it a major American writer again asserts his identity through hunting. And there are other important resemblances and connections between Faulkner and Hemingway. Like Hemingway, Faulkner was interested in that social frontier inside society inhabited by gangsters, gamblers, whores, jockeys, and boxers. (He briefly compares the contest between the dog, Lion, and the bear, Old Ben, to that between Dempsey and Tunney.) In *Death in the Afternoon* Hemingway praised Faulkner for his description of whorehouses, and Faulkner wrote the screenplay for Hemingway's *To Have and Have Not.* They shared feelings for the vanishing wilderness and against the city and its encroachments on the wild.*

The affinity between the two writers, and the hegemony they jointly exerted in the 1950s and 1960s, was a striking feature of the literary scene in those years. Their power to influence the general reader and the average writer was perhaps as great in the 1930s and 1940s (in Hemingway's case) and a little later (in Faulkner's). But it was after that that observers began to realize how deeply imprinted by these two were the new serious writers, who were typically Jewish and urban by origin (e.g., Saul Bellow in *Henderson the Rain King* and Norman Mailer in *The Naked and the Dead*). When such young men turned away from the great European modernists they had studied to ask what was specifically and significantly American in the writing of their own time, it was Hemingway and Faulkner they picked on, even though these two were the reverse of Jewish and urban. No doubt this was partly because certain influential critics, for instance, Lionel Trilling and Edmund Wilson, had long been pointing to these two as the preeminent *American* writers. No doubt it also had something to do with the imperialist adventures America engaged in in foreign policy, in the decades after 1945, when it felt itself the guardian of world order.

What this meant for literary America in the 1950s and 1960s was that the adventure novel, which Hemingway and Faulkner adapted and wrote, became a genre of serious literature as it had never been before. The old identification of the writer with the Brahmin caste, of the novel with civilization, and the old opposition of both to adventure, was suppressed. It was an American moment like that English moment 50 years earlier when Kipling

---

*See, for example, Boon's trip to Memphis for whiskey and Faulkner's treatment of the railroad line and logging camps in "The Bear."

seemed to impose the adventure tale upon the critics and to change the ideological profile of literature. As the Englishman was suddenly persuaded to think of himself as essentially a man on horseback—long after horses had ceased to be a mode of transport in England—so the American was persuaded to think of himself as essentially a hunter long after the frontier had been closed. It was when horsemanship, in the one case, and marksmanship in the other, had ceased to be practical skills and become proofs of status, that literature made them marks of national identity and racial myth.

On the first page of "The Bear," we read:

> He was sixteen. For six years now he had been a man's hunter. For six years now he had heard the best of all talking. He was of the wilderness, the big woods . . . of the men, not white nor black nor red but men, hunters, with the will and hardihood to endure and the humility and skill to survive . . . those fine fierce instants of heart and brain and courage and wiliness and speed were concentrated and distilled into that brown liquor which not women, not boys and children, but only hunters drank (185–86).[2]

The passage recalls not only Hemingway and Roosevelt but also Twain (in the emphasis on men) and Parkman (in the emphasis on "fine fierce instants"). The new, Faulknerian note (besides the rhetoric of repetitions and negations) is the sacramental image of the whiskey, half hieratic, half blasphemous, like a Black Mass.

The story's principal anecdote is of the day they hunt and kill the bear, Old Ben. It is narrated fully and excitingly, so that the act of killing (Boon's knife working inside the bear's body, searching for the heart to pierce it) is very real, as well as full of terror and splendor and of the multiple other resonances Faulkner has given it. Those resonances are created narratively, by all the smaller anecdotes, of previous unsuccessful hunts of Old Ben, and of Lion and the fyce, and so on. They are created rhetorically, by the legendary and mythical suggestion of the phrasing, the sentencing, the order, the perspective; and thematically, by the allusion to myth and ritual, the sacred and the primitive. The first half of "The Bear" is a compound of hunting anecdotes of various kinds, and includes several more remotely related anecdotes, some of them comic, like Uncle Ash's expedition, and the final image of Boon Hogganbeck, hammering his disintegrated gun together in order to shoot the squirrels and furiously forbidding Ike to touch them.

Hunting stories are important to Faulkner for the same reason they are to Hemingway: because they bring into focus the values the writer wants to endorse. Both of them declare the same masculinism (the difference between men and women, and between men and boys, is highly prized) and misogyny (which is explicit in Faulkner's story of Ike's marriage and implicit in Hemingway's treatment of his own marriage in *The Green Hills of Africa*). This "masculinism" is also a matter of caste ideology; unless we realize that, it will seem too crude to be of interest. The caste of hunters is essentially a caste of men-and-only-men (*Men Without Women* is a Hemingway title); the hierarchy within the caste, and the group identity with which it looks out at other social groups, both depend on "manhood."

Most strikingly, perhaps, the two writers share the cult of power within the cult of the hunt—a power acquired by the hunter through his love of the animals he hunts or hunts with (this love is more boldly dramatized in Faulkner). When Sam Fathers speaks of Old Ben to the boy as "the head bear. He's the man," his eyes have "a quality darkly and fiercely lambent, passionate and proud" (122). And when Boon first sees Lion, he says "Jesus. Jesus.—Will he let me touch him?" and Sam replies, "You can touch him. He don't care. He don't care about nothing or nobody." Then the boy watches as Boon "touched Lion's head and then knelt beside him, feeling the bone and muscles, the power. It was as if Lion was a woman—or perhaps Boon was the woman. That was more like it" (213).

Boon persuades the dog to sleep in his bed, and Ike at first finds that demeaning (for the dog); but when he becomes a man he understands: "Sam was the chief, the prince; Boon, the plebeian, was his huntsman. Boon should have nursed the dogs" (215). Thus there are important status divisions within the caste of hunters; though all hunters are involved in the cult of power. Lion is Major de Spain's dog even more than he is Boon's or Sam's; the reason the Major never returns to the camp after that hunt is that Lion died in it. (This is made clear in another version of the story.)

One can compare Faulkner's interest in the power of Lion with Hemingway's in the Old Man's big fish or in Francis Macomber's lion. (If we think of Parkman's interest in the Indian, or Dana's in the ocean, we are struck by the specifically animal nature of the modern authors' figures; it gives them what feels like their greater rawness, "funkiness," authenticity; but, in fact, the cult of power in nature links the moderns back to the early nineteenth century, before the hiatus represented by Twain.) The striking difference between the two twentieth-century authors is that where Hemingway's interest is ethical, Faulkner's is mythical (or anthropological). From the beginning of the story, he presents Ike's initiation as a theme parallel to and equal with the hunt; the boy was brought to the woods when he was ten "to earn for himself from the wilderness the name and state of hunter provided he in his turn were humble and enduring enough" (187). This initiation is called an apprenticeship, but—like Dana's in *Two Years Before the Mast*—it is presented as something more total and sacramental. "Then for two weeks he ate the coarse rapid food . . . which men ate, cooked by men who were hunters first and cooks afterwards; he slept in harsh sheetless blankets as hunters slept" (190). Sam takes him on a three-hour ride into a trackless section of the wilderness to show him "the print of the enormous warped two-toed foot" (194); and when he kills his first buck, Sam marks his face with the hot blood (the scene, only alluded to in "The Bear," is fully presented in "The Old People," in *Go Down Moses*).

This buck has been greeted by Sam as "Chief" and "Grand Father," but he must be killed nevertheless, for Ike will be alien to the big woods till he has drawn blood. The buck's blood makes him kin with it, with Sam, and with the earth— "Consecrated and absolved him from weakness and regret." He learned from Sam "things that had been tamed out of our blood for so long."[3]

Finally, Ike is taught to lay aside his gun and watch and compass and enter the wilderness as a creature of nature himself; and so he is allowed his personal vision of Old Ben: "Then it was gone. It didn't walk into the woods. It faded, sank back into the wilderness without motion as he had watched a fish, a huge old bass, sink back into the dark depths of its pool and vanish without even any movement of its fins" (202). Faulkner, like Hemingway, has a preference for huge old creatures that stand still and stare; in this, as in so many matters of hunting sensibility, Parkman provides a precedent—in the buffalo that he confronts and kills at the end of *The Oregon Trail.*

These elements of mystery and myth surround the actions of the hunters but are restricted to the writer's mind and largely external to *theirs.* In their minds the hunt is linked—if to any ideas at all—only to the aristo-military caste and its huntsmen-servants, *General* Compson and *Major* de Spain. The latter leads a hunting party almost as strong (except that not all the men are armed) as those he led as a commander in the Civil War—"in the last darkening days of '64 and '65." Boon Hogganbeck is a feudal retainer (like Callum Beg, in *Waverley*), "brave, faithful, improvident and unreliable; he had neither profession job nor trade and owned one vice and one virtue; whisky, and that absolute and unquestioning fidelity to Major de Spain and the boy's cousin McCaslin" (220). The idea of sacrament, or initiation, does not enter the Major's mind any more than it does Boon's. But for the reader all these ideas, ethical and mythical, are interwoven and indissociable, including the misogyny: "If Sam Fathers had been his mentor and the backyard rabbits and squirrels his kindergarten, then the wilderness the old bear ran was his college and the old male bear itself, so long unwifed and childless as to have become its own ungendered progenitor, was his alma mater" (203).

This idea, of an Old Man who explains the wild to a young one, which recurs significantly in Hemingway's fiction too, goes back to the nineteenth-century stories about the frontier, to Natty Bumppo himself. Henry Nash Smith has pointed out how many such Old Hunters appeared in dime novels. The change brought about by Hemingway and Faulkner is that they sometimes make the Old Man an animal.

When hunting is thus mythically treated, it can assert racial identities and differences without arousing political conflicts. Sam is defined essentially in terms of his Chickasaw and Negro ancestry; Boon, of his white and Chickasaw blood; and Uncle Ash, of his Negro costume (the old quilt from his bed wrapped around his head "till he looked like nothing the boy had seen before") (221). There are racial conflicts between the characters—between Uncle Ash and Boon, for instance; but they are saved, by being mythically treated, from the contemporary-political formulas and ideological suspicions and tensions that Faulkner sought to avoid.

Men are seen mythically, in part because they are assimilated into animals, and vice versa. Old Ben is treated as a man; a foolishly brave hound is "just like folks," Sam says (193); and the difference between Lion and the other hounds is one of social status. Courage and endurance, loyalty and indifference—all the crucial qualities from Faulkner's point of view—are incarnated in the fyce, in Lion, and in Old Ben. At the same time, the men are so simplified as to lose ordinary consciousness and self-consciousness; Boon, for example, has the mind of a child.

And if the men are made like animals, the animals are made to belong to the world of myth. Old Ben's legend is "a corridor of wreckage and destruction beginning back before the boy was born, through which sped, not fast but rather with the ruthless and irresistible deliberation of a locomotive, the shaggy tremendous shape" (187). And Lion's "big head, the chest almost as big as his own, the blue hide beneath which the muscels flinched or quivered to no touch since the heart which drove blood to them loved no man and no thing . . . implied not only courage and all else that went to make up the will and desire to pursue and kill, but endurance, the will and desire to endure beyond all imaginable limits of flesh in order to overtake and slay" (229).

In creating this world of myth and rite, legend and initiation, Faulkner is developing a side of Kipling (*The Jungle Book*, for instance) different from one Hemingway worked. But he owes even more to Conrad, to whose work his own is so akin in style and structure; this similarity is perhaps most strikingly apparent in their landscape descriptions.[4] Together Conrad and Kipling may be said to have created the imperialist novel in English—with its techniques of oblique narration, shifting viewpoint and parodic characterization—devised it in order to tell stories in the service of the British empire's master class.

Of the two, Conrad developed the most thoroughly Latinate rhetoric that became Faulkner's—the ominous repetitions, the exaggerated sentencing, the hints of double meaning, and the overhanging sense of doom that dwarfs characters and events and lets every innocent phrase boom like the echo in the Marabar caves. The legendary and the grotesque are combined, both in the design of the symbols and in the way they are narrated. Take, for instance, the tin coffee pot in which Ike, in later years, keeps his savings (288). This is mentioned, as it were in passing; but then follows a five-page anecdote (a parenthesis within the enormous sentence that constitutes Part IV) about how his uncle gave him at birth a silver cup with gold pieces but stole them back ("borrowed" them) one by one, so that all Ike inherited was this tin pot with some pennies in it. This is the sort of satiric-romantic legend that might have occurred in a Scott novel, but its distorted prolongation and parenthetical insertion into "The Bear" announces the intermediary influence of Conrad. (The episodes about the Intended in *Heart of Darkness* seem to me similar in effect.)

Less obvious (in this story) but more beneficial is the influence of Twain and the frontier anecdote; the minor and comic hunting anecdotes are of this kind. (The major anecdote, the killing of Old Ben, we cannot imagine Twain writing.) In "Spotted Horses" and "Old Man" Faulkner develops such anecdotes into a major mode of comedy, finding quite brilliant high literary effects that correspond to that low genre. In "The Bear," however, they are mainly techniques for rendering violence into Disney-like comedy.

There is, for example, the anecdote of the Texas paint pony that Ike and Boon try to harness: "They lost the first wheel against the post of the open gate only at the moment Boon caught him by the scruff of the neck and flung him into the roadside ditch so he only saw the rest of it in fragments; the other wheel as it slammed through the side gate and crossed the backyard and leaped up onto the gallery and scraps of the cart here and there along the road and Boon vanishing rapidly on his stomach in the leaping and spurting dust" (224). Some effects of Faulkner's violence (those to do with Lion and Old Ben) are a part of the cult of power, but these cartoon moments—of solid things and bodies fragmenting or exploding like half-glued constructions—are full of the kind of excitement found in Twain. A similar story is told about Boon, who had never hit anything with a gun except a Negro woman—when he was shooting at a Negro man; the latter had "outed with a dollar and a half mail-order pistol and would have burned Boon down with it only it never went off, it just went snicksnicksnicksnicksnick five times and he broke a plate-glass window that cost McCaslin forty five dollars and hit a Negro woman who happened to be passing in the leg only Major de Spain paid for that; he and McCaslin cut cards, the plate-glass window against the Negro woman's leg" (227). That is a classic frontier anecdote, in which bodies and feelings are just materials for the effects of violent humor.

All I have said so far about the story refers to its first half. The second half, also about 60 pages long, is about the history of the McCaslin family over 150 years of slave owning and plantation working. If the first part was a narrative, with mythic dimensions, the second is a monologue, full of bitter reflection and moral renunciation. If the first part may be said to celebrate adventure by narrating it, the second must be said to condemn power, the heritage of adventure, by brooding over it.

The narrative substance is the story of Carothers McCaslin—who fathers a daughter upon a slave and then fathers a son upon that daughter—and of the attempts of his white children and grandchildren to share some of the old man's wealth with the descendants of that incestuous and miscegenous union. It is a story of oppression and degeneration, of personal and social misery, and it leads Ike, who meditates upon it, to renounce his heritage entirely and to become a carpenter, like Christ. It is the owning of land as much as of slaves that seems to him wrong. The men who bought and sold the land of his plantation, whatever their race, "knew better" than to think they could own what belonged always only to God. "He made the earth first and peopled it with dumb creatures, and then He created man to be His overseer on the earth . . . to hold the earth mutual and intact in the communal anonymity of brotherhood" (247).

Ike relinquishes everything and buys carpenter's tools, "because if the Nazarene had found carpentering good for the life and ends He had assumed and elected to serve, it would be all right too for Isaac McCaslin" (296). This relinquishment is symbolically a repudiation of his whiteness, a self-alignment with the Negroes. It is associated with Ike's conviction that the Negroes will endure: "They are better than we are. Stronger than we are" (282). Endurance is also linked to humility, which he also attributes to Negroes. Ike tells a black man that the future is his: "Granted that my people brought the curse onto the land: maybe for that reason their descendants alone cannot resist it, not combat it—maybe just endure and outlast it until the curse is lifted.

Then your people's turn will come because we have forfeited ours" (247).

These qualities are crucial ones for Faulkner. "She endured" is the final word on Dilsey, who is the final value in *The Sound and the Fury*. Endurance here is a key virtue for white characters, but their claims to it can never be as self-evident or as confidently asserted as the claims of the Negroes. Only rarely does Faulkner come to the point, as he does here, of symbolically repudiating his race and caste heritage. Ike McCaslin enters a new caste. To be Christian, in the sense of relinquishing property and power and repudiating the social enterprise is not, of course, to enter a caste of any ordinary kind. It is the reverse, choosing to be outcaste, in Hindu terms a saddhu or sannyasin. But inasmuch as we use the word more generally for any social grouping, the Christian is a (theoretical) caste. Our (theoretical) imagination has a space for those who choose that mode of life, but it is a space that is nowhere coextensive with that we assign to the hunter. Yet Faulkner wants to link the two categories, and that marks his failure, on the prophetic as well as the aesthetic level.

Ike's repudiation of his heritage is, presumably, Faulkner's as well, and it is bound to remind us of the renunciation of another great novelist—Tolstoy, who gave up his family heritage as land owner and serf owner, and there are some striking similarities. One can see the McCaslins as a grotesque version of the Tolstoys and their half-built mansion as a caricature of Yasnaya Polyana; and one can view Ike's carpentry as parallel to Tolstoy's cobbling. But Faulkner's repudiation is only a gesture compared with Tolstoy's, a half-gesture. Later in his life, repenting his sudden radicalism, he wanted "The Bear" to be reprinted without the second half; and he was prudent to do so. Even literary critics usually favorable to Faulkner have condemned Ike's action harshly.[5] The world of literary criticism and the world of Oxford, Mississippi, joined ranks against Faulkner's offer to change himself, in a moment of weakness quickly repented. Even within the passage there is much that is incompatible with the idea of such a change, for example, a strong endorsement of the South's part in the Civil War and a condemnation of the North, especially of Reconstruction. Much of this rhetoric is inherited directly from Thomas Dixon's *The Klansman* and could not conceivably be more alien to the Christian ideas allied to it. We read

of "that rank stink of baseless and imbecile delusion, that boundless rapacity and folly, of the carpet-bagger followers of victori-
ous armies" (267). Amongst the men of the North, Faulkner tells
us, the farmers of the Midwest were already looking to the
Pacific coast, the New England mechanics owned no land, and
the traders "were attached to the continent only by their counting houses" (275). Such people could have been induced to fight
for a cause only by the romantic defiance and brilliance of the
South, whose leaders brought no equipment or armament to the
fight but only "love of land and courage—and an unblemished
and gallant ancestry and the ability to ride a horse" (277).

The feeling in such passages is vividly aristo-military, with its
scorn for "the sons of middle-aged Quartermaster lieutenants
and Army sutlers and contractors in military blankets and shoes
and transport mules who followed the battles they themselves
had not fought and inherited the conquest they themselves had
not helped to gain" (278) but had inherited by means of "fierce
economic competition." This feudal caste-enmity is associated,
in this "Christian" half of the story too, with masculinism and
misogyny. Ike's marriage, and the story of Percival Brownlees,
are narrated from a point of view as rankly masculinist as anything in the adventure half. In fact, Ike continues to hunt, even
while he is a carpenter. Hunting, and the violence involved and
the cult of power included, is still felt to be morally pure and
spiritually strong. Only ownership is repudiated. Even in Christian society, the hunters will be the supreme caste; only they will
own nothing, and they will be exempt from other social functions. Faulkner seems to say that it is good for men to win power
but bad for them to hold it.

It is no doubt because of these paradoxes—this self-
contradiction in political and religious terms—that the general
tone of the story is so tragic. In the second half of the story,
brooding over his family's horrible history, Ike breaks out,
"Don't you see? This whole land, the whole South, is cursed,
and all of us who derive from it, whom it ever suckled, white and
black both, lies under the curse" (267). Nothing can be done
about it. When Sam knows the dog has been found who will
finally track and kill Old Ben, he foreknows his own death: "It
was almost over now and he was glad" (208). The boy Ike
"should have hated and feared Lion. Yet he did not . . . It was

the beginning of the end of something, he didn't know what except that he would not grieve. He would be humble and proud that he had been found worthy to be a part of it too or even just to see it too" (218). The something that is about to end is evidently a great performance, a great play, a tragedy.

It is surely the reason for the extraordinary profusion of images of death that surround Old Ben, Lion, and Sam. First the men who have hunted Ben come to look at Ben's corpse and at Lion as he lies dying. Then Boon loosens the floor boards so he can carry Lion on his mattress, out to the gallery to see the woods for the last time. Then nearly a hundred swamp dwellers arrive to pay their last respects. Then Lion dies and is buried by a funeral procession bearing lanterns and lighted pine knots. Then Ike refuses to go back to the city with the other hunters; he must stay behind to see to Sam's death. Then all the others have to return because Boon has buried (and perhaps killed) Sam. At the very end of the story there is the axle-grease tin by the grave; in it Ike puts food and tobacco, when Sam is buried, and, on a later visit, tobacco, candy, and a bandanna.

What all these emblems announce is that life is tragic. They announce fatality, irremediability, and, therefore, the irreconcilability of opposite claims; claims that, from our point of view, could be named, on the one hand, as love of adventure, love of the hunt, the source of all that is best in life and in men; and, on the other hand, the sense of sin involved in land ownership and slavery and all racial and class power. Adventure is good, but empire is bad; the means are good, but the end is bad. Hunting, and the power it makes available, is the source of everything good; but the power itself, once acquired, is the source of everything evil. That is why identification with powerful animals does not bring the expansion of self that it did in nineteenth-century adventures. There is an intensification of self, a concentration and assertion, but it comes in the form of a bitter consciousness of limitation and paradox and a gnarled self-stylization (as a shabby Southern aristocrat, for example) that is close to self-caricature.

Chapter 13   MAILER'S
WHY ARE WE
IN VIETNAM?
(1967)

Despite its title, this is a story not about the war or politics, but about a hunting adventure. At the age of sixteen, a rich Texan, D.J., and his friend Tex accompany D.J.'s father on a millionaires' safari in Alaska to shoot deer and bear. The boy finds the atmosphere of the hunt "phoney" and quarrels with his father. He and Tex slip away into the wilderness, where they spend a night without the protection of weapons. That experience, acting on their intense mutual competitiveness and their ambivalent sexual feelings toward each other, turns them into comrade-killers, who two years later, at the end of the novel, go off to Vietnam.

Mailer's novel may be said to represent the response of American Jewish urban writers to the adventure tradition that—associated with the WASP caste and the preurban landscape as it is—seems so alien to them. It is, in his case, and in the general one, a parodic and yet an affirmative response. One finds something like Mailer's use of adventure in Bellow's *Henderson the Rain King* and in Malamud's *A New Life*, but Mailer's treatment is both the most parodic and the most committed to its own version of the same values. Moreover, there are clear enough political parallels to Mailer's adoption of "American" values—for example, *Commentary*'s endorsement of Ronald Reagan.*

It was also Mailer's generation of writers who introduced the Jew into war novels and into peacetime army novels like James Jones's *From Here to Eternity.* Before 1945, Jews stood on the opposite side of the American imagination from adventure and

---

*Mailer dedicated the novel to *Commentary* editor Norman Podhoretz.

armies; but in many novels about World War II a Jewish soldier was a central figure; and a great many of those novels were written by Jewish writers such as Mailer himself, Herman Wouk, and Irwin Shaw. According to Alfred Kazin, 1945 was the pivotal year for the career of Jewish-American writers. They began to write about adventures and about themselves as adventure heroes, although there was always a note of irony, of self-parody that seemed especially Jewish.

This is not, however, the first time in our study of adventure that we have met this kind of parody, which expresses loyalty as well as mockery. Different though the two writers are, Mailer can remind us of Twain in his temperamental ambivalence—Mailer speaks of trapping the Prince of Truth in the changing of a style—and Twain gets at his truth the same way. This similarity relates to their talent for theater, that is, for dominating, challenging, and scandalizing a live audience with their personalities, refusing—or seeming to refuse—to deliver what the audience has paid to hear, delivering what they have to give, and shattering the social mold of the occasion to make it more existential. That last is, of course, Mailer's word; Twain established this mode of American parody within the limits of laughter. Although Mailer is ostensibly more political and philosophical, the two are more alike than such terms would suggest.

Like the other adventure writers, Mailer has always taken a political interest in *Machtpolitik* and a sexual interest in sexism. His answer to the feminists' charges against him is entitled *The Prisoner of Sex,* and the phrase sums up my argument about him—in its hint of grotesquerie as well as in its confessional truth. Mailer can see beyond the obvious limits of his male persona, but it is his fate (his chosen but immutable fate) to stay within them, to describe the prison yard rather than any landscape beyond. I could call this chapter "The Prisoner of Adventure"—a phrase that, like the other, is a division of "The Prisoner of Manliness."

Mailer's Jewishness explains the greater seriousness of his thrust, compared with Twain, just as it explains the greater intellectual and emotional ambition of his writing. Like the other Jewish writers of his generation, he carries the burden of Israel's emergence as a nation-state at the center of the modern world-system. He cannot be content to be a nonhero or antihero in Twain's style; in fact, Mailer is the tragic clown who claims to be more serious than those who are playing the classical tragic parts. This is made clearest in *Armies of the Night,* an account of his drunken speech the night before the 1967 march on the Pentagon, and his performance on the actual march. He was challenging the men of action (both the police and the revolutionaries) on their own ground—transforming it into his own ground by his parody of himself and them. This challenge clearly runs parallel (in the zigzag fashion typical of Mailer) to the emergence of Israel as a nation-state and the emergence of the Jews as a warrior nation after a long past of passive-ironic apoliticism. Israel is as new a nation as America was when it began to write its adventures. But Jewish-American writers are now citizens of a world empire—a state that has ceased to be a nation in that pristine sense. Thus they have especially acute, and tangled, feelings about adventure.

Both as Americans and as Jews, then, writers like Mailer have extraliterary reasons for following the southerners discussed in the last chapter, in paying their allegiance to the adventure tradition in fiction. But there are literary-intellectual pressures upon them as well. Between 1930 and 1960 there were, after all, only two major organs of highbrow opinion in America: the *Kenyon Review,* which spoke for and to the southern writers; and the *Partisan Review,* which spoke for and to the Jewish metropolitan intellectuals. The second journal was more political, and—in its early years—more left-wing, but one of the striking features of that piece of history is the degree to which the two magazines agreed about literary matters, in spite of ideological differences that would have seemed to prevent concurrence. Critics like Trilling, Kazin, Howe, and Podhoretz were effectively allies and colleagues of Ransom, Tate, Brooks, and Warren; all agreed about the importance of Hawthorne, Melville, Hemingway, and Faulkner. When Twain was led back into the corral of American literature, lassoed with the silken lariats of symbolist interpretation, they were wielded by Lionel Trilling, of all people. This agreement of the critics no doubt explains why this rich crop of fiction (and essays) was signed by both southern aristocrats and sons of the ghetto, these adventures in which sons of the ghetto and the shtetl affiliate with the cossacks of the American West and choose Natty Bumppo or Davy Crockett as fathers in the spirit.

Not that Mailer, at least, is imperialist, or a Reaganite reactionary, in any simple sense. While Hemingway's work treats hunting as an antidote to the poisons of civilized life, and Faulkner's presents it as a ritual of spiritual renewal, Mailer's *Why Are We in Vietnam?* is an accusation. The novel offers itself as a diagnosis of American imperialism and names adventure as its fatal germ, its corruptive beginning. The hunt is the accusing answer to the question in the title.

The war is mentioned only in the last few lines of the book, when it is announced that the two central characters are leaving home, going "off to see the wizard, in Vietnam." The event being honored at the dinner party in Dallas, which—Mailer reminds us several times—is the setting and stimulus under which D.J. thinks about the meaning of that hunt two years before. The hunt provides the narrative with its main action; it also provides the men preparing for war with their main motivation. They need the inner power to kill. We are told, for instance, that D.J., the hero, and Tex, his friend,

> For present period in their eighteen- and nineteen-year old life are super-hot business cause they got illicits going . . . For instance, they are digging corpses in Tex's father's funeral parlor . . . They are not hunter-fighter-fuckers for nothing, no, nor with enclaves of high ability in karate, football, sports car, motorcycle, surfboard . . . without having to snoop here and there for powers which they get from crime, closet-fucking, potential overturns of incest . . . plus ghoul surgery on corpses which is demonological you may be shit-and-shure, and derives from their encounter with all the human shit and natural depth of their Moe Henry hunt two years ago (W156–57).[1]

A number of motives are named, notably, the identity of the boys as hunter-fighter-fuckers and their consequent need to snoop here and there for powers. But it is the last one—their experience of the hunt—which the narrative stresses.

What they discovered in Alaska, partly by reflection on the human ugliness of the hunt, and partly as a message from the land itself, was that,

> yeah God was here, and He was real and no man was He but a beast . . . In the field of all such desire D.J. raised his hand to put it square on Tex's cock and squeeze . . . who had never put a hand on Tex for secret fear that Tex was strong enough to

turn him around and brand him up his ass . . . [and Tex] was finally afraid to prong D.J. because D.J. once become a bitch would kill him . . . yeah, now it was there, murder between them under all friendship, for God was a beast, not a man, and God said, "Go out and kill—fulfill my will, go and kill" . . . and as the hour went by and the lights shifted, something in the radiance of the North went into them, and owned their fear, some communion of telepathies and new powers, and they were twins, never to be near as lovers again, but killer brothers, owned by something, prince of darkness, lord of light, they did not know (W202–04).

And that is the mind-set with which they—and many like them, the nation's elite, the natural leaders—were going into the army. That is why we are in Vietnam.

Saying that God is a beast, Mailer takes Hemingway's and Faulkner's message that a more-than-human power manifests itself in animals only one step farther. Mailer declares God's law—for these boys—to be, "Go forth and kill." In several of his books, Mailer describes or implies a Faustian contract, whereby a man acquires primal powers by giving away decency and self-restraint—by selling his soul. This is not a simply conscious or voluntary process. It can be seen as a matter of fate. The boys, wanting these aristo-military powers, acquire them by "demonological" means, but also through the event in Alaska, of which they seem passive recipients, in which they exchange love for the power to kill.

The book makes dozens of links connecting the hunt with war, or more generally with America's military-industrial complex—links that are both symbolic and realistic because they are parts of society's own symbolic system. We are told that Rusty, D.J.'s father, and his rival, Cunningham, would have burned up the Brooks Mountains "trying to light a light of love in Big Luke's eye," except that Cunningham has to withdraw to negotiate a contract for the space program(W47). When Rusty asks for a really reliable gun—and thus betrays the risk-ethos of hunting—he alludes to the obliteration bombing in World War II. The helicopter that supports the hunters, and the gaping wounds they inflict on their defenseless prey, remind us of Vietnam, for the hunt is a competition in virility that rehearses in purer form the participants' competition at work and America's competition in international politics. Such competition, in a virility measured largely by the ability to kill, is the essence of D.J.'s key relationships, with Tex and with his father. In order to succeed, all three have to sacrifice other values and better qualities.

Another example of Mailer's Faustian contract, more directly related to war, can be found in his first novel, *The Naked and the Dead.* The story begins with a poker game played on board ship before landing on a beach. We see the men of the platoon interact in the game, and, in particular, we watch Sam Croft, the platoon sergeant. In his case, the contract is quite unconscious. Croft is a man who relies almost completely on his instincts, which tell him more than other men know, in compensation for the blindness in his soul.

During the game he has a sudden sure feeling that he will win; he is positive that one of the next two cards he draws will give him a full house. Moreover, watching another soldier, Croft thinks to himself, "That boy is too careful . . . And then with a passionate certainty he thought, 'Hennessey's going to get killed today . . .' This time he was sure" (*N*29). At the end of Part 1, Hennessey has in fact been killed, and Croft "brooded over the event all day . . . Hennessey's death had opened to Croft vistas of such omnipotence that he was afraid to consider it directly. All day the fact hovered about his head, tantalizing him with odd dreams and portents of power" (*N*40).

In the capsule section on Croft, Mailer says that *"there was a crude unformed vision in his soul but he was rarely conscious of it"* (*N*156). But there is also, relatedly, a rage smoldering in him, which feeds on itself. Like Henry Fleming in *The Red Badge of Courage,* Croft feels a tension in his throat when his rage becomes conscious. "He hungered for the fast taut pulse he would feel in his throat after he killed a man" (*N*143). Having taken a Japanese prisoner, Croft gives him some food and a smoke, and the man relaxes, feeling secure. Then "Croft felt a tension work itself into his throat and leave his mouth dry and bitter and demanding. His mind had been entirely empty until now, but abruptly he brought up his rifle and pointed it at the prisoner's head," and shot him (*N*195). Like Hemingway, Mailer is always asking where men find the inner energy they need to kill others.

All three of the twentieth-century adventure writers come close to discussing the subject, to focusing on adventure as a discursive topic, and even to relating it specifically to modern imperialism. Hemingway and Faulkner may seem to differ crucially from Mailer in that they argue an opposition between hunting and the ills of modern civilization, while he argues a causal connection. But the difference is not really black against white. Hemingway and Faulkner also imply a connection. The design of "The Bear," after all, juxtaposes the hunt with the plantation and so suggests the natural twinship of huntsman and landowner; and Hemingway was both hunter and war correspondent—the two roles are natural twins again. He and Faulkner fully accepted the ills of civilization. On the other hand, Mailer cannot be said to *condemn* either the hunt or the war: however ominous the tone of the book and the context in which the hunt is set, it is clear that he too accepts these evils as man's fate.

Of the two precursors, it is Faulkner whose presence is more obviously felt in *Why Are We in Vietnam?* It is, after all, the story of a boy's initiation, it occurs during a bear hunt, and it involves his laying aside gun, binoculars, etc., to enter the wilderness as a creature of nature. Thus the substance of the narrative is strikingly like that of "The Bear." And though the prose Mailer designs for D.J. is a far cry from Faulkner's grand rhetoric, there is a resemblance between D.J.'s humor and the frontier anecdote Faulkner often employs in the first part of "The Bear." The grotesqueries of frontier humor and those of a white-negro disc-jockey come from the same part of the social map—both are frontier rebels against the classical canons of prose.

More than once in *Advertisements for Myself* (1959) Mailer acknowledges his debt to Faulkner—the long influence of *The Sound and the Fury* in his *Barbary Shore* and *The Deer Park*. "Faulkner's style—which is to say, his vision—was to haunt my later themes like the ghost of some undiscovered mansion in my mind" (*A*79). And indeed one can trace the exaggerations of Mailer's style, some of the violence of his sensibility, and his homemade fantastic metaphysics, to that source.

As for his persona as a writer, and the contests in virility at the center of his plots, those Mailer plainly got from Hemingway. The whole idea of *Advertisements for Myself* derives from Hemingway, so he implies. Hemingway

knew in advance, with a fine sense of timing, that he would have to campaign for himself, that the best tactic to hide the lockjaw of his shrinking genius was to become the personality of our time. And here he succeeded . . . he's known the value of his own work, and he fought to make his personality enrich his books. Let any of you decide for yourselves how silly would be *A Farewell to Arms* or better, *Death in the Afternoon*, if it had been written by a man who was five four, had acne, wore glasses, spoke in a shrill voice, and was a physical coward. (*A*18–19).

Mailer admits that all his early work was written in imitation of Hemingway. But what is more important is that Hemingway invented the identity of the adventurer-writer, which Mailer chose to make his own.

Moreover, the eight-novel sequence he planned after *Barbary Shore*, and long worked on, was to revolve around the adventures of a mythical hero called Sergius O'Shaughnessy, who appears in *The Deer Park* and in "The Time of Her Time," in which he runs a bullfighting school. In one section of *Advertisements for Myself*, Mailer refers to himself as the General, a very Hemingwayesque touch. He also describes himself as "one of the few writers of my generation who was concerned with living in Hemingway's discipline"; this is what we might call the military-manly discipline. Mailer even shared Hemingway's belief that "even if one dulled one's talent in the punishment of becoming a man, it was more important to be a man than a very good writer" (*A*247). Thus the religion of manliness survives in twentieth-century literature. Mailer's writing of adventure novels depends crucially on Hemingway's influence, however unlike particular Hemingway novels *Why Are We in Vietnam?* may be.

The central character of the later novel, D.J., presents himself to the reader in such a self-contradictory way that we learn very little about him; we are teased with the suggestion that he may be black and not white, a New Yorker not a Texan, old not young. We are also invited to associate the voice of the Intro Beep with William Burroughs: we are told that the voice represents "the expiring consciousness" of recently executed nerves (*W*26). Much of this turns out to be semantically trivial—merely an extra trumpet playing another motif alongside the main theme—for the story concerns the Texan D.J. It does mean that the writer's energies, and ours, go into something other than "knowing the character."

Apart from his theological theories (to which we must return later), we see D.J. mostly through his conflicts with his father and mother and with Tex. It is in terms of these relationships, these experiences, that he defines himself and enters manhood. Despite the monologue form, we rarely see him alone, as we do see his precursors, Holden Caulfield and Huckleberry Finn.

His relationship to his mother is ancillary to the major conflicts with his father and with Tex, but it is important to understanding him. In the two anecdotes we hear of his childhood she saves him from his father's wrath. At five he runs screaming from his father into his mother's arms: "little man save by cunt, virility grew with a taint in the armature of the phallic catapult" (W137). At thirteen, "it took a week of negotiations by his ma to bring him out of the hideout in Mineral Wells where she'd stashed him and into audience with his father again" (W42). Thus, while "full of daddy-love, Tex got that mean glint in the eyes for which Texans are justly proud and famous . . . D.J. has got the sweet smile of my-momma-loved-me-and-I'm-sweet-as-a-birthday-cake kind of mean look" (161). The Old Man figure, Big Luke the guide, who knows the wilderness is not shown in direct contact with the hero, as he is in Hemingway, Faulkner, and earlier adventure writers. Instead the crucial events take place between son and father, boy and friend (and, of course, Man and God). Mailer's mind is much more thoroughly psychoanalytical (and magical) than that of the earlier writers.

Rusty, the father, head of Pure Pores, a division of CCCC and P, is defined in terms of corporate life and products. But he is also a "heroic-looking figure of a Texan, 6 ½, 194, red-brown lean keen of color . . . like a high-breed crossing between Dwight D. Eisenhower and Henry Cabot Lodge." He is also said to be "an unlisted agent for Luce Publications, American Airlines Overseas Division, and the IIR—the Institute for International Research—shit!, Spy Heaven they ought to call it" (W31, 34). Thus he represents the ruling class of America in several of its aspects. The variations in tone announce the son's ambivalence: his wish to judge and destroy his father versus his wish to respect and love him.

When D.J. offers to tell us why he is so angry with his parents, it is because he has, while high on pot, "seen his [father's] face disintegrate" (W35–36). Rusty's eyes showed that America is run by a hidden mastermind, a plastic asshole in his brain to shit out the corporate management of thoughts. Rusty is the most dependable human product America turns out, but he's not fully a man. D.J. has to go to Big Luke for true fathering (W37).

Rusty is caught up in business competition and status anxieties, and the hunt is corrupted by them. Their guide is reserved 18 months in advance, not because of his expert marksmanship or the scars he's won fighting bear (his back is like an old seam of welding grown over with vines and thorns) but because he has been the guide for Charley Wilson, J. Edgar Hoover, George Humphrey, and other celebrities.

D.J. and Tex watch Rusty drop points in his contest with Big Luke, and they transfer their loyalty to the latter—"a sweet old bastard who's so tough that old grizzly bears come up and kiss his ass" (W38). D.J. tells us that "Big Luke got a presence, not much of a face . . . but Big Luke sends out a wave every time he has a thought" (W54). He is another Pop or Natty, defined in Mailer's terms. He "got eight clients out of the Brooks Mountains once in a record September blizzard" and "fought a grizzly or two barehand to a kind of draw" (W46). But the essential point about him, what the boys want to learn from him, is presence: "what made Big Luke the Man was that he was like the President of General Motors . . . he had like the same *bottom;* man . . . 'cause he was a *man!* You could hang him and he'd weigh just as much as Charley Wilson or Robert Bonehead MacNamara, I mean you'd get the same intensity of death-ray off his dying as you'd get from some fucking Arab sheikh who had 10,000 howlers on horses to whoop and scream for the holy hot hour of his departure to Allah" (W47). (Ten thousand of the Africans who attached themselves to Hemingway, or 10,000 Boon Hogganbecks blindly devoted to Major de Spain, or 10,000 Nazis at Nuremberg.)

The other two adults on the hunt, Rusty's subordinates at work, Bill and Pete—who are anxious to please him—are, respectively, assistant to the procurement manager and personnel director for the production manager. Moreover, all Rusty's feelings on the hunt are oriented to the thought of what people will say of his performance afterward. What will they say if, for example, he comes home with caribou antlers instead of a bear skin? "He don't believe in nature; he puts his trust and distrust in man. 5% trust, 295% distrust" (W53). Rusty also represents

White Anglo-Saxon Protestantism, and he is full of WASP anxieties, as we learn in Intro Beep 7. Seventeen anxieties are listed: women are free; niggers are free; the yellow races are breaking loose; Africa is breaking loose; the adolescents are breaking loose, including his own son; the white men are no longer champions in boxing; the Jews run the eastern wing of the Democratic party; and so on.

However, when Rusty and D.J. slip away from the others ("They are off on a free, father and son"), Rusty shows a different side to his nature, and they achieve a temporary harmony (W124). He knows the names of the flowers they see, his sweat smells good to D.J., he can instruct his son in hunting and in the lore of the wilderness. D.J. addresses him as sir, even as Daddy.

But D.J.'s mood is very unstable; as soon as they sense that a bear is near, and D.J. "breathes death—first time in his life—[he] . . . is hip to the hole of his center which is slippery desire to turn his gun and blast a shot into Rusty's fuck fat face" (W136). The savage beating Rusty gave him when he was five has left a deeper and fiercer trace than he was aware of.

Then the mood shifts: "the murder was outside them now, same murder which had been beaming in to D.J. while he was thinking of murdering his father, the two men turned to contemplate the beast" (W138). (This is a rehearsal of the later decisive shift in the boys, from dread to mutual murder, and from that to common murder.) But in the killing of the bear, Rusty behaves badly, and D.J. doesn't speak to him on the way back to the others. Then, talking to the guide afterwards, Rusty behaves worse; he claims the bear as his. "Whew. Final end of love of one son for one father" (W147). That is why, when D.J. gets ready for Vietnam, two years later, "between D.J. and Rusty it is all torn, all ties of properly sublimated parental-filial libido have been xed out man, die, love, die in a diode, cause love is dialectic, man, back and forth, hate and sweet . . . it's all torn, torn by the inexorable hunt logic of the Brooks Range when D.J. was sixteen, wait and see" (W126).

Now Hemingway and Faulkner do not present us with the idea that on a hunt a father and son might learn to hate each other to the point of murder. Their message points in an almost opposite direction, implying that on a hunt old quarrels end and feuds are reconciled. It is true that Mrs. Macomber murders her husband; but she is a woman, and she does it because Mr. Macomber had just *become* a man; *that* is Hemingway's implicit message. But could she not have been a man? Could there not have been the same intensities of feeling between two men, aroused by the question of virility? What did Karl feel about Hemingway in Africa? Clearly, Mailer is only taking such work as Hemingway's one step farther.

D.J. and Tex, on the other hand, deeply respect, fear, and love each other: "They is crazy about each other" (W179). It is clear that the link between them is in some sense sexual attraction. We hear D.J. defined early as "a latent homosexual highly over-heterosexual," and his mother is dominant in his home, while Tex's father is dominant in his (W14). That suggests at least one reason why D.J.'s mother is anxious to separate the boys at all costs. But the link between them involves all the strands that combine in what we call love; they name it to themselves as comradeship; they are adventure comrades. When, unarmed, they encounter an arctic wolf, they jointly give off waves of murderous fierceness, so that it slinks away. They do everything together. But being American boys, they cannot think of loving each other except in terms of a power struggle, of aggressive rape. Thus, spending the night alone in the Arctic Circle, deprived of every civilized restraint and support, they become aware of something hitherto hidden in their feeling for each other. It is sexual desire, aroused by ontological anxiety, by each one's need to establish his personal power in terms of the other's weakness, to transgress against each other, and against the ultimate sanctity of their feeling for each other. It is an anxiety and drive so strong that D.J. calls it murder. This is what Mailer implicitly declares to lie at the root of all adventure comradeship. (We should remember that Mailer belongs to the same generation as Leslie Fiedler, whose *Love and Death in the American Novel* puts a sexual interpretation on Huck Finn's relations with Jim, Natty Bumppo's with Chingachgook, and similar relations in Hemingway and Faulkner.)

Unlike Faulkner, but like Hemingway, Mailer organizes his demonstrations of courage and virility in the form of contests; one man's courage and virility are (often) acquired at another man's expense. "Comedy is the study of the unsound actions of the cowardly under stress," says D.J., "just as tragedy is the equal study time of the brave under heroic but enigmatic, reverberating, resonant conditions of loss" (W81). Men study each other's courage. The bear roars as it charges, and hours later D.J. can still hear that roar "echoing out of the ashy pores of Rusty's monumentally shaken skin" (W106). Even Big Luke, the guide, who is said to stand outside the system of anxieties, has the same testingness and demandingness, as far as others are concerned. If you had "naught but a smidgeon of flunky in you it would still start . . . in Big Luke's presence to blow sulfur water, steam, and specks of hopeless diarrhetic matter in your runny little gut, cause he was a *man!*" (W46).

More essential than the challenges of men, intermediary between them and the full presence of God in the North land, are the animals. *Why Are We in Vietnam?* has the same anthropomorphic sense of animals we found in Hemingway and Faulkner. They think and feel as men do. Luke explains the bear's psychology this way: "He remembers the bullet, that bullet maybe tore his intestine, that is a terrible pain. A bear feeling such pain, sir, is in my opinion, struck as if by lightning and so picking up in certain ways the intelligence of man" (W66). But, more important, man can pick up the spirit of a beast—the zoomorphic sense of men is the heart of Mailer's message. When D.J. shoots a goat, "*Wham!* the pain of his exploding heart shot like an arrow into D.J.'s heart, and the animals had gotten him" (W99). When Tex shoots a wolf, which had "lived to rip one piece of flesh from another piece" (W60), Luke gives them each a cup of its blood to drink, and D.J. gets down on his hands and knees, "looking up into that upper Yukon wolf mouth, those big teeth curved like tusk, and put his nose up close to that mouth, and thought he was looking up the belly of a whale, D.J. was breathing wolf breath . . . he was ready to get down and wrestle with the wolf, and get his teeth to its throat, his teeth had a glinty little ache where they could think to feel the cord of the jugular . . . D.J. was up tight with the essential animal insanity of things" (W69).

Besides the wolves, we see the caribou and the eagle, but above all the bear: "Some giant wolf in D.J.'s heart, some prehistoric wolf all eight feet big began to stir new boils and springs and pools in the river of D.J. . . . he had to get him a wolf in the form of a bear" (W119). When Rusty and he shoot theirs, "Something in that grizzer's eye locked into his, a message, fellow, an intelligence of something very fine and very far away, just about as intelligent and wicked and merry as any sharp light D.J. had seen in any Texan's eyes any time" (W146). All this is nature, and it is contrasted, as it is in other adventures, with the forces of civilization—the guns the hunters bring, the motel they stay in, the commercialization and technologization of the hunt. This is symbolized in the helicopter and, above all, in the ugly wounds: "toilet-plunger holes seen in caribou, and shattered guts and strewn-out souls of slaughtered game-meats all over the Alaska air" (W175). We are asked to think here of the cruel damage caused by military technology in Vietnam, but the explicit references are all to animals. "Big Luke brought that animal back to feed us. Its guts, belly and lungs were one old jelly flung together by the bullets . . . we had the meat for lunch, and it wasn't exactly gamy, it tasted loud and clear of nothing but fresh venison steeped in bile, shit, and the half-digested contents of a caribou's stomach . . . that was Luke's message to us" (W98). This passage carries on, and adapts, the image of the hyena from *The Green Hills of Africa.* But now the men are hyenas.

An important motif of the story is Texas, which, though still full of the frontier myth, the hunting myth, is in fact no frontier but the metropolis from which men like Rusty must go out to Alaska to renew their virility, their Americanness. Now only Alaska is America, "that sad deep sweet beauteous mystery land of purple forests, and pink rock, and blue water, Indian haunts from Maine to the shore of Californ, all gutted, shit on, used and blasted, man" (W205). Texas is evoked in all the characters, but above all in Tex. D.J. will face God's anger rather than "the contempt and contumely of the State of Texas personified by Gottfried Tex Hyde Jr." (W143). He is "half German and half-Indian on his father's side, Redskin and Nazi all in one paternal blood, and his mother . . . jes old rawhide Texas ass family running back through fifty two shacks" (W17). He is a killer because one of his mother's ancestors died at the Alamo; and when those men died ("they was the best bunch of sinewy high bounding zap and God streak fuckers") their buddies and relatives were their spiritual beneficiaries (W166). Tex himself is tall,

got a whippy old body, 6-1, 168 pounds, all whip leather, saber and hide even when he seventeen. He and D.J. are lookalikes, except for expression, cause D.J. is full of mother-love received in full crazy bitch perfume aromas from Hallie, whereas Tex is full of ape shit daddy-love . . . a most peculiar blendaroon of humanity and evil, technological know-how, pure savagery, sweet aching secret American youth, and sheer downright meanness as well as genius instincts for occult powers (he's just the type to whip asses at the Black Masses) as well as being crack athlete (W162).

It is clear enough that Tex represents the military, executive, aggressive energies of the American empire, while D.J. is his conscience, consciousness, and sensibility—his literary better half, who is fascinated by him, dependent on him, imitative of him, but full of ambivalence about him.

In addition to the familiar elements of American adventure, *Why Are We in Vietnam?* has features not found in earlier adventures. The image of the disc jockey, both as representative of the city's technology and as unreliable narrator, brings a different dimension to adventure. (One might find the origins of that unreliability in Kipling.) This idea is surrounded by contributory features like the allusions to drugs and to tape recorders in heaven. Also new are the stress on the corporation as characterizing America, and on technology as an omen of dishonor.

But above all we have to add in Mailer's metaphysics of the body, of its smells and excretions, and the existentialist theology of dread that he ties to it. Like Artaud, D.J. feels the Lord slipping into him, installing tape recorders in our bodies, stealing our souls: "We are all, after all, agents of Satan and the Lord" (W28). This metaphysics of the personal body is extended to become a theory of the physical earth, which is seen as a living body with sexual orifices that create the electromagnetic field, which is particularly strong within the Arctic Circle. Above the circle every mind, even vegetable and mineral, is tuned in to the same place (W115). All of America's dreams can be felt in the air, and those dreams are messages of greed; consequently, a ring of vengeance "rings out of the air" (W205). D.J. is full of beauty and of "the sorrow of the North, the great sorrow up here brought by leaves and wind, some speechless electric gathering of woe" (W196). Magnetism potential and electricity are the actual of the Prince of Darkness, D.J. suggests (W172). In this whirl of tentative cosmology and eschatology, Mailer most resembles Melville and Twain (the most ambivalent of adventure writers), but his emotional scheme is much more erotic and—because of its stress on virility—closer to Hemingway and Faulkner.

The most striking formal characteristic of *Why Are We in Vietnam?* as an adventure is that it is so schematic and fabulous; it makes such open use of its literary predecessors. It is a story told in answer to the question asked in the title, a fable made up in answer to it. As a result, we are not so engaged by its characters and events as by what they stand for—or, more exactly, by the process by which they come to stand for it, above all, the process of literary borrowing and allusion to Hemingway and Faulkner. It is the sort of book that provokes literary critics to say that it is not about the Vietnam war at all but about the adventure tradition.

From the point of view of this study, the importance of this feature is that it inhibits the expansion of the self that occurs in earlier adventures; there is no contagion of power and excitement from the main character to the reader. As for the writer, he cannot be located, except as the fabulist, the literary technician. Nor can we say what he believes about, for example, caste. On the other hand, Norman Mailer, the author of *Advertisements for Myself* and several lesser books, has talked very frankly about just such subjects. He is, in fact, one of the writers most committed to escaping the limitations of the Brahmin identity by entering into the aristo-military caste. One can deduce that he is in basic agreement with his character's sense of God (as a beast). It is a savage theology he is proposing.

It is worth noting that in each of the twentieth-century writers we have considered, the expansion of the self in adventure has been blocked, both for him and for his readers. Twentieth-century America is less morally self-confident that nineteenth-century America. The reason *seems* to be different for each writer; if in Mailer it is the didactic *use* of adventure, as a blackboard diagram of imperialism, in Faulkner it is the parody of the self that was affirmed, and in Hemingway it is the prescription of adventure as an antidote for social evils. In each case the enthusiastic message of adventure is ironically circumscribed and limited. Thus one suspects that some more general and fundamental law is acting within all of them, some guilt about American imperialism which forbids expansive movement.

One may also suspect that this blocking effect is more apparent than real, that these twentieth-century adventures *do*, after all—though in a different way—expand the self of reader and writer. There is, after all, a strong excitement in the self-definition of all three writers (an excitement generated in the act of writing), and the reader who brings sensibility to his reading will receive the discharge of that excitement. It may be that in these twentieth-century writers, two of the concerns we have asked about, self-expansion and caste identity, are more closely connected than they were earlier. When adventure becomes aesthetic, the artist becomes the great adventurer. It is now the identity each one writes from, the writer's identity he has strenuously constructed for himself (becoming more than a mere Brahmin)—this identity, rather than the animals they *name* as the locus of power—that is the source of the reader's contagion.

Does this mean that adventure can be purely or mainly aesthetic, that it can be separated from its roots in the political excitement of imperialism? Can adventure writing carry the same intensity of meaning in a cultural situation in which it does not derive from and in turn promote national greatness? Surely not. Of course, there are adventure tales that are innocent in this sense; nonetheless, the ones we have considered are interesting just because they do have such roots.

Chapter 14   CONCLUSION:
CASTE-THINKING
IN AMERICA

It is time to draw some general conclusions about adventure in America and what these adventures tell us about the meaning of being an American. First, however, we should remind ourselves of the other kinds of American literature—confining ourselves to prose narratives—that critics have thought to be central. If adventure, contrary to my claim, is only peripheral to American literature, the conclusions to be drawn from analyzing it will be narrow in their scope.

During the period I have covered, great numbers of novels of the domestic kind were published in America—novels that raised such questions as Which suitor will our heroine choose? How should she deal with sudden poverty? With sudden wealth? With a too-sophisticated friend? In England the domestic novel became a great literary tradition in the hands of writers like Jane Austen, George Eliot, and, later, D. H. Lawrence. In this country it flourished in terms of publication statistics but not in terms of artistic quality—at least not until the last quarter of the nineteenth century, when we find distinguished work by Henry James, W. D. Howells, and Edith Wharton. It is significant that two of these three writers, James and Wharton, chose to live in Europe and felt America to be an uncongenial atmosphere for their kind of novel. Their kind of imagination never felt 100 percent American. In any case, in scope of subject matter and in time range of publication, this tradition cannot compare with the one we have studied.

A little later, Willa Cather combined a similar kind of fiction with an interest in the American frontier. Hers was not the hunters' frontier, which was so important to the adventure writers, but the farmers' frontier (with the settlements not far behind), a setting in which women could be the central figures of a narrative. To Cather's name we could perhaps add those of Sarah Orne Jewett and Hamlin Garland; even then we would not have a sequence of books comparable with those of the adventure writers either in range of publication dates or in political centrality.

A different sort of novel, which has on occasion seemed to critics much more serious than the adventure, can be represented by Crane's *Maggie, A Girl of the Streets*, and Dreiser's *Sister Carrie*. These are, again, stories centered around women, but not this time around marriage. Instead, they are in some sense about the big new cities of the twentieth century and their harsh cultural environment—about the harsh cultural significance of modern commerce and industry.

In the last quarter of the nineteenth century and the first quarter of this one, these two kinds of novel seemed more important to critics than the adventure, although in the years between 1925 and the present, works of these genres were often either adversely judged or neglected. It is natural that present-day critics should attempt to rewrite the history of literature in their favor and to teach courses in American literature composed of such texts. That is only fair because in the 1920s and 1930s that history was rewritten in their *disfavor* when young critics like Trilling and Wilson in New York, and Ransom and Tate in the South, steered readers away from both these kinds of narrative.*

The taste formed by such critics, which was still dominant when I first read American literature, espoused Hemingway and Faulkner, among contemporary writers, and Hawthorne, Melville, and James, in the past. It did not praise adventure—indeed, Trilling both temperamentally and theoretically preferred the novel of manners—but in effect that taste promoted the identification of art, so far as American literature went with adventure. This was disguised by the critics' sophisticated language of myth and symbol, folk legend, and ironic ambivalence; but in fact the stories that lent themselves to that sort of artistic elaboration and critical exposition were adventure stories.

---

*A good place to see the reformation of taste is in Trilling's early essays, collected in *The Liberal Imagination*.

It is, therefore, natural that nowadays critics and teachers of American literature (especially feminists) should reverse that tendency and replace those texts with others in which women are more important. Moreover, there has always been a literary tradition, in a transcendent sense of "literary," that was hostile to adventure. Literary study consists largely of an institutionalization of ideas opposed to those in vogue in the corridors of power; literary canons are always, to some degree, countermyths designed to contradict the myths that energize the larger society.

What I am proposing, on the other hand, is the opposite-seeming tactic of stripping away from adventure the aesthetic and critical rhetoric—the elaborations of both form and point of view devised by novelists and critics—in order to look directly at their implicit message of imperialism. To turn away from such texts toward others—those about "strong women"—can do more to build up the communal pride and energy of readers who want to resist imperialism and to change the meaning of "America." Intellectually, however, there is more to be said for a dialectical engagement with these powerful texts—a reading that makes readers grapple with an inimical discourse—that imposes on them the discipline of making a generous and balanced response to ideas they dislike.

Of course, this effort is only feasible if the writers and their stories are impressive enough in intelligence and moral seriousness to engage the reader in such a dialogue. It seems to me, as I have tried to show in the preceding chapters, that many of them are. And if they are, this writing is historically and politically privileged, above the competing strains in American narrative; for it expresses in the flattering form of adventure the myth that energized America's political and historical policies and shaped America's behavior toward other states and other peoples. This national myth is not expressed in other kinds of American literature. As readers grapple with *this* discourse, they grapple also with the imaginations of those among their own contemporaries who deal in power. They grapple also with American history—and in spite of everything, with American literature. More fully in America than in, for example, England, adventure has commanded the participation of talented writers, however ambivalent and reluctant that participation sometimes was. Read dialectically, then, this sequence of books can be called the great tradition, the central tradition, in American liter-ature.

There is, of course, an alternative tradition, a sequence of narratives about the author's retreat from society into the Ameri-can landscape and a life of intercourse with nature, of which *Walden* is the most famous example and which Annie Dillard, among others, is continuing today. In historical range and in literary distinction this form *can* be compared with the adven-ture; and it expresses what "America" has meant to many *readers* (I mean men and women of letters) both American and foreign. But to me it seems that such reading is, nowadays, inspiring in a weak sense. Because it does not invite a dialectical response, it can only build up a conspiracy of complacency between the reader and the writer (or teacher and critic). Of course, some-thing like a conspiracy is inevitable; literary study must always represent "us," the contemplative culture, against "them," the world of action. But we surely owe it to ourselves to make that representation as honest and objective and self-critical as possi-ble. Critics who accept that principle should, I believe, direct their literary criticism toward the adventure in American litera-ture.

BEING AMERICAN, AS LITERATURE HAS DEFINED IT

What then *is* the American tradition in literature, if we accept the adventure as its dominant category? First of all, it is anti-Christian, in the sense that it challenges the radical Christian commitment to peace. That challenge is explicit in the first three writers I discussed—Cooper, Irving, and Bird. In their books we saw the Quakers, the Moravians, the Shakers, and nonviolent Indians being criticized in various ways. The reader is taught that peace cannot be a serious commitment for the citizens of the newly independent United States; at least not for men. (Women will, of course, continue to believe in it. That division of men from women may seem merely old-fashioned, but as late as 1967, Norman Mailer, in *Armies of the Night,* saw his wife as Christian and nonviolent; he saw this not conventionally but paradoxi-cally, and in a burst of passionate insight. He did not, however, assign to himself, the adventurer, any comparable affiliation.) For all three early writers, the general culture hero is the pioneer, the frontiersman, the solitary hunter, while the *reader* is specifically represented by a regular army officer, Captain Bonneville, Captain Middleton, Captain Forrester. Officer or pioneer, the hero is a man of blood.

Adventure then is antifeminist, in that it assigns only peripheral and ancillary roles to women. Women are the objects of lust and pity, seizure and rescue, but they are not subjects who themselves act. They are prizes, measures of success, rewards and responsibilities for men. In matters of emotion, they are apparently subjective centers, but their own passions usually make them more passive—they faint, fail, or freeze in a crisis. The effective emotions, those which are embodied in action, are those they inspire in men. Indeed, the caricature female in the stories (for example, the Indian hag, the hideous torturer of white male prisoners) suggests a panic and disgust inspired by women not confined to passivity, women who work, who act, who labor—women who are not mere prizes.

That this view of women belongs to the adventure form rather than to individual writers is proven by the case of J. F. Cooper, who presents some of the feeblest of all "heroines" of adventure, but who was also able to conceive of women as powerful presences in his domestic novels of manners, and even introduced such a powerful presence as Elizabeth Temple into *The Pioneers.* Cooper's handling of Elizabeth is somewhat inept, and she is out of place in a story of adventure, but her conception is a striking image of vigorous and indeed intimidating judgment.

Still, the adventure tradition, because it is masculinist and nationalist, is antifeminist, whatever opinions its individual writers may have held. Adventure is the imaginative concept that links the personal-identity concept of manhood with the political concept of nationalism. All three concepts define themselves against alternatives: the nation is defined *against* empire (both the latter's passive subject peoples and the corrupt exploiting power itself); adventure is defined *against* the routines of everyday economic duty, and against the artifice of privileged and mannered society; and manliness is defined *against* effeminacy (or womanliness) and against childishness (or boyishness). All these are aggressive and energetic ideas.

Because "adventure" carries with it the implication of the other two concepts, we can say that it is also importantly expansive or expansionist. No doubt every positive and asserted identity expands itself at the expense of other people, or at least of other possibilities within the personality; even humility is aggressive when it is asserted. But manliness/adventure/nationalism are more assertive than other identities. We have already sufficiently pointed that out in regard to manliness. It remains to remark on the expansiveness of nationalism, hidden or implicit as it is.

The great story of the growth of the United States in the nineteenth century, of its "natural" self-expansion from the Atlantic to the Pacific—the story so often told by Hollywood in terms of wagon trains and railroad tracks—is sung to the tune of increasing power. It expands *against* other competitors, against the Native Americans, against nature itself. And it expands economically as well as politically. Take away the message that everything is getting bigger and better (for the American people, not for their competitors) and the story would lose its excitement, deflate, and collapse.

This truth is clear enough in the three early narratives, by Cooper, Irving, and Bird, but we associate it more particularly with the second three, by Dana, Melville, and Parkman. It is clear in these three cases that the adventure of the individual author, although primarily a personal self-proving, the occasion of his becoming a man, is also part of society's adventure of becoming the continental American nation. Dana looks over California, as a space for that nation to expand into (at the expense of the Spanish Americans, the Indians, and the Kanakas). Parkman goes west on the Oregon Trail, along with the adventurers and the migrants making the trek to the new lands. Melville reports on the South Sea islands, already invaded by American traders and missionaries, as well as by representatives of British and French imperialism.

We also notice, in all six of these narratives, the authors' claims that their own social group should be the dominant caste in American society; for Melville was not a trader or missionary, Parkman was not a migrant, and Dana was not a sailor. They were gentlemen, members of the responsible class in America, and they wrote as gentlemen, for gentlemen. The group's overt claim is to be representative, to be American. However, because their social function is to give orders and to lead others, in war and in peace, the implicit result of legitimizing their claim is to grant them dominance. It is from this point of view that we first discern the hairline but deep split within adventure, between literature and popular legend. For in popular legends (such as Paul Bunyan or Mike Fink) the gentlemanly caste has no role except to be outraged and outfaced by the demotic and democratic heroes. Literary adventure, on the other hand, welds together the popular legend and the genteel romance (in which the central figures always represent the gentlemanly class).

In the second half of the book which covers the second group of six writers, we note the same themes as before, with the addition of some new ones. In the case of Kit Carson, we see the power of the literary adventure to shape real life. Carson was seen by his contemporaries as an old guide (he was in fact quite young) instructing the genteel young hero Frémont; and he came to see himself as a legend, his image mirrored in the popular press, his name echoed in the hills and towns of the West. In Theodore Roosevelt, we see literary adventure intervening as an imaginative force in politics. Roosevelt saw himself as one of those adventurous American gentlemen, like Dana and Parkman. He felt that he had made himself an American hero through his adventures, and he made his contemporaries see him in that guise—they consequently voted him into the White House.

Mark Twain's interest is of a different kind, exemplifying all the splits and antagonisms in American culture. One of the keenest conflicts was that between the genteel class and literature, on the one hand, and the frontier class and adventure, on the other. Genteel readers—Twain's wife's family, for instance—felt remote from adventure. Twain, of course, embodied both options, and his enormous popularity represented the conventional reconciliation of the two. It was also his genius, and his fate, to make obvious the falsity of that reconciliation and the force of the antagonisms that lay beneath it. His life story reminds us of the career of the adventure genre—of the intellectual tragi-comedy of adventure's uneasy enshrinement within American culture.

The final three narratives represent the American literature of the generation just past, and they show a striking recurrence to the stories and motifs of the first group, in spite of differences in the intellectual idioms of the various writers. Hemingway, Faulkner, and Mailer tell hunting anecdotes about the process by which one becomes a man in America and about the responsibilities of manhood and, implicitly, of nationhood. Manliness, nationalism, and adventure are as closely linked in *Why Are We in Vietnam?* as they were in *The Pioneers.* However, during the intervening 150 years, America has become an empire, and white Americans are now seen—by Hemingway and Faulkner too—not as newborn innocents, but as rich and wicked world aristocrats, as lords of the earth. Contemporary concepts of adventurism and male chauvinism announce a skeptical resistance to the old values of adventure and manliness, which these writers uneasily echo. Nonetheless, in the end it is the old values these narratives endorse. Thus what American literature tells us about the culture as a whole (insofar as adventure is its dominant category) is that America has been a peculiarly masculinist society and that its writers have reflected, have served, that society, even in their most sophisticated and critical writings.

However, the foregoing summary cannot stand without a qualification or a comment. Put that way, the literary record seems to call for a militant reaction on the reader's part, a distancing of oneself from the American tradition. Yet I believe that such a response would not be appropriate for several reasons. First of all, since adventure and the world of action are so intimately related, an activist cannot afford to cut himself or herself off from adventure. (Gandhi used the idea and rhetoric of adventure to call his Satyagraha movement into being.) Second, to cut oneself off from one society in order to join another is valid in the world of action and actuality, but, insofar as one is a reader and critic of literature, one is acting within the culture of contemplation, where the morality is different. To triumph rhetorically over male chauvinism in a classroom full of English majors is too easy; and to turn one's back on what is inimical is a moral failure, if the subject is important. The virtues of truth are appreciation and criticism, and these virtues find their function in full engagement with a difficult problem. An activist (a man like Gandhi, say), a nonreader, would be justified in narrowing his/her vision and limiting imaginative participation in opposite points of view, in the interests of effective intervention. But a reader belongs in the culture of truth; and his/her duty—in this matter of American literature—is to enter into a dialectical engagement with adventure.

CASTE-THINKING IN AMERICA

Finally, if American action has been linked especially to adventure, adventure, in turn, seems to have been just as strikingly linked to caste, in a number of ways. The connection, made primarily by American gentlemen, was not *just* an attempt to show the gentleman to be an American adventurer; it was not *just* one class's ideological tactic to advance its own interest. In fact, although other links between the two ideas are vaguer they are equally important and even more pervasive. Those who lived adventures on the frontier, as well as those who wrote about them, were always much concerned about questions of caste; it was part of their group psychology and was based on occupations and social functions.

The adventurers and writers saw society and themselves and other people in caste terms (as the hunter, the merchant, the Brahmin, and so on), not as equal members of a working class striving ever upward in constant competition. They saw everyone, including themselves, as playing a fixed role vis-à-vis others, and achieving (or failing to achieve) a destiny defined in caste terms. Their accounts of St. Louis, or of a trapper's rendezvous, are peopled by a motley mosaic of contrasting types, like a caste-divided city in India. Their image of America was a rodeo, or Buffalo Bill's Wild West.

It was not, I think, hard to show in the preceding chapters that the authors made striking use of such categories in many of their narratives. But I want to argue something more—that their use of caste images was not accidental but logical. Perhaps most of us, when we notice those images, explain them away as old-fashioned rhetoric with no real significance, as intended ironically or at least dialectically (in opposition to other values), or as merely idiosyncratic. We tend to dismiss as an accident the coincidence of their use by so many of these writers.

Such explanations, however, satisfy only so long as they remain unselfconscious and unquestioned. They have to be rejected once we see how important and various are the uses to which adventurers (using that term for both adventure lovers and adventure writers) put caste categories. It then becomes clear that caste-thinking is highly congenial to men of action; so much more congenial than orthodox "serious" thought that it may be said to be natural and necessary to them. In this last section, therefore, I shall discuss some of the other ways in which caste-thinking is appropriate to adventure and adventurers. We have already looked at the matter of command and the authority our writers ascribed to gentlemen.

Let us begin with that bonding together of frontier groups that fascinates Mark Twain in *Roughing It* and *Life on the Mississippi.* What strikes Twain and provokes some of his most brilliant writing is the power that accrues to certain occupational groups—for example, river pilots and stagecoach drivers—who, though not ostensibly high on the social register, yet dispose of authority, in matters to do with their vocations, with a brutal absoluteness that is almost unparalleled in the rest of society. Although the examples are not as immediately relevant to the connection between caste-thought and adventure in the sense of dangerous fighting, they are very relevant to the testing of young manhood, another of adventure's themes. Clearly these drivers' and pilots' authority derives not from some formal union they enter into or some economic advantage they possess—much less from any educational or intellectual advantage—but from their vocational identities. (In our own time groups like construction workers and automobile mechanics enjoy something of this power.) When it is written about, it is usually with humor, but rarely with Twain's insight and passion.

This example also reminds us that one source of our resistance to thinking in caste terms is a typically modern presupposition that a concern with caste always derives from a mean concern for status and serves the dominance of the rich and powerful. This presumption is a part of our ideology, but it is unjust; caste has at least as much to do with vocation, and above all with vocation-based identity—the range of attributes and tastes ascribed to people on the basis of their work or their parents' work. (These ascriptions are made by individuals themselves as well as by outsiders.)

In India, the two meanings are made explicit; "caste spirit" can refer to the communal pride inspiring any vocational group, however poor and oppressed it is, as well as to a passion for precedence and a concern with social hierarchies. (Hindus use the term *jati* for the first idea of caste, and *varna* for the other.) It is the first meaning that gives a caste member the sense of social identity that Twain wrote about. At the same time, the other meaning is not entirely irrelevant to what he is talking about; the cutting edge of a frontier *jati*'s social style also owes something to its consciousness of ranking low in the *varna* system. The members of all such *jatis* are likely to be suspicious of superior claims by, for instance, Brahmins. Modern Americans can use the two meanings only humorously or ironically.

Another important use of caste categories for adventurers and adventure writers (as for other people) is that they enable them to distinguish human types from each other, and to name the conflicts that interest them. Indeed caste thought is just a vivid case of a more general type of thinking we might call "residual," because it makes use of residual categories—that is, those left behind by the march of intellectual history and applied to problems left out of our consciously serious thought. Our serious thought about society, I am suggesting, employs Marxist or Weberian terms;* but insofar as we think organically about society, we often use categories such as geography, caste, race, or ethnicity to explain and define our social experiences and theories. Adventure writers, it is my impression, use these categories more than other people, perhaps because adventure thought is always "unofficial"—in the service of the dynamic world of action and in rebellion against the static world of thought. †

We may also note that adventure writers often assert the reserves of savagery that lie just below the surface of even the most civilized and intellectual men. They like to depict people reverting to primitive violence. Atavism is caste thinking, not only as a technique (adventure novelists often used it as a plot device at the end of the nineteenth century) but also as a faith; it declares the value of activities and aptitudes that modern thought tends to suppress and repress. Nationalism, too, insofar as it was an organic theory of society was a return to premodern thinking. All these ideas serve the purposes (the imaginative purposes) of men

---

*I use Max Weber to stand for modern sociology at its most severe and scholarly.

†We find geographical terms for instance, used in Judge Hall's *Letters from the West* (published in 1828 but begun as early as 1819); they are, I believe, very important documents in the history of American self-definition.

of action, but they have no status in the modern theory of society and human nature. What this suggests is a profound opposition between all modern thought about society and the "residual" ways of thinking represented by adventure, nationalism, and caste.

Adventure may even be said to embody an alternative philosophy of history. In our discussion we have associated it with imperialism, but this could be misleading. In fact, an adventure sensibility—one oriented toward the colors and varieties of culture—may be found associated with anti-imperialist politics. Some of the great British adventurers, like the poet Wilfrid Blunt, were anti-imperialist. And though Lévi-Strauss's *Tristes Tropiques* is a major document of Europe's remorse for three hundred years of world domination, it is as much a cult of travel and adventure as Theodore Roosevelt's *Through the Brazilian Wilderness* (which covers the same geographical ground). There is a cleavage within the modern philosophy of history that creates an alliance among everyone on the same side of it—in this case, among all those with a passion for anthropology, geography, and "otherness," whatever their politics.

This cleavage may be said to result from the ax blow of the question What is the most important event in modern history? Theodore Roosevelt and Lévi-Strauss would both answer, Europe's conquest of the rest of the world. Sartre and most Marxists (and most modern intellectuals) answer, Europe's industrialization of its economy. The first answer implies that international militarism, force, and hegemony are the primary phenomena of history; the second puts the stress on intranational production and consumption, social justice, class conflict. The first implies that we can be saved from the nightmare of mutual destruction only by a steady-state economics, a no-growth population, a stable society. The second holds that the triumph of the people and the progress of the human mind will save us. The first speaks of castes and even accepts class differentiation as a useful force that builds social structures; the second speaks of class and implies that such differentiation is the enemy of justice and the source of internecine strife. The first (e.g., Rousseau, as expounded by Lévi-Strauss) asks people to identify with the Other, the form of humanity most unlike themselves; the second asks them to identify with those around them, to speak always as "we," not as "I." The first writes adventure fiction and travel books (*Tristes Tropiques* is an apotheosis of the travel book); the second writes domestic/political novels, and nonfiction like *The Condition of the Working Class in England in 1844.* The one is represented by Rousseau and his remorse, Lévi-Strauss and his Buddhism; the other by Marx and his revenge, his call to action, to praxis, to political rising. The first sees the world in synchronous structures, splendid panoramas of triumph and ruin; the second sees history, progress, change, production, purpose.

Intellectually speaking, the second has won the big battles, in serious fiction and literary criticism. It has engrossed all the seriousness for itself, so that even brilliant men, like Twain and Mailer, have not been able to present the other side seriously— nor even, perhaps, to believe it themselves. It is time to give the first answer some attention. That is another reason why we should begin to think about adventure.

NOTES

1. Introduction: Adventure, Manliness, Nationalism

[1] Herman Melville, *Moby Dick* (Boston, 1956), p. 101.

[2] John Ferling, "The American Soldier," *American Quarterly* 33(1):26–45.

[3] As quoted in ibid., p. 44.

2. Cooper's *The Pioneers* (1823)

[1] Page numbers in parentheses refer to quotations from *The Pioneers*, Leon Howard, ed. (New York, 1959).

[2] Preface to ibid., p. 12.

[3] J. F. Cooper, *The Pilot* (New York, n.d.), pp. 20–26.

3. Irving's *A Tour on the Prairies* (1832)

[1] Page references in parentheses are to the following editions: *Astoria* (Norman, 1954), abbreviated *A; A Tour on the Prairies* (Norman, 1956), abbreviated *T*; and *The Adventures of Captain Bonneville* (Boston, 1977), abbreviated *CB*.
tain Bonneville (Boston, Twayne 1977), abbreviated *CB*.

[2] William Goetzmann, *Exploration and Empire:* the explorer and the scientist in the winning of the American West (New York, 1966).

[3] Francis Parkman, *Vassall Morton* (Boston, 1856).

[4] Ibid.

4. BIRD'S *NICK OF THE WOODS* (1837)
[1] Page references in parentheses are to *Nick of the Woods,* Curtis Dahl, ed. (New Haven, 1967).

[2] Quoted in Arthur K. Moore, *The Frontier Mind* (Lexington, Ky., 1957), p. 68.

[3] See Ronald T. Takaki, *Iron Cages* (New York, 1979), p. 88.

5. DANA'S *TWO YEARS BEFORE THE MAST* (1840)
[1] Page references in parentheses are to *Two Years Before the Mast* (New York, 1969).

[2] D. H. Lawrence, *Studies in Classic American Literature* (New York, 1964), p. 115.

6. MELVILLE'S *TYPEE* (1846)
[1] Page references in parentheses are to the George Woodcock edition of *Typee* (London, 1972).

[2] Jonathan Swift, *Gulliver's Travels* (New York, 1950).

7. PARKMAN'S *THE OREGON TRAIL* (1849)
[1] David Levin, *History as Romantic Art* (Stanford, 1959).

[2] Quoted in Robert L. Gale, *Francis Parkman* (New York, 1973), p. 72.

[3] Howard Doughty, *Francis Parkman* (Westport, Conn., 1978), pp. 4,5.

[4] Page references in parentheses are to Francis Parkman, *The Oregon Trail* (New York, 1950).

[5] Quoted in Doughty, pp. 69–70.

[6] Quoted in Levin, p. 35.

[7] Quoted in Gale, p. 99.

[8] Francis Parkman, *The Parkman Reader*, S. E. Morison, ed. (Boston, 1955), p. 333.

[9] R. W. Emerson, "Power", in *Prose Works of R. W. Emerson*, vol. II (Boston, 1870) p. 352.

[10] Quoted in Gale, p. 85.

8. CARSON'S *AUTOBIOGRAPHY* (1856)

[1] Page references in parentheses are to Kit Carson's *Autobiography*, (Lincoln, Neb., 1966).

[2] Allen Johnson ed., *Dictionary of American Biography*, vol. VII (New York, 1928).

[3] References to the Lakeside Classics edition, Milo Milton Quaise, ed., (Chicago, 1935) are indicated by the prefix *LC*.

[4] Quoted in Henry Nash Smith, *The Virgin Land* (Cambridge, Mass., 1950), p. 86.

9. TWAIN'S *ROUGHING IT* (1872)

[1] Page references in parentheses are to *Roughing It* (New York, 1962).

[2] Mark Twain, *Life on the Mississippi* (New York, 1961), p. 92.

[3] Ibid., p. 93.

[4] Ibid.

[5] Mark Twain, *A Connecticut Yankee in King Arthur's Court* (New York, 1963), p. 56.

[6] Francis Parkman, *The Oregon Trail* (New York, 1950), p. 262.

10. Roosevelt's *Autobiography* (1913)

[1] Page references in parentheses are to the following works: Theodore Roosevelt, *Rough Riders* (New York, 1900), designated *RR; Theodore Roosevelt's Autobiography* (New York, 1920), designated *A;* Theodore Roosevelt, *Literary Essays* (New York, 1926), designated *LE;* Theodore Roosevelt, *African Game Trails* (New York, 1924), designated *AT;* and William H. Harbaugh, *Power and Responsibility* (New York, 1963), designated WH.

[2] G. Edward White, *The Eastern Establishment and Western Experience* (New Haven, 1968), p. 90.

[3] Ibid., p. 92.

[4] Quoted in ibid., pp. 92–93.

[5] See the stories of the Roman centurion and the Norman knight in Kipling's *Puck of Pook's Hill* (New York, 1906).

[6] E. Digby Baltzell, *The Protestant Establishment:* aristocracy and caste in America (New York, 1964), pp. 11–12.

[7] Henry Nash Smith, *The Virgin Land* (Cambridge, Mass., 1950), p. 55.

[8] W. H. Hudson, *The Purple Land,* Theodore Roosevelt, ed. (New York, 1916), pp. ix–x.

[9] Theodore Roosevelt, Introduction to *Captain Macklin* by Richard Harding Davis (New York, 1920), pp. vii–viii.

11. Hemingway's *The Green Hills of Africa* (1935)

[1] John Lenihan, *Showdown* (Champaign, Ill., 1980), p. 6.

[2] Jeffrey Richards, *Swordsmen of the Screen* (London, 1977), p. 25.

[3] Page references in parentheses are to: Ernest Hemingway, *The Green Hills of Africa* (New York, 1935); and Ernest Hemingway, *Death in the Afternoon* (New York, 1932), designated *DA.*

[4] Rudyard Kipling, "A Conference of the Powers," in *Many Inventions* (New York, 1941); Ernest Hemingway, *The Hemingway Reader*, Charles Poore, ed. (New York, 1953), p. 569.

[5] As quoted in Poore, ibid., p. 542.

12. FAULKNER'S "THE BEAR" (1942)

[1] Quoted in Robert L. Gale, *Francis Parkman* (Boston, 1973), pp. 68–69.

[2] Page references in parentheses are to William Faulkner, "The Bear," in *Three Famous Short Novels* (New York, 1961).

[3] William Faulkner, *Go Down Moses* (New York, 1942), pp. 182, 167.

[4] See, for example, *Heart of Darkness* and *The Secret Sharer* (New York, 1971), p. 102.

[5] See the critics cited in *Bear, Man, and God*, Francis Lee Utley, Lynn Z. Bloom, and Arthur F. Kinney, eds. (New York, 1964).

13. MAILER'S *WHY ARE WE IN VIETNAM?* (1967)

[1] Page numbers in parentheses refer to Norman Mailer, *Why Are We in Vietnam?* (New York, 1973), designated *W.*; *The Naked and the Dead* (New York, 1948), designated *N*; and *Advertisements for Myself* (New York, 1959), designated *A*.

BIBLIOGRAPHY

Baltzell, E. Digby. *The Protestant Establishment: Aristocracy and Caste in America.* New York: Vintage, 1966.

Bird, Robert Montgomery. *Nick of the Woods.* Edited by Curtis Dahl. New Haven: College and University Press, 1967.

Carson, Kit. *Kit Carson's Autobiography.* Lincoln, Nebraska: University of Nebraska Press, 1966.

Conrad, Joseph. *Heart of Darkness* & *The Secret Sharer. Collected Works of Joseph Conrad,* Garden City, N.Y.: Doubleday, 1925.

Cooper, James Fenimore. *The Last of the Mohicans.* New York: W. A. Townsend, 1859.

——. *The Pilot.* New York: W. A. Townsend, 1859.

——. *The Pioneers.* Edited by Leon Howard. New York: Holt Rinehart & Winston, 1959.

——. *The Water-Witch.* New York: W. A. Townsend, 1861.

Dana, Richard Henry. *Two Years Before the Mast.* New York: 1969.

Davis, Richard Harding. *Captain Macklin.* Introduction by Theodore Roosevelt. New York: Scribners, 1920.

Defoe, Daniel. *Robinson Crusoe.* New York: Norton, 1975.

Doughty, Howard. *Francis Parkman.* Westport, Conn.: Greenwood Press, 1978.

Emerson, Ralph Waldo. "Power" in *Prose Works of R. W. Emerson.* vol. II Boston: Fields, Osgood and Co., 1870.

Faulkner, William. *Go Down, Moses.* New York: Random House, 1942.

——. *Three Famous Short Novels.* New York: Random House, 1961.

Fiedler, Leslie. *Love and Death in the American Novel.* New York: Dell, 1966.

Gale, Robert L. *Francis Parkman.* Boston: Twayne, 1973.

Goetzmann, William H. *Exploration and Empire: The Explorer and the Scientist in the Winning of the American West.* New York: Knopf, 1960.

Harbaugh, William H. *Power and Responsibility: The Life and Times of Theodore Roosevelt.* New York: Octagon Books, 1975.

Hemingway, Ernest. *Death in the Afternoon.* New York: Scribners, 1932.

———. *The Green Hills of Africa.* New York: Scribners, 1935.

———. *The Hemingway Reader.* Edited by Charles Poore. New York: Scribners, 1953.

———. *The Sun Also Rises.* New York: Scribners, 1953.

———. *To Have and Have Not.* New York: Scribners, 1937.

Hudson, William H. *The Purple Land.* Edited by Theodore Roosevelt. New York: Dutton, 1927.

Irving, Washington. *The Adventures of Captain Bonneville.* Boston: Twayne, 1977.

———. *Astoria.* Norman: University of Oklahoma Press, 1964.

———. *A Tour on the Prairies.* Norman: University of Oklahoma Press, 1956.

Kipling, Rudyard. "A Conference of the Powers" in *Many Inventions.* New York: Doubleday, Doran & Co., 1941.

———. *Puck of Pook's Hill.* New York: Doubleday, Doran & Co., 1941.

Lawrence, D. H. *Studies in Classic American Literature.* New York: Viking, 1964.

Lenihan, John H. *Showdown: Confronting Modern America in the Western Film.* Champaign: University of Illinois Press, 1980.

Levin, David. *History as Romantic Art.* Stanford, Cal.: Stanford University Press, 1959.

Mailer, Norman. *Advertisements for Myself.* New York: Putnam, 1959.

———. *Armies of the Night.* New York: New American Library, 1968.

———. *The Naked and the Dead.* New York: Rinehart, 1948.

———. *Why Are We in Vietnam? A Novel.* New York: Putnam, 1967.

Melville, Herman. *Moby Dick*. New York: Norton Classics, 1967.

——. *Redburn*. New York: Viking, 1983.

——. *Typee*. Edited by George Woodcock. London: Penguin, 1972.

——. *White Jacket*. New York: Grove Press, 1956.

Moore, Arthur K. *The Frontier Mind: A Cultural Analysis of the Kentucky Frontiersman*. Lexington: University of Kentucky Press, 1957.

Parkman, Francis. *The Oregon Trail: Sketches of Prairie and Rocky Mountain Life*. New York: New American Library, 1950.

——. *The Parkman Reader*. Edited by Samuel Eliot Morisson. Boston: Little Brown, 1955.

——. *Vassall Morton*. Boston: Phillips, Sampson & Co., 1856.

Richards, Jeffrey. *Swordsmen of the Screen: From Douglas Fairbanks to Michael York*. London: Routledge & Kegan, 1977.

Roosevelt, Theodore. *African Game Trails*. New York: Scribners, 1924.

——. *Literary Essays*. New York: Scribners, 1926.

——. *Rough Riders*. New York: Putnams, 1900.

——. *Theodore Roosevelt, an Autobiography*. New York: Scribners, 1920.

Smith, Henry Nash. *The Virgin Land*. Cambridge, Mass.: Harvard University Press, 1950.

Swift, Jonathan. *Gulliver's Travels*. New York: Modern Library, 1950.

Takaki, Ronald T. *Iron Cages: Race and Culture in Nineteenth-Century America*. New York: Knopf, 1979.

Trilling, Lionel. *The Liberal Imagination: Essays on Essays and Society*. New York: Harcourt Brace Jovanovich, 1979.

Twain, Mark. *A Connecticut Yankee in King Arthur's Court*. New York: New American Library, 1963.

——. *Life on the Mississippi*. New York: New American Library, 1961.

——. *Roughing It*. New York: New American Library, 1962.

Utley, Francis L., and Lynn Z. Bloom and Arthur F. Kinney. *Bear, Man, and God: Eight Approaches to Faulkner's The Bear*. New York: Random House, 1964.

White, G. Edward. *The Eastern Establishment and Westward Expansion*. New Haven: Yale University Press, 1968.

INDEX

120, 121
Turner, Frederick Jackson, 16, 156
Twain, Mark, 14, 18, 24, 58, 76, 84;
his accounts of South Sea
islands, 99; *The Adventures of
A Connecticut Yankee in King
Arthur's Court*, 133, 143; *The
Adventures of Huckleberry
Finn*, 133, 148, 171–172, 186;
*The Adventures of Tom
Sawyer*, 133; animals in work
of, 50; and culture/anticulture
heroes, 130; and Faulkner, 194;
and Hemingway, 171–172, 173,
174; humor of, 133, 134, 136,
137–138, 139, 144, 149–150;
and Kipling, 170, 182; *Life on
the Mississippi*, 133, 139–140,
141, 143, 148, 226; and Mailer,
200, 214; and Mormons, 62,
137; *Roughing It*, 15, 16, 119,
133–150, 223, 226; his years in
Carson City, 129
Two Years Before the Mast, *see
under* Dana, Richard Henry
Typee, *see under* Melville, Herman
Tyranny, in Dana's *Two Years
Before the Mast*, 77–78

Unitarianism, 103–104, 185

Van Buren, Martin, 49
Vancouver, George, 90
Venereal disease, in Melville's
Typee, 98
Verne, Jules, *20,000 Leagues Under
the Sea*, 31
Victoria, Queen, 119

War, portrayals of: in Mailer's *Why
Are We in Vietnam?*, 199, 202–
205; in T. Roosevelt's *Autobi-*

ography, 158; in Parkman's *The
Oregon Trail*, 103, 105–106
Warren, Robert Penn, 201
Washington, George, 101
Washington Post, 154
WASP heroes and adventures: in
Bird's *Nick of the Woods*, 56, 60;
in Dana's *Two Years Before the
Mast*, 76, 82, 83; and Jewish urban
writers, 199; in Mailer's *Why Are
We in Vietnam?*, 209; in Mel-
ville's *Typee*, 95, 97, 99
Wastefulness of frontiersmen, in
Cooper's *The Pioneers*, 26, 27
Wayne, John, 121, 167, 168
Weber, Max, 227n
Wharton, Edith, 217
White, William Allen, 158, 162
Whittier, John Greenleaf, 136, 144,
185
Why Are We in Vietnam?, *see
under* Mailer, Norman
Wilson, Charley, 208
Wilson, Edmund, 188, 218; *Axel's
Castle*, 186
Wister, Owen, 134, 162; *The Vir-
ginian*, 161
Women, depictions of, 220–221;
in Cooper's *The Pioneers*, 34–36,
221; in Melville's *Typee*, 97–98
Wood, Leonard, 152
Woodcock, George, 90, 92
Wordsworth, William, 51
World War I, 168
World War II, 203
Wouk, Herman, 200

Yale University, 162
Yeats, William Butler, 186
Young, Ewing, 127

Zola, Émile, 161

Born and raised in London, Martin Green has
lived in France, Turkey, and the United States.
The author of fourteen books, including *The
von Richthofen Sisters* and *Children of the Sun,
Von Richthofen Sisters* and *Children of the Sun,*
Green is professor of English at Tufts University.